STRONGER

THE DESTRUCTION OF VILNA JEWRY
1941–1945: AN EYEWITNESS ACCOUNT

THAN IRON

Mendel Balberyszski, *z"l*

MENDEL BALBERYSZSKI

STRONGER
THE DESTRUCTION OF VILNA JEWRY
1941–1945: AN EYEWITNESS ACCOUNT
THAN IRON

Revised and Edited by
Theodore Balberyszski

Translated from the Original Yiddish Edition by
Abraham Cykiert
and Theodore Balberyszski

gefen גפן
publishing house בית הוצאה לאור
JERUSALEM ◆ NEW YORK   Est. 1981

Typesetting and Cover Design by S. Kim Glassman

ISBN: 978-965-229-485-2

1 3 5 7 9 8 6 4 2

Gefen Publishing House, Ltd.
6 Hatzvi Street
Jerusalem 94386, Israel
972-2-538-0247
orders@gefenpublishing.com

Gefen Books
600 Broadway
Lynbrook, NY 11563, USA
1-800-477-5257
orders@gefenpublishing.com

www.gefenpublishing.com

Printed in Israel   Send for our free catalogue

This English edition is dedicated to the memory of our parents,

Mendel and Leah Balberyszski.

They did not despair when seemingly all hope was lost, and struggled with all their strength to ensure the survival of their children and the continuation of their heritage.

Contents

PART ONE
Germany Invades the Soviet Union

PART TWO
In the Small Ghetto

PART THREE
In the Large Ghetto

PART FOUR
In the Concentration Camps of Estonia

PREFACE TO THE ENGLISH EDITION
by Dr. Theodore Balberyszski

On September 1, 1939, I was a happy, carefree eight-year-old child. By September 22, 1944, I was a thirteen-year-old adult.

The lost years of my childhood were drowned in an orgy of sadism, brutality and inhumanity which no child could be expected to understand and from which no child could be left unaffected. That I survived the savagery and was able to return to a normal life is due entirely to my parents' efforts to shield me and my sister as much as they could from the events around us and, when that became impossible and our family was separated, it was my father's strength, tenacity and wit that saved me time and time again from the murderer's clutches and imminent death. I could only admire his will to live, to maintain his humanity, dignity and moral strength. *Stronger Than Iron* bears witness to that. It is the story of my family, one of the many thousands who formed the great and thriving Jewish community in Poland until the outbreak of the Second World War and the tragic period of the Holocaust. It is a chronicle of days and nights, of months and years, recorded by my father behind the walls of the ghettos, behind the barbed wire of concentration camps, in the darkness of hiding places – always in the shadow of death, always with the uncertainty of living to see another tomorrow. It is a record of events for historians to study. It is yet another brick in the great monumental indictment of the German people and their accomplices. It is also an expression of the innermost thoughts and feelings of a single individual possessed by the idea of saving his family from destruction and of helping his fellow Jews in their darkest moments of need. It is above all the story of a man who would not give up and who would not be broken when seemingly all hope was gone, a man whose will to survive and bring this story to the judgment of future generations was stronger than iron.

My father started writing this book immediately after the liberation and in 1946 his booklet *The Liquidation of the Vilna Ghetto* was published in Polish by the Jewish Central Historical Commission in Lodz, Poland. Even earlier, in 1940, he wrote at the request of the Vilna Historical Commission *My Travels from Lodz to Vilna in 1939*, an account of the perilous flight of thousands of Jews, including himself, from German-occupied Poland toward Vilna, which was then under Lithuanian rule. Throughout the years of the German occupation he made copious notes of events as they unfolded, as witnessed by him or as reported by others. He kept these notes in a little suitcase which my grandmother Liba held on to. Tragically, the little suitcase disappeared when she was suddenly separated from the rest of the family during the final hours of the Vilna Ghetto. Immediately after liberation from the German camps in Estonia my father and I returned to Vilna and my father was given access to the official documents from the Vilna Ghetto housed in the Vilna State Museum. Over a period of some five months (December 1944–May 1945) he studied and copied them as documentary material for his story of the destruction of Vilna Jewry. The project was postponed when we received news that my mother and sister had survived the Holocaust and made their way back to Lodz, Poland. It took some time for us to obtain the necessary travel permits, but by the end of 1945 our family was reunited and eventually left Europe and settled in Australia to start a new life.

The original Yiddish version of this book was written in the 1950s and published in 1967 in Israel. The Holocaust was still fresh in the collective mind of humanity. The atrocities committed by the Germans and their helpers were universally condemned but the level of consciousness was low. Anti-Semitism, although existent, was confined to the fringes of society.

Rehabilitating their shattered lives and bringing their Holocaust stories to the attention of a world that allowed it to happen became the major objective of many of the Holocaust survivors, the remnants of European Jewry. Since then a voluminous Holocaust literature has been published: numerous accounts written by survivors of ghettos and death and concentration camps; protocols from legal proceedings against German criminals and their helpers; and official German documents obtained from German military and other archives. These served as documentary material for Holocaust historians, and several monumental studies dealing with Hitler's "Final Solution" and the Holocaust were published during that period, including several books, diaries and memoirs dealing with the destruction of Vilna Jewry. Of the latter, however, *Stronger Than Iron* is the only comprehensive and uninterrupted eyewitness account of the events leading to the destruction of Vilna Jewry from the first day of the German occupation of Vilna until the day of liberation of the eighty-four survivors in the Klooga Concentration Camp in Estonia.

Since we were herded into the small ghetto on September 6, 1941, the book contains the only historical record of the establishment of the small ghetto and life there from its very first day of existence until its liquidation. It records for history's judgment a historic meeting between the Judenrate of the two ghettos that revealed profound differences between them about the role of the Judenrat and the nature of its cooperation with the German authorities. It also reveals that on September 15, 1941, the Judenrat of the small ghetto refused the German demand to deliver fifteen hundred Jews to the gate of the ghetto. This decision did not save any Jews. Eventually the inhabitants of both ghettos were led to their deaths. But the Jews in the small ghetto had to be hunted down by the Germans and Lithuanians themselves – none of them were delivered by the Judenrat or the Jewish police. This extraordinary act of moral heroism deserves to be recorded in history and *Stronger Than Iron* is the only narrative of the destruction of Vilna Jewry that does that.

*   *   *

The murder of the remnants of the survivors of the Vilna Ghetto in the concentration camps of Lagedi and Klooga on September 18–19, 1944, brought to an end the glorious history of the Jewish community of Vilna which over the centuries of its existence had become the pride of European Jewry. Although there are indications that Jews may have settled in Vilna, the capital of the Grand Duchy of Lithuania, as early as the mid-fourteenth century, the first historical documents that refer to the Jewish population of Vilna date back to the year 1568 when the Jews were granted permission to engage in commerce and crafts, subject to some limitations. Over the next two centuries the Jewish population of Vilna grew and prospered.

By the early eighteenth century Vilna was already established as a flourishing center of religious studies with a vast array of Talmudic scholars active in numerous institutes of religious learning (*yeshivot*), religious schools and synagogues. Elijah ben Solomon, known as the "Genius of Vilna" (*Vilna Gaon*) and one of the greatest Talmudic scholars of his time, headed the *Mitnagdim* (opponents to Hassidic Judaism) which added great impetus to religious learning in Vilna and throughout Lithuania. After the 1795 partition of Poland and the incorporation of Vilna into the Russian Empire, the city became an important center of Jewish culture that served the needs of the Jewish communities throughout the so-called Jewish Pale of Settlement, the area in which Jews were confined.

Vilna's cultural activities continued to flourish in the nineteenth century. It became an important center of the Haskalah, which led to the establishment of Jewish secular educational institutions, teachers' seminaries, secondary schools and vocational training schools and fostered a new generation of Jewish writers, Yiddish and Hebrew, whose books were published and printed in the city. By the end of the nineteenth century and until the outbreak of the Second World War the Vilna Jewish community witnessed a resurgence of Jewish social and cultural activities that brought it to the forefront of Jewish life in Europe. The city boasted flourishing institutions of research and education, including the Jewish Scientific Institute, YIVO, with its magnificent collection of cultural treasures, the Jewish Historical and Ethnographical Society with its library of original manuscripts by renowned Jewish authors and the Straszun Library with its collection of rare manuscripts, Judaica items that could be found in the hundred synagogues that existed in Vilna. Over the years the Vilna Jewish community became a magnet to many actors, who established a Yiddish theater; to journalists, who founded some six daily newspapers in Yiddish and Hebrew; and to artists and musicians, some of whom became world famous.

Vilna became home to intensive political activities as well. The socialist Bund Party was founded in Vilna and became a major force in Jewish life, competing only with the Zionist Movement, which also took root in the Vilna Jewish community and enjoyed widespread popularity. The community was led by a Jewish Council which coordinated the activities of all welfare, health, religious and sports organizations. By 1939 Vilna was the crown jewel of Jewish Poland and Lithuania with cultural wealth accumulated over the course of centuries of vibrant Jewish life.

The destruction of that vibrant Jewish life and the annihilation of the seventy thousand Jews of Vilna were yet another link in the German master plan to eradicate from the face of the earth any vestiges of Jewish tradition, Jewish culture and centuries of Jewish achievement.

*   *   *

My father loved Vilna, the "Jerusalem of Lithuania" as it was called. He was born and raised there, as was his father and grandfather. He knew every street, every corner, every house, every one of the many synagogues and houses of prayer, every one of the schools, libraries and houses of learning. All of them had a meaning to him, all of them symbolized to him the richness of the Vilna Jewish community, the centuries of Jewish tradition and Yiddish culture. But above all he loved the people of the city. He was a man of the people and felt close to them. He was deeply involved in Jewish public life and recruited many to various communal causes and they became his friends. Some of them were eminent communal leaders, such as Dr. J. Wygocki, Dr. Grigori Gierszuni and Advocate Yoseph Wietsman, who were all attracted by their young friend's intellect, energy and enthusiasm. Others were ordinary Jews – artisans, small businessmen and young professionals who made up the bulk of Vilna's Jewish population and who appreciated my father's drive and his direct, honest talk. He was a man of strong ideas which over time evolved into a weltanschauung, a philosophy of life steeped in Jewish tradition and universal values. Honesty, decency, compassion and a desire to help his fellow Jews in times of need were the values he cherished and it is those values that he brought with him to the gates of the small ghetto.

At the request of the Judenrat my father organized a housing department which was charged with the almost impossible task of finding accommodation both for the nine thousand Jews herded into a few small streets and for the various institutions that the Judenrat decided to establish. He did this with his customary energy and efficiency. He was greatly impressed by the members of the small ghetto Judenrat, which consisted of five ordinary Jews, none of them former leaders of the community or party activists – just people like him, steeped in Jewish tradition who understood the enormity of their responsibility and were determined to do what was needed without compromising their integrity or morality. My father was particularly proud of their decision, during the first week of the ghetto, to refuse to deliver Jews to the Germans without having an official document that would stipulate the workplaces to which those Jews were to be allocated.

The concept of a ghetto Judenrat was new to all and not clearly understood. It was obvious that there was an immediate necessity to establish an administration that would organize all communal activities – housing, food supplies, health services, education, and law and order – in order to manage the thousands of people enclosed between the walls of the ghetto. It also became quite evident that the Judenrat would have to represent the ghetto and maintain relations with the German authorities. One of its key functions would be to supply organized labor groups to the various workshops and factories outside the ghetto. What was not understood is that the Germans expected full cooperation of the Judenrat and the Jewish police in the transmission of German orders to the Jews of the ghetto and in the delivery of Jews into the hands of German murderers, with no questions asked. In other words, the Judenrat would do their bidding.

During the first weeks of the ghetto's existence most Jews hoped they would now be safe behind the walls, providing an organized labor force to the Germans and Lithuanians who were desperately in need of workers. But immediately after the September 15 and the Yom Kippur "cleansings," my father began to realize that "cleansings" meant the killing grounds of Ponary and that it was no longer possible to continue living in a state of denial. He was supported in this by I. Lejbowicz, chairman of the small ghetto Judenrat, who was probably the first among the leadership of the two ghettos to give public expression to the terrifying thought that was on many people's minds. The idea that "cleansings" meant death confronted the Judenrate with a terrible moral dilemma, at least those who had decided on a policy of cooperation with the German authorities: how to justify the rounding up of Jews by Jews and their delivery to the Germans at the ghetto gates. The response of the large ghetto Judenrat, under the leadership of A. Fried and Jacob Gens, was that one must sacrifice some in order to save many. The small ghetto Judenrat did not disagree with the tragic reality but decided that Jews could not be the ones to deliver other Jews to be sacrificed.

After the liquidation of the small ghetto and our transfer to the large ghetto, my father understood that the large ghetto Judenrat's proclaimed policy of "work to live" meant that the Judenrat was willing to select and deliver to the Germans Jews destined for death. "My hope is to save the ghetto," said Ghetto Chief Gens to my father. "You may save the ghetto," replied my father, "but it will be without Jews." But the policy continued. An ugly side effect of that policy was rampant favoritism and corruption. Once the Judenrat and the Jewish police were given the authority to select "who will live and who will die," a brisk trade developed in the coveted, life-saving yellow work permits. People with financial means were willing to pay small fortunes for a permit and many Judenrat officials and policemen enriched themselves through such transactions. Many Judenrat department heads also used the work permits to accommodate their party comrades, irrespective of their qualifications for the positions involved (most of the Judenrat administrative positions were held by members of the Bund and the Zionist parties who reorganized themselves within the ghetto walls). My father was enraged by the moral degradation of the self-interested and corrupt individuals, among whom were many he had known for years. He could not understand how they could sink so low. To trade in Jewish lives was the depth of depravity and he was sickened by it. But that did not stop my father from continuing to observe life in the ghetto and to record the many instances of courage, moral heroism, and the determination to survive.

*   *   *

Stronger Than Iron must be read on several levels. It is first of all an account of the struggle of one family, one of many thousands, to survive the tragic years of the German occupation of Vilna. It follows the story of that family from the moment German motorcycles passed by their home on Wielka Street on June 24, 1941, and continues through the liberation of my father and myself by the Soviet Army in the Klooga Concentration Camp on September 25, 1944. It describes the routine of daily life in Vilna after German occupation, inside the ghettos and in the concentration camps. It describes the daily struggle to avoid the Lithuanian "street catchers" and the many miraculous escapes during the ghetto "cleansings." It describes the humiliations, the hunger and brutality that were part of our everyday life. Above all, it describes my parents' supreme efforts to retain their human dignity in spite of everything.

But *Stronger Than Iron* is not just a personal journey through the gates of the Nazi hell. It is also a record of observations about ghetto life in general, about responses of the ghetto population to the various events taking place, about the ghetto leadership. My father was an astute and intelligent observer who noticed and noted reactions of the people in the streets. He was not an impartial observer; he did not have the luxury of observing from the outside. Rather, he was very much an insider, totally involved in ghetto life. He held strong views and did not hesitate to express them when dealing with particular events. Not being a member of the ghetto establishment, he was not a witness to everything that was happening in the ghetto. Therefore he had to supplement his own observations with those of others who were, and fortunately many years of friendships with Vilna Jews provided him with numerous sources of reliable information. In order to give expression to the true atmosphere and feelings of Jews in the streets of the ghetto he did not hesitate to include some of the plentiful rumors and colorful comments about various ghetto personalities.

In addition to these subjective views, *Stronger Than Iron* also includes an objective and factual description of the two ghettos, including the establishment of the Judenrat, the ghetto police and the ghetto administrations. It provides a detailed description of the various Judenrat departments and their struggles to deal with the insurmountable problems of daily life in the ghetto. The original Yiddish edition contains some ninety documents dealing with the daily activities of the Judenrat departments, which provide important documentation about ghetto life and source material for historical research.

*   *   *

The starting point for my father's original Yiddish edition is the year 1938, with the arrival of the German Jewish refugees in Lodz, Poland. It spans a period of almost seven years, until September 1944. Although the period 1938–1941 is critically important to an understanding of German plans for the destruction of the Jewish people and includes two years of their implementation (1939–1941) in lands under German occupation, it was necessary to reduce the scope of this English translation and confine it to the story of the destruction of Vilna Jewry. This edition, therefore, deals with the events of June 1941–September 1944, with the knowledge that by doing so the wide panoramic spread of the original work is lost.

Some semantic problems also needed to be resolved. Many Holocaust writers refer to the German activity of removing Jews from the ghettos using the German word *Aktion*. Jews in the Vilna Ghetto used the Polish word *czystka*. The English translation of the word *czystka* is "cleansing." Rather than use the German term, this English edition uses the term "cleansing" and plural "cleansings." Also, the names of the ghettos in the few books that were written on the subject were ghetto No.1 and ghetto No. 2. But, again, the Jews of the ghettos knew them as "*Di kleine ghetto*," meaning the small ghetto, and "*Di groise ghetto*," meaning the large ghetto. This English translation, therefore, retains the terminology used by the Jews of the ghetto and by the original Yiddish edition. Providing correct English spelling to family names written in Yiddish is not a simple task. Especially when one deals with Polish names that contain sounds like *cz*, *rz*, and *sz* – and sometimes all three in one name. To solve this problem, other references were consulted and if the names were identified the spelling given in the reference is used. Many names that appear in the book were not found in other references and they are spelled in a manner that permits an English reader to pronounce them phonetically. Apologies are due for whatever errors crept in.

Finally, the editor and the translators have made every effort to be as true and faithful to the original text as possible. Because the English edition is a considerably shortened version, some modifications were inevitable. Whenever these were made, however, the modification does not affect the essence of the text and, above all, it maintains the spirit and the atmosphere of the text. Painting the atmosphere of the period and giving expression to the mood of the people at various stages of the tragic events was one of the outstanding achievements of the original *Stronger Than Iron*. It is our fervent hope that the English edition does not fail in meeting this challenge.

Tel Aviv, April 2009

Acknowledgments

I am grateful to Professor Dov Levin, preeminent scholar of the history of Eastern European Jewish Communities and director of the Oral History Division of the Hartman Institute of Contemporary Jewry at the Hebrew University of Jerusalem, and to Professor Dina Porat, director of the Stephen Roth Institute for the Study of Contemporary Anti-Semitism and Racism at Tel Aviv University and a distinguished historian of the Holocaust, for their intense encouragement to publish a translated version of my late father's original work. Having used the original Yiddish version in their research and academic work they firmly believed that an English edition would be of great value to the new generation of Holocaust historians and students and the new generations of descendants of Holocaust survivors who are not fluent in the Yiddish language. Their encouragement is in no small measure responsible for my undertaking the three-year-long project that has now come to fruition.

I owe a great debt to Dr. Laurence Weinbaum, lecturer in Holocaust History at the Ariel University Center of Samaria, executive director of the Research Institute of the World Jewish Congress in Jerusalem and chief editor of the Israel Journal of Foreign Affairs, who has reviewed the manuscript "as a labor of love" and has let me impose on his knowledge and his time. He has contributed expert advice and many constructive comments. I have profited greatly from his incisive mind, though, naturally, he bears no responsibility for any errors that may remain in this work.

Translating and abbreviating a massive Yiddish volume into English while preserving the spirit of the original version is not an easy task. I was most grateful, therefore, when Mr. Abraham Cykiert consented to cooperate in this undertaking by translating significant sections of parts 2 and 3 of the English version. Mr. Cykiert, a survivor of the Lodz Ghetto and Auschwitz, settled in Melbourne, Australia, after the war. He was a talented and widely acclaimed poet and playwright in Yiddish and English and a leading community activist. Tragically, Mr. Cykiert passed away in March 2009 after a long illness.

I would also like to acknowledge the most efficient assistance that was provided by the staff of Gefen Publishing House and particularly the efforts of Ms. Tziporah Levine, a dedicated and highly professional language editor who did all she could to render the book into fluent English.

The original idea for the translation of the book came from my family and particularly my sister Deborah. They felt that it would be a fitting memorial to our parents who did so much to ensure that our family tradition would continue. Employing the persuasive powers of the younger generations (grandchildren and great-grandchildren), I could not but consent.

In undertaking to revise and edit the English translation of my father's book I was fully aware of the complexities involved and of the intellectual effort that would be required. And, of course, I was quite prepared for that. What I was not prepared for was the intense emotional experience that I would have to go through during the days, weeks and months in which I was engaged in the project. I neglected to consider the fact that I was not an uninvolved editor or translator. I was, in effect, a participant in all the events I was describing from the very first day until the very end. And although I was describing events that took place over sixty years ago, and which over the years had been shunted off to the distant recesses of my mind, in reliving them day after day they burst forth in full force of remembrance. The effect was immediate. The memories affected my behavior, they impeded my ability to carry on with the daily routine and I was in danger of becoming a difficult and withdrawn person. My wife, Anat, noticed the ongoing transformation and showed the wisdom, patience and presence of mind to support me during the many moments of crisis. Through her quiet, unobtrusive efforts I was able to complete my work without succumbing to the emotional stresses it created. Therefore, I owe the greatest debt of gratitude to my beloved wife, Anat.

Theodore Balberyszski

The two forewords were written by Dr. Nachman Blumental and
Dr. Joseph Kermish for the original Yiddish edition of Stronger Than Iron,
published in 1967. They are included in this English edition as a tribute to
the memory of two distinguished historians and Yad Vashem researchers
who contributed so much to Holocaust research.

FOREWORD

by Dr. Nachman Blumental, z"l

There are people – and they make up by far the largest segment of society – who live on the edge of the communities to which they belong. They live their own lives, as individuals and within their families, and come into contact with the world around them only to the extent that life forces them to do so. For in today's world it isn't really possible to live in isolation, completely detached from society. But their outlook on life is self-centered. Such people are said to be carried along by the wave of events. Their participation in those events is purely passive and submissive. They belong to organizations – professional, political or social – and take part in meetings and various activities but they do so as followers, at times against their will, against their own convictions. They participate because they are swept along by the crowd around them and feel obligated to take part or at the very least, that they are fulfilling their duty to society.

But fortunately there are people – though few in number – who have an entirely different worldview, an entirely different approach to life and society. Their approach is active, I would say even aggressive. They do not wait until they are called or invited to join an activity for the benefit of their fellow men. They go by themselves and in many cases they themselves create, organize and act. They create the idea, the purpose to which they believe one should devote oneself of one's own free will. And the purpose is for the benefit of their society, because such people look for the welfare of their fellow men first.

Their efforts are driven, at least at the outset, by an inner compulsion to accomplish things without even having a clear rational understanding of their aims. They act because there is a need. They act because something must be done! That is the essence of their being. Only as time goes by does the urge to act crystallize itself into an intellectual and programmatic framework, a worldview, which makes one understand where the initial urge came from.

Mendel Balberyszski, the author of the memoir before us, belongs to this category of people.

From the earliest years – as far as our author's memory goes back – Mendel Balberyszski devotes himself to public service for the benefit of all. He is a social-cultural activist in the best sense of the word, devoting his time and energy to the well-being of his fellow Jews. Back in 1922, while still a university student, Balberyszski stood up to a bunch of hooligans out to start a pogrom in the Jewish quarter of his native Vilna. Balberyszki was beaten but fought back for as long as he could – long enough to give time to other Jewish youth to come out into the street and to prevent the pogrom. He acted that way because he had to react. That urge to react when confronted with injustice to Jews – his own people, his professional colleagues, the small artisans, the small businessmen, the poor – would accompany him throughout his life. He could not do otherwise. It was innate in his psychological makeup.

Over time this life view became a conscious commitment. In times of need and trouble Balberyszski felt it is his duty and responsibility to help the community. As a communal leader he believed he should be among the first to provide help at the least sign of danger or distress. He felt obliged to do all he could for the larger community.

Read the book and you will find numerous examples of such efforts – starting from the peaceful times in Vilna and Lodz before the war, through the years in the Vilna Ghetto and until the last stage in the Klooga Concentration Camp. In times of greatest difficulties the author's thoughts are devoted to the question: and what will happen to my fellow Jews? His healthy understanding of human nature, his love of people and his years of experience and efforts on behalf of the community in normal times guided him in his work. They also stood him in good stead during the inhuman times of the Hitler era.

There were occasions when Balberyszski broke down and let tears roll down his face… No wonder! The Hitler period managed to destroy many strong individuals – but not Balberyszski. He kept his humanity. He kept his morality. He would recover from each crisis and continue his efforts and his life. From the beginning of the horrific period until the end.

After surviving the Holocaust Balberyszski renewed his communal activities in a far corner of the world – Australia. This book is a part of his activities in that distant land and we now pass it on to the reader. The book provides a panoramic view of Jewish life during the final years of the Tsarist regime in Russia, the First World War, independent Poland and Lithuania, through the Third Reich and the end of the Second World War. We see this history through the eyes of a man of the people – he was indeed a leading member in the Jewish Democratic Party (Folkspartei) – a man who can observe and pass on his observations to others. And since the author was not "a private person" but a community leader his observations are not "private" and encompass a much wider scope. We have in front of us a mosaic of Jewish life in Vilna, in Lodz and other townships where the author had intimate connections.

In this memoir we get an insight into the life of a Jewish community leader in what until not so long ago were centers of Jewish culture, Jewish national life, Jewish greatness – that all came to a tragic end.

The memoir also enables us to understand the struggle of an individual for his life, for his beliefs, against enemies who were determined to destroy the Jewish people – his people – and himself.

The book should be read keeping these two points in mind.

FOREWORD

by Dr. Joseph Kermish, *z"l*

The memoirs of Mendel Balberyszski, *Stronger Than Iron*, describe "events as they happened before [my] eyes" during the Second World War, including the two years of German occupation of Vilna. But it is the story of the destruction of Vilna Jewry that dominates the wide-ranging narrative of the book.

The author, a leading communal personality in prewar Poland, always had the courage to tell the truth. As a keen observer he started writing down his observations of events from the early days of the outbreak of the war – as witnessed by his booklet, *My Travels from Lodz to Vilna in 1939*, which he delivered to the Jewish Historic Commission soon after his arrival in Vilna in October 1939. The commission was at that time collecting rare documents and materials about the destruction of Poland and about the early tragic fate of the Jewish population.

The scholarship on Vilna Jewry is meager given the importance of the community. This can be explained, in part, by the fact that the destruction was so thorough that very few survived to bear witness. Those who did made serious efforts to present the story of the "Jerusalem of Lithuania" during the period of the ghetto. But none of these writers gives a complete picture of the destruction of their community. Balberyszski's book fills many of the voids. His book, for example, contains a heartrending and almost unknown chapter about the herding of Vilna Jews into the small ghetto. The small ghetto existed for forty-six days (from September 6 until October 21, 1941), during which time nine thousand Jews were taken to their deaths. Balberyszski is also a crucial eyewitness to the tragic events leading up to the final liquidation of the large ghetto.

Personal grief and suffering did not blunt the sharpness of his memory. *Stronger Than Iron* describes daily routine alongside extraordinary incidents;

it records ghetto life, including the fate of individuals and institutions. But much of the narrative is devoted to the author's thoughts about the fate of his community, about people and their behavior in times of danger. Much space is devoted to his own feelings, not only in terms of his personal suffering but also in terms of the survival of his people. In the darkest days he found words of encouragement and hope.

The author's descriptions bring to life the atmosphere and mood as the barbaric events unfolded. Restraint and integrity create a feeling of confidence in the author, who balances the positive and the negative but gives expression to both. He describes and clarifies a number of negative occurrences – for example, the activity of the Judenrat during the *aktionen* or "cleansings" (as explained above), the decision that Jews would decide who would live and who would die, the trading in lifesaving work permits, the moral degeneration of many members of the Jewish police and the social injustice prevalent in the ghetto.

But the author notes with great satisfaction many instances of Jewish tenacity and spiritual strength. He rejoices at every manifestation of a determination to live, to survive at all costs and under all conditions, inhuman as they may be. He relates the inspiring moments in the cultural activities of the ghetto. "The strength of the bond uniting the Jewish family," writes the author, "the devotion of a husband, a wife and children to each other in those tragic times, was a mass phenomenon."

The extraordinary moral and spiritual resistance of the Jews of the Vilna Ghetto as well as the healthy cultural life in the ghetto gave them the strength to live and not to be broken. This affected any thoughts of armed resistance and resulted in the forests around Vilna, and elsewhere in Lithuania and Byelorussia being filled with hundreds of partisans from the Vilna Ghetto.

The author's description of ghetto life is strengthened by numerous official ghetto documents that describe the organization of ghetto life. During a five-month period (December 1944–May 1945), the author was given access to the ghetto archives of the Vilna State Museum which enabled him to copy original documents of the various ghetto Judenrat departments, including tables describing many aspects of ghetto life. One document details the composition of the ghetto administration and provides information about its various departments and activities, including: the works department and the distribution of the work force; the approval department and food distribution; the public kitchens; the health department, with special emphasis on the sanitary-epidemiological activities; cultural activities, particularly the activities of the library; and historical research. Unfortunately very few documents from the Vilna Ghetto survived. That is why the documents and materials published by the author are of such great importance. An astute reader and researcher will find valuable new materials in this book.

Mendel Balberyszski's book is one of the most important sources for the history of destruction and resistance and a most impressive monument for the "Jerusalem of Lithuania" during the storm of carnage and barbarism that wiped out one of the most influential Jewish centers in the world – a center with seventy-five thousand Jews and priceless cultural treasures.

Preface to the First Edition

My book is entitled *Stronger Than Iron*, for a human being had to be stronger than iron to endure the savage brutality and hatred of the Germans and their Lithuanian helpers, who were determined to implement a policy of the extermination of Vilna Jewry.

One had to be tough as iron to absorb the blows of the "good" German during the slave labor; to survive when the body was swollen from hunger; to overcome disease and lice and to work from dawn till night in rain, snow, blizzards, winds, frost and heat.

One had to be tough as iron not to collapse physically as well as morally when witnessing the pain of an old mother, of one's wife and most importantly of one's little children who all of a sudden, from a beautiful, cultured, materially secure life, were thrown into the abyss of need, confinement, dirt, hunger and horrible suffering.

Yes, it was necessary to be tough as iron to witness the pain and fear of death reflected in the eyes of every family member and especially of the children who were forced, before their time, to comprehend what even adults who had already lived a full life were incapable of understanding.

Yes, to be tough as iron was crucial in order to not to lose one's humanity when witnessing the barbaric destruction of a people.

This is not a history book and certainly not the history of the Hitler era or of the German master plan to eliminate the Jewish people. This book is a look at the tragic events that led to the destruction of the centuries-old Jewish community of Vilna, through the eyes and experiences of a single family. It is my hope that it will provide material for the use of future historians. I write of events as they happened before my eyes in chronological order. I write about day-to-day life in the early days of the German occupation, through the ghettos and the concentration camps until our liberation. I write about what I saw and experienced, and in some cases I recount events that I myself did not witness, but which were described to me by other eyewitnesses

I especially studied and collected official ghetto material I received after the liberation from the Vilna State Museum founded by S. Kaczerginski, of blessed memory, who perished before his time. I copied them in Vilna over the course of five months (December 1944–May 1945). I do not glorify anyone nor memorialize anyone. As the tragic story of the destruction unfolds I express opinions about certain events and record the impressions that certain incidents and actions made on me in those moments.

I had no official position in the ghetto administration and was not an active member of any committee or council. I was thus spared the agonizing moral dilemmas associated with such activities. I had strong convictions that guided me through a lifetime of public service and I hope that they would have helped me make the right decisions in any circumstances. But they were never put to the ultimate test.

It was destiny's will that my wife, our two children and I survived the Holocaust. My mother, Liba (nee Schwartz) was torn away from us, literally in the last moments during the liquidation of the Vilna Ghetto. Apparently, she was killed in Majdanek. My brother and his family were murdered in Ivye (Byelorussia). One sister, Sara Margovitzky and her family, were killed in Taganrog (Soviet Union); a second sister, Braina Posner, and her family were killed in Lepel (Byelorussia). All the members of my wife's family also perished: her brother, Aba Ashkenazi and his family, in Utian (Lithuania); her sister, Chana Levin with her husband and son, in Kovno (Lithuania). The family of my brother-in-law, Yerachmiel Rachmilewicz, also perished. My aunt Rivka Schwartz, my cousin Dora Papp and her husband Dr. Leon Papp, my cousin's daughter Shoshanna Kulbis and the families of my Aunt Zawel, all fell victim to the Germans and their henchmen.

This book honors the memory of my friends and mentors Dr. Jacob Wigocky, Dr. Grigori Gierszuni, Professor Noah Prylucki, and Advocate Yoseph Wietsman. They dedicated their lives to the service of the Jewish people and perished during the German occupation of Vilna.

May this book be a living memory to the six million brothers and sisters who perished at the hands of the murderous German nation and their allies. Honor to their memory!

Mendel Balberyszski
Melbourne, Australia
February 1966

PART ONE

Germany Invades the Soviet Union

CHAPTER 1

The First Two Days

On Sunday morning, June 22, 1941, the German army crossed the northern frontier of Lithuania in a sudden attack on the Soviet Union. Within hours German tanks crossed the river Nieman and advanced at full speed toward Vilna. On that morning several of my colleagues and I were in our pharmacy taking advantage of the peace and quiet of a Sunday to catch up with some work. We were totally unaware of the morning's developments and paid little attention to the air-raid sirens that were heard around ten in the morning and the distant explosion sounds that came soon afterwards. We ascribed them to military exercises that were common in those days and continued with our work. Suddenly a young man, clearly very agitated, entered the pharmacy and interrupted our work. He asked for some bandages, adding that he hoped our stock of bandages was large enough.

"Large enough for what?" I asked, rather surprised by the comment.

"Haven't you heard?" he asked. "We are at war! Earlier this morning the Germans invaded the Soviet Union. Listen to the radio – Molotov is about to speak."

I felt as if a heavy stone were falling on my heart. Once we heard the Soviet Foreign Minister Molotov confirming the stranger's words I realized that we were about to witness a new disaster. It became clear that we were in a new war with the enemy we had managed to escape a short time earlier.

Throughout the morning, one by one, my colleagues left to join their families and I was left alone.

A torrent of thoughts raced through my mind, bringing me back to September 1939. My family and I were living at that time in Lodz, Poland, where we had moved from Vilna in the late 1920s. I had accepted a position as director of pharmacies for a health fund in the Lodz district, continued my communal activities in a number of Jewish social and political organizations and with my wife and two little children settled into a comfortable middle-class life in a vibrant Jewish community. This all came crashing down on September 1, 1939, when Germany declared war on Poland and German troops crossed the Polish border. I knew, of course, what to expect from German occupation. For several years prior to the outbreak of the war I headed a Jewish organization, Notein Lehem, a social welfare organization which provided support and assistance to thousands of Jewish refugees who were expelled from Germany by the Nazi regime. From them we learned of the anti-Jewish edicts, of persecution, of humiliation and of the executions. I was also very outspoken in public forums and in the press, speaking and writing against Nazi Germany and calling for coordinated actions to oppose it. I was under no illusion, therefore, as to my fate when the Germans would occupy Lodz.

Many Jews decided to leave Lodz immediately by whatever means of transportation they could find. When within a day or two there was no transportation available thousands went on foot, headed eastward. The German advance toward Lodz was rapid and it was a matter of days before they occupied the city. I had little time left and a decision had to be made: to stay with my family in Lodz or to join the thousands walking eastward in an attempt to reach my native Vilna. If I were to stay in Lodz my fate would be sealed. If I managed to get to Vilna, I could use all the high-level contacts I had developed over several decades with the Lithuanian authorities (Vilna had become part of the independent state of Lithuania) to find a way of getting my family out of Poland. I remember the heartrending discussions with my wife, and the tears of my children as I stood with a little suitcase in my hand, hugging and kissing them goodbye on the night of September 6, 1939. *Will we ever see each other again?* was the unspoken thought in everybody's mind.

But miracles do happen! It took me twenty-four days of grueling hardship, harrowing experiences and many escapes from death by German bombs and bloodthirsty anti-Semites to reach Vilna. (The events of those twenty-four days were described in a booklet, *My Travels from Lodz to Vilna in 1939*, submitted to the Vilna Historical Commission.) It took another two months of relentless and vigorous activity to obtain the documents that would allow my wife and children to leave Poland and travel to Lithuania. On December 30, 1939, we were reunited at the Kovno railway station.

And now, less than two years later, the nightmare was repeating itself! The scenes we saw in Lodz at the outbreak of the Second World War were again before our eyes in Vilna. Streams of frightened people, mostly Jews, were leaving the city moving eastward. I stopped one man and asked where he was going but got no answer. The same with the second one. No one knew where to go except for a vague idea of wanting to go east.

I left the pharmacy and went home. We knew by now that the Germans were advancing rapidly and it wouldn't be long before they arrived in Vilna. Once again we were faced with the question: to run or not to run? To run meant leaving Vilna, where our family had lived for generations. To run with a wife, two children and an old mother? Not long ago we had run from Lodz and with extreme luck managed to get to Vilna, settle in and start our life again – and now to leave it all and run? Our minds were in turmoil, things were chaotic and we could not decide. I decided to seek out the advice of my dear friend and mentor, Professor Noah Prylucki. I had met Professor Prylucki while studying in Warsaw and had been greatly impressed by his erudition, depth of knowledge, personal warmth and deep commitment to the well-being of the Jewish people. We became close friends and for years his home was my second home.

I found Noah Prylucki's household in the same disarray as my own. "Noah, what should we do?" I asked. His wife Paulina replied for him: "Mendele, we must run immediately. Noah should not remain here a second longer. They will tear him to pieces." Prylucki himself was calm and composed: "With the first bomb that Hitler dropped on the Soviet Union he dug his own grave. His end will come swiftly, a very dark end." I insisted: "Yes, but what should we do now, for the moment?" "For the moment," he replied, "I am waiting for a group of writers and we will run together."

*   *   *

Professor Noah Prylucki was one of the preeminent Jewish intellectuals in pre-war Poland. Born in Berdichev in 1887, he grew up in Kremenets and Warsaw. He completed studies in jurisprudence at Warsaw University and became a distinguished literary critic, linguist and expert on Yiddish and its various dialects. He was one of the founders of YIVO, the Jewish Scientific Institute, and together with his father, Zvi Hirsh Prylucki, they founded the Jewish newspaper *Der Moment*, of which he became the chief editor. In 1916 Prylucki founded the Jewish Folkspartei (known also as the Jewish Democratic Party), which was based on ideas developed by the great Jewish historian Simon Dubnov. The Folkspartei became in time the home for small Jewish businessmen, artisans and intelligentsia and in elections to the Polish parliament (the *Sejm*) in November, 1922, Prylucki was elected as a representative of the Folkspartei.

With the outbreak of the Second World War in 1939, Prylucki and his wife Paulina left Warsaw and managed to reach Vilna. In Vilna, with the support of the Joint Distribution Committee, he immediately organized the Jewish Historical Commission, to which he invited a number of Jewish writers and journalists. The objective of the commission was to document the events following the German invasion of Poland and the exodus of Jewish refugees. When Vilna became part of the Soviet Lithuanian Republic, Prylucki was appointed Professor of Yiddish Literature at Vilna State University, a position he held until the arrival of the Germans.

Soon after the occupation of Vilna, German as well as Lithuanian authorities began to take a personal interest in Noah Prylucki. One July morning, two Lithuanians came to his home demanding that he give up his radio – which, incidentally, was a gift he had received from my brother-in-law. His wife Paulina said she would immediately send the radio, a large, box-shaped machine, with the building caretaker. "Not good enough," replied the Lithuanian official. "Right now, no delay!" "Well, please come with me," said Paulina. "I will take it myself; the professor is ill and weak and cannot walk very well." The Lithuanians would not accept that. "No, the professor has to come with us and carry the radio." They rejected any further suggestions Paulina made. Prylucki had to leave the house and walk with them, carrying the radio. Along the way the Lithuanians "enjoyed" themselves and callously tormented the sick man. He arrived back home more dead than alive, but Paulina was relieved to see him return at all.

At that time, July 1941, a new German specialist arrived in Vilna. He was Dr. Pohl from the Institute for the Study of the Jewish Question, established by Alfred Rosenberg, Hitler's Reichsminister for Eastern Territories, in Frankfurt-am-Main. The objective of the institute was to study "the vanished Jewish Race." Dr. Pohl knew Yiddish and Hebrew well. He had attended the Hebrew University in Jerusalem and published several texts dealing with the Talmud. He came now as an expert to assess Jewish cultural treasures collected over centuries in the "Lithuanian Jerusalem," i.e., Vilna. The treasures had of course become "German property" and the German specialist came to plunder the vast Jewish libraries and art collections and to decide what would be sent back to the institute and what would be destroyed.

He started with YIVO, the prestigious Jewish Scientific Institute. Noah Prylucki was brought to YIVO under guard, where the German doctor already waited for him in "his" office. Dr. Pohl demanded that Prylucki prepare a complete list of all unique and unusual documents available in the YIVO libraries. To carry out this work, Prylucki was brought under guard every morning and taken back under guard every evening. I visited Paulina a few times during that period and each time she expressed her anxiety over the close relations between her husband and Dr. Pohl. She had a premonition that the relations between the two would not end well; her premonitions were unfortunately fulfilled.

One evening Prylucki didn't come home from YIVO. The next morning Paulina made anxious inquiries about the whereabouts of her husband and was told that he had been taken to spend the night at the Gestapo and would be accommodated there until he finished his work. Paulina was permitted to see him at YIVO and to bring him food and clean clothes. This went on for several days, until one morning when Paulina came and was told the professor no longer came to YIVO to do his work.

Various rumors began spreading within the community. One rumor was that he had been taken to the Alfred Rosenberg Institute Headquarters to continue his scientific work. However the truth was sadly different. A prisoner released from the Lukishki prison had seen Prylucki in jail badly beaten up. Prylucki was lying on the floor of the cell with a bloody head bandaged with a rag that looked like a piece of a torn shirt.

In December 1947 I read an item that appeared in a foreign Jewish newspaper which said: "The Polish Court in Pomerania has sentenced to death the Pole Konstantyn Gajzewski, a coworker of the Gestapo in Vilna. He was found guilty of having murdered members of the Jewish Scientific Institute YIVO. One of his victims was the famous Yiddish writer Noah Prylucki."

Years later, on March 18, 1965, the Warsaw Yiddish paper, *Folks sztyme* (Peoples' voice), no. 43, published some information and documents found in Vilna about Noah Prylucki. Among the documents was a "Prylucki File, Act 1–2," dated July 1, 1941. It stated that all Jewish members of the Vilna University were relieved of their positions retroactively to June 22. "The order was signed," read the notice, "by the rector Mikolai Birzyszko, who as a Lithuanian Nationalist bourgeois began serving the murderous occupiers of Lithuania." In the file there was a notice of Prylucki's professorial title, given to him by Vilna University. The title document had been crossed out with two red lines to cancel its validity. Beside it was a hardboard paper yellowed with age – his registration for the Gestapo work. He fell into their hands on July 28. In the line "released" was a cynical notation in ink: "Liquidated on

August 12, 1941, 'Unterstumfuehrer' Polenzieven." The "case handler" of "Case Prylucki" had personally sent the great man to his death.

This is how Noah Prylucki, one of the most prominent personalities of Polish Jewry, distinguished writer and linguist, a man who dedicated his life to the well-being of his people, admired for his calm wisdom, came to end his life in the hands of German murderers and their local accomplices.

Besides Prylucki, Pohl "engaged" a large group of Jewish scholars and other personalities for the work in YIVO, including the writer and journalist Zelig Kalmanowicz and the librarian Herman Kruk. Their work was to collect and catalog books, manuscripts and works of art from Jewish libraries, museums and private homes. Whatever Pohl considered to be unique and valuable was to be crated and sent to the Rosenberg Institute – the rest was to be destroyed. On occasion, Jewish workers hid priceless, irreplaceable documents and books and smuggled them into the ghetto for the ghetto archives and the museum that came into existence after the war.

Prylucki's wife Paulina came to a similarly tragic end. She was forced into the large ghetto on September 6. She managed to take a few minor things that her failing health enabled her to carry. She had already sent her husband's major works, together with some domestic items such as furniture and tableware to their Lithuanian friends to protect them for the future. What she brought to the ghetto was of very little practical value. She became immediately destitute. At that time I was living in the small ghetto. During the six weeks that the small ghetto existed I looked out for Paulina and managed to see her twice. She complained bitterly about her loneliness, her living conditions and the inhuman treatment from her neighbors. She was particularly bitter about the younger writers who had once been her husband's students. They ignored her and left her destitute without means for daily survival. Both times I saw her I left her some money; after my second visit, I never saw her again.

When we managed to save ourselves from being herded to Ponary at the liquidation of the small ghetto and reached the large ghetto I learned of the sad end of Paulina, a woman who was a unique personality in her own right.

A few days after the small ghetto was liquidated and stood empty, the Judenrat of the large ghetto announced that anyone who wanted to could move over to the liquidated ghetto and receive comfortable accommodation there. Those who took up the offer would be permitted to take over the items left by the people who had been removed. Many Jews accepted the offer and went to the small ghetto. It was not surprising. At the time we were all completely disoriented and resigned and hardly knew what we did or why we decided on anything. Many went voluntarily, among them a few well-known members of the prewar community.

The Jewish police of the large ghetto wanted to get rid of what they termed "illegal Jews" – Jews who had no valid work permit. They were particularly interested in eliminating the older and sick people living in the provisional old-age home. The Jewish police of the large ghetto forced out old and lonely people who had no one to save them. Among those driven out to the small ghetto was Paulina. To drive back Jews to the small ghetto after its liquidation was one of the many cynical exercises of the Judenrat in the large ghetto. As soon as the population in the small ghetto was once more large enough for the Gestapo to become interested, they arrived and with whips and dogs dispatched the whole population to Ponary.

Shortly before this happened the people of the small ghetto realized that they had been tricked. They sent notes to the large ghetto to friends to help them return but it was of no use. There was no way back. Paulina also sent pleading notes, which I have not seen but was told about. But there was no one interested in her fate.

Within two months of the German occupation of Vilna the famous Prylucki family had ceased to exist.

I returned home with no decision. At dusk there was a second air raid and a bomb landed on the house across from us. In panic we ran out of our apartment and took the children down to the caretaker of the building who had his dwelling in the basement, which was now considered to be safer than our own apartment. While all this was taking place, overloaded trains kept leaving eastward with masses of people desperate to flee. By late evening the whole town was in turmoil. Offices began to evacuate their employees. Autos were nearly unavailable. Despair took hold of us as we saw disaster right before us and no way to escape.

The next few hours brought additional bad news. The situation grew far worse – beyond our own black fantasies. As time passed, the air raids became more intense and the darkness of the night was cut with rays of light reaching endlessly toward the dark skies. After each movement of the search lights came new explosions with more fatalities and victims. Confusion and chaos reigned throughout that terrible night.

The tenants of our building congregated in the yard and kept together. The disaster united Jews and non-Jews. For the moment no one gave a thought about tomorrow. A single thought invaded our brains: to survive the air raids.

We put all the children for the night in the caretaker's basement while we remained in the yard and reached all kinds of conclusions about what lay ahead of us. The Jewish neighbors were no longer ready to run and I was dead tired. "Whatever will be will be," I said as I left the yard and went to bed.

At dawn the air raids started once more, accompanied now by ominous news that the German army had already crashed through the Soviet forces and were marching forward at high speed. We tried very hard not to believe the dark rumors, but when we saw the panic and the speed with which officialdom began to evacuate the city our hopes kept draining away. From the experience of 1939 we already knew that running away was useless without some mechanical means of transport.

Despite the situation, in the morning I left for my pharmacy. The whole length of the road was full of wanderers but a change had taken place overnight. On the first day the marching throngs were peaceful and only slightly restless but now, on Monday morning, a change took place that made the blood run cold, particularly among the Jews. The Lithuanians began coming out onto the streets and stopping retreating Soviet soldiers. There were now Lithuanians shooting at the retreating soldiers and torturing the families that soldiers left behind.

The impudence of the Lithuanians on the second day of the war, their attacks on the Red Army and the way they had already started to plunder the abandoned dwellings told us that the situation was hopeless; the front was crumbling.

As the hours passed, the barbarity of the Lithuanians grew. They began to show their beastly faces. They now stopped the carts carrying Soviet families and beat or killed helpless women and children. The same Lithuanians who a week earlier had sung praises to the "liberators" and their "good friends," as they used to call the Bolsheviks, now took revenge for their "fatherland." During the morning the Lithuanians became unruly and aggressive to the point of threatening a general pogrom. By midday the streets suddenly became empty and a dead silence fell over the roads that had earlier been filled with chaos and confusion.

In the meantime, wild scenes took place at the railway station and around the bus terminals that were still partly under government supervision. Flooded with people attempting to save themselves from the approaching hell, the fists of the strong dictated who would be able to leave. Knowing what they could expect from the Germans the younger Jews in particular rushed to escape. Seeing no hope of gaining access to any means of transport, thousands of them began fleeing on foot toward Minsk.

Around dusk the bombardment stopped. We didn't know what this meant but we kept to our rooms. Looking carefully out into the street we saw Lithuanians who seemed to have surrounded some central streets. The streets were eerily silent.

Out of the silence we suddenly heard loud shouts. We moved carefully toward the window and began to follow what was going on. The windows of our apartment faced Wielka Street, a major thoroughfare in the center of the city. As far as we could see, the street was totally empty. But from the city hall a few Lithuanians started to appear with belts and white cloth in their hands. Soon they were a group of fifteen or twenty and assembled themselves into a column. When the formation was completed they began raising their white cloth and shouted out in as if in victory: "*Valia, valia* (Long live, long live)!" The cry paralyzed us; we remained glued to our places.

It was not long before we heard the sound of approaching motorcycles. They sped by in front of our window like demons. Two soldiers rode on each motorcycle. One was driving while the other held his machine gun at the ready to shoot. They were followed by tanks draped in huge red covers with white circles in the center that prominently displayed the black swastika. The artillery was not far behind and heavy trucks with soldiers closed the procession. The soldiers and, even more so the officers, had a smug, arrogant expression on their faces. They were welcomed by scores of Lithuanians who greeted them with enthusiastic shouts of jubilation.

We remained at the window, watching the endless military columns. At last, tired and frightened, we left our lookout posts, each of us retreating to a different corner. After coming back to our senses we summarized the situation: only yesterday the war started and today the Germans had already reached our city. Such a swift collapse of the Soviet Army was something that no one could have foreseen.

Our talk was futile, totally useless. We knew we were standing before a reality that had only one meaning. We had fallen into the claws of the beast. Would we be able to escape? The only comfort we derived was that at least this time our family was together, not torn apart as it had been in Lodz in 1939. There was an additional ray of comfort: a sister and brother-in-law were on the other side. What an irony of life! Only eight days earlier NKVD agents had arrived at our house in the middle of the night and rounded up my sister, brother-in-law and their little daughter, given them an hour or so to pack up their belongings, herded them into trucks and deported them deep into the Russian interior. Their crime was being "an anti-Soviet element"! During the two days of June 14 and 15, 1941, some five thousand Jews met the same fate. Communist cruelty thus saved them from the horrors of Nazi occupation.

Pain, apprehension and fear accompanied us unseen through the unlit rooms, as we looked from time to time at the mob outside. The endless parade of the German army was continuing with tanks, field guns, motorcycles and trucks, all mechanized. Not a single foot soldier was to be seen. Buried under our other fears lay our worry over the fate of my brother and his family in Ivye and the fate of my wife's family in Lithuania. The greatest worrier among us was my mother, her eyes sore from constant crying. She cried over everybody and everything. *What will happen tomorrow? What about Lodz, Poland, Lithuania? Has it all reached the end?* A new chapter in our life was approaching.

A brutal period, the cruelty of which the world had never seen the like of before, was beginning. All our notions about evil, suffering, brutality, human hate, pain and sadism, all our understandings about the greatest and most shocking fate that can befall humanity were to pale and count for nothing compared to what we were to go through in the next three years.

As I write these lines three years after liberation, I can begin to clarify many details that we did not know at the time. However one detail remains in my mind as an unsolved riddle, a puzzle beyond understanding! Where did we get the energy to remain alive throughout our years of torturous suffering? And how did living human beings manage to awaken in themselves those wild instincts of sadism, to endlessly torture and murder other human beings the way the Germans and their many collaborators of other nationalities did while performing their "ideological" mission?

The Hitler period sealed the fate of some seventy thousand Jews in Vilna, a large portion of them refugees from other parts of Poland who had sought sanctuary there. The period lasted from June 24, 1941, till July 13, 1944. By the most optimistic assessment only one thousand Jews survived. Those who appeared in Vilna after the war – two thousand to twenty-five hundred in total – were returnees from the Soviet Union. They had to be thankful that just a week before the Germans attacked Russia they had been deported deep into the Soviet Union.

The Lithuanian killers, encouraged and supported by the German chief murderers and their trained killer dogs, within a period of three years destroyed not only the Jews of Vilna but also all the entire Jewish population of Lithuania.

It is difficult to understand the Lithuanian cordiality and the warm welcome they extended the occupying Germans. It may be true that they carried a deep-seated animosity toward the Soviet Union. But all things considered the Lithuanians had lived reasonably well during the Soviet period. They had little reason to greet the Germans with such great joy. They achieved nothing from the German occupation – not liberation, and certainly not independence. Yet they were the only nationality in Vilna that greeted the Germans with jubilation.

With deep restless thoughts, in total silence, each of us moved to a different corner of the dark apartment. We fell on our beds awaiting the first morning under German rule.

CHAPTER 2

Conditions under the German-Lithuanian Administration

The Anti-Jewish Regimen Begins

On Tuesday, June 24, 1941, Vilna was a ghost town. Streets were empty and the few individuals who dared to go out moved about aimlessly, going nowhere. There seemed to be no authority. Everything was closed and locked; everybody remained at home waiting for some unknown development.

The day was dramatically different from the previous two days. All day Sunday and on Monday morning a vast number of people – the majority young Jews, government officials and Soviet soldiers with or without their families – had filled the streets and used all their energies to find places in any means of transportation leaving the city eastward in the direction of Minsk. The majority however had had neither the power nor the good fortune to find any transport and had been forced to flee toward the prewar Soviet border on foot. Now, on the third day, Vilna was under German occupation and strangely calm.

Sometime during the third day we received news from unknown sources that heavy fighting was taking place around Kovno and other parts of Lithuania and that Kovno was still not in German hands.

In spite of the strange calm, I decided to go to the pharmacy as usual. The streets were empty of civilians but flooded with German military might. In the pharmacy I met my Jewish coworker Miron and a few non-Jewish colleagues. The cashier, Shlisim, a Lithuanian, did not show up and there was little work done that day.

Shlisim came the next day to inform me that he resigned from his position since he had signed up to join the newly organized Lithuanian police force, to be known as the Militia. In answer to my question why he, a peaceful man, had of all things decided to join the Militia in such a turbulent time he replied that he could hardly make a living on the salary in the pharmacy and the Militia had offered him unusually good conditions and opportunities.

We closed the pharmacy to the public and remained open only for emergencies. We spent our time talking over and over the new situation. I used some of the free time to visit the Kantorowicz family, the prewar owners of the pharmacy, which the Soviets had nationalized; they had been allowed to remain in part of their apartment. The family consisted of an old mother, her married daughter and son-in-law Maks Kantorowicz and their two children.

I also dared to visit Noah Prylucki. I found him and his wife engaged in burning stacks of papers in their kitchen. The material he was feeding to the flames consisted of very precious and valuable historical records he had collected in the course of his work for the Historical Commission since he arrived in Vilna less than two years ago. He had started the collection with the help of the Joint Distribution Committee Directors Giterman and Bekelman. With their help he had created the Historical Commission, to which he recruited writers from Vilna and many prewar members of the famous Jewish Writers and Journalists Club of Warsaw. Most writers had described their experiences of the first weeks and months of the war. Beside the vast amount of material that the Pryluckis were now feeding to the oven (concerning the destruction of Poland and the tragedies of Jews during the first weeks of the German occupation), they were also consigning to destruction an irreplaceable treasure of folkloristic work. Among the documents destroyed on that day were published Soviet orders to the people in the part of Poland that they had taken over by dividing Poland between the Soviet Union and Germany; collections of the first yellow Stars of David and white armbands ordered to be worn by Jews under German occupation; some saved Jewish religious relics that had been received; and Nazi German publications.

The Pryluckis also had to get rid of a large number of Soviet books they had managed to collect since arriving in Vilna. For obvious reasons, there was no time to hide them. Nobody pretended   Noah Prylucki's status as a famous and important Jewish personality would not be known. While feeding the flames, Prylucki told me that on Monday a number of young Jewish writers came to him and asked him to join them on the way out of Vilna. They had no transport. "Well, I ask you," he said in his calm way, "how far would I and Pauline have managed to reach on foot? Obviously it was ordained right from the beginning…"

The future was soon to show how justified his words were. To move out of Vilna on foot had been mostly useless and mindless. Many did not get far before they had no longer any need to run – with the compliments of the German death machine they remained close to where they had started…

After leaving the Pryluckis I managed, with some risk, to visit also my friend Dr. Wygocki. Dr. Jacob Wygocki was a Zionist and a venerable personality in the Jewish leadership of Vilna, acting as head of the Jewish Council of Vilna. The elderly man told me hair-raising stories about what he and his wife had gone through during the last few days. His daughter, Mme. Burstein, a well-known Soviet writer, and her adult daughter, an artistic director of the famous Berioska Soviet dance ensemble, had come from Moscow on a visit to Vilna a month earlier. They were well known in the Vilna artistic establishment and had come to collect the necessary papers to bring their elderly parents to Moscow. The idea of taking their parents to Moscow was not new and the doctor himself was not against it; he only always asked, "what's the hurry." When pressed to say why he delayed the move he used to say: "It is not so easy for me to say goodbye to Vilna where I have spent a considerable number of years of my life."

Dr. Wygocki had mentioned a few times that he would use his time in Moscow to persuade the Soviet decision makers to change their opinion about Zionism. "I am thinking of writing a memorandum on the matter," he said. "I will try to convey it to Stalin. They have to recognize Zionism and to support the idea. Zionism is absolutely not against the interests of the Soviet Union… On the contrary, the Soviet Union should help us Zionists." Of course, he always remembered to add, "the matter has to be handled diplomatically, without the help of the Jewish 'advisers' in Moscow."

It is worth noting that these conversations took place in 1941. During each conversation the doctor was self-assured and fully convinced of his argument.

At times he gave me the impression that at any moment he would sit down and write his memorandum. Later, in 1947, when the Soviet diplomats began their pro-Zionist declarations in international forums and became strong supporters of Zionist aspirations I recalled the words of the wise doctor.

When I visited the Wygockis once more a few days later the doctor told me that his next-door neighbor was taken away after a thorough search of his house. "Having seen that," the doctor said, "I have destroyed the book I had written about the fourth partition of Poland. In my present state of health I don't think I would survive German imprisonment. I had written about them the way they deserved to be presented and they certainly would not like it."

My visits to Professor Prylucki and Dr. Wygocki only increased my concerns, and the successive days brought additional terrible news. Within days the majority of those who had left Vilna on foot began to return, bringing horror stories of their experiences at the prewar border of the Soviet Union. After suffering the torments of the mass exodus on the road – constant air attacks, hunger and thirst – they were not allowed to enter the Soviet Union proper. By the time they gave up trying and decided to make their way back home they found themselves cut off by the advancing German armies. A considerable number of returnees who fell into the hands of the German murderers were dealt with the German way – with the bullet.

Those who managed to avoid death passed through seven portals of hell before they reached Vilna again. Only a small number managed to break through and enter the Soviet Union proper; at least for the moment they were safe. At the border crossing Soviet passports and communist party identifications issued in Vilna were useless and ignored. The Soviet Union was too afraid of spies infiltrating their borders to allow entry to individuals from a country with which they were at war.

Following their occupation of the city, the Germans formed a joint German-Lithuanian Administration and left the management of Vilna in the hands of the Lithuanian Vilna City Committee, led by Professor S. Zakievicius. His committee had already organized its own militia. All shops remained closed except food stores and bakeries. This caused long queues at those shops that were open and provided the first signs of what we Jews could expect. It was not a good omen. The overexcited, "liberated" Lithuanians started throwing Jews out of the queues. However, as most Jews had no food reserves in their homes they were forced to risk and repeat the same thing day after day – to join the queue in the hope of obtaining the minimum. Often, Jewish queue joiners returned home not with bread or food but with tears, hunger and deep humiliation. In many cases the Poles suffered the same fate. Our family suffered less in this respect than others. My non-Jewish colleagues prepared food parcels at the pharmacy for me and my family. When it became unsafe for me to carry the parcels in the street, my colleagues brought the prepared parcels to our home.

At the same time new rumors began swirling in Jewish circles. Jews were apparently being taken off the streets and led away to some unknown destination. Within days the rumors intensified. It was said that those taken off the street were taken "to work." But nobody knew to what kind of work or how long this work was going to last, or anything else about those who had suddenly disappeared. The situation became more strained from day to day. The knowledge that Jews were being taken off the street caused panic in Jewish homes.

Within less than a week since the war had started we found out that all Jewish medical staff had been fired from hospitals, ambulances and all other medical institutions. Rumors about the future also reached us pharmacists. One early morning my friend, Dr. Tenenbaum, appeared in the pharmacy with a rucksack on his back, accompanied by his son. He greeted me by saying: "I was thrown out of the hospital where I had been working. I'm afraid to remain in the city. We're going to people we know who own land outside the town; we believe there it will be more peaceful. We came to say goodbye." We embraced and said goodbye – forever.

The rumors that the Jewish pharmacists would also share the fate of the medical staff became a reality. The general manager of our district, my colleague Adler (originally from Minsk, he lost his life in the ghetto at an early stage) was replaced by a mediocre Lithuanian pharmacist by the name of Narbut. As soon as Narbut took over I received an order to hand over the pharmacy to my

Lithuanian colleague Balkowski, who became director in my place. Another order followed within hours that all Jewish pharmacists were to be relieved of their positions from the first of July. Colleague Balkowski excused himself, telling us that it had all been arranged behind his back and without his knowledge. Miron and the other Jewish pharmacist, Reintjun, no longer came to work on the stated day. The same order was received at all pharmacies in Vilna and pertained to medical bulk stores as well as to individual pharmacies; no Jewish workers were any longer allowed in the pharmaceutical industry. I was the only exception and was asked to remain for an additional three days in order to hand over the inventory and stock to the chosen Lithuanian. Within a matter of a few days all Jewish medical and pharmaceutical personnel became unemployed.

Initially, I did not take it too seriously. "What does it all mean?" I debated with myself. "How long can Vilna last without the few hundred Jewish doctors, pharmacists and Jewish nurses? And, in general, how will the city go on without the Jewish working element?" I was convinced, or was trying hard to convince myself, that in a short time the authorities would change their attitude. "They will send for us in the end," was the thought of many.

By the hour the situation in town became more insecure; people began to seriously worry about those who were taken off the street and – disappeared. On top of this worry came the constant torturing news of German victories along the whole length of the Russian front. The fatal news was the last nail in the coffin of our hopes. The news cut into our psyche as if it were cutting into our flesh. Those who had not managed to reach Minsk kept returning daily in small groups, bringing more frightening stories about the growing lawlessness of the Lithuanians. The situation became desperate. We started praying for the moment when a German administration would take over, no matter what its character, so that there would be an end to Lithuanian anarchy.

I couldn't stay in the house. I couldn't take being locked up, inactive, within the four walls. I got in touch with Dr. Wygocki and Noah Prylucki and on their advice I began to seek ways to make some contact with the Lithuanians. The most difficult part was going outside, to take the risk of venturing out into the street.

My first visit was supposed to be to the rector of the Vilna University, Professor Mikolai Birzyszko, an old Lithuanian liberal activist and a personal friend of mine. He was now living in a new house in a new street in the Buffalo Hills. It was quite a long way from where we lived.

On a Sunday morning I decided to go to see the rector. I reasoned that at that time the Lithuanian dogcatchers, who were now hunting for humans, would not be in the street. To my disappointment the rector was not at home. His wife Bronislava came to the door. She did not offer me her hand in greeting nor did she invite me to enter. Standing in the doorway she asked with a touch of coldness in her voice why I had come and what it was that I wanted.

The manner of her greeting disturbed my prepared thoughts. Was this the same woman who only a year and a half ago did much to save my wife and two children from Hitler's claws? She herself also had a personal reason to be grateful to me for some medical assistance that I rendered her in the past. Yet this was her way of receiving me?

Apparently she noticed my confusion and in a calmer voice repeated her question asking why I came at such an improper moment. "I came on the advice of Dr. Wygocki and Professor Prylucki to speak with the rector about our present situation," I said as calmly as I could manage.

"The rector is not at home," she replied, "and about your situation, well… what is there to say. It is very bad and it will be even worse. What is happening now can be considered child's play compared to what you may expect."

I managed to regain some of my composure during the few seconds of her talk.

"We know," I said, "what we may expect from the Germans. But in the meantime all our troubles come not from the Germans but from the Lithuanians. They pull Jewish women out of the queues at the bread and food distributions. It is Lithuanians and not Germans who take Jewish people off the street and we don't know what happens to them. Lithuanians and not Germans enter Jewish homes to plunder and steal under the pretext of making searches and seeking Bolsheviks. All this is taking place through your Lithuanian Committee. It is they who give all the orders – "

She interrupted me: "Our Lithuanian Committee bears no blame in all that goes on. These are the orders of the Germans and we have to execute them. The chairman of the Lithuanian Committee is Professor Zakevicius, my son-in-law. He is a decent man and a liberal…"

That Professor Stasys Zakevicius was her son-in-law was news to me; it encouraged me: "If this is the case, you surely could try to influence him to execute the German orders less brutally, even to mitigate them a little."

"Oh, no," she replied with a certain finality. "We cannot do anything in your case; everything is done according to the order of the Germans. By the way, you Jews deserve what you are getting. You were not satisfied with the buttered rolls you were getting from us Lithuanians. You considered life wasn't good enough in Lithuania. You ran to welcome the Red Army with open arms. We well remember your large manifestations in Kovno and in Vilna. We remember very well your provocation in Vilna. The way you tore down the Lithuanian National Emblem from the front of the magistrate in Vilna. No, we cannot intervene. It is bad and it will be much worse… No, for all Jews we will not intervene, however if anything bad should happen to Dr. Wygocki, for him we would go to the end of the world."

Neither of us noticed how we came to be sitting and talking at the small table outside the door. I told her that we had all been thrown out of work and I no longer worked at the pharmacy where I had been commissar and administrator. "You see," she came back quickly, "you too were a commissar."

"Yes," I said, "but wasn't your husband a commissar at the university?"

We ended our conversation in a more relaxed way. She asked me for some medications for her daughter that she was unable to obtain. I promised to do my best to see that she would get it through my Polish colleagues. I fulfilled my promise a few days later.

With a disturbed mind and heavy heart I left. Cautiously I reached the house of Dr. Wygocki. I recounted the details of our conversation. His reaction was significant: "If *she* speaks like that, if people to whom Jews have shown so much humanitarian goodwill when they were in serious need speak like this, it is bad, very bad."

With the same cautiousness I reached also Noah Prylucki. My report made a devastating impression on him. "Bitter, bitter," he said. "The conversation should be written down and kept somewhere hidden." The anarchy in the town grew. Jewish homes were plundered by Lithuanians, passing Germans, as well as ordinary robbers who all took advantage of the "temporary situation." This was the condition in Vilna until Friday, July 4.

Conditions Worsen

On June 25, 1941, the Vilna City Committee published notices stating: "To ensure peace and order in the city sixty Jews and twenty Poles were taken hostage. Communists, youth that belonged to Communist organizations, past Russian and/or Polish soldiers and officers should present themselves immediately at the police headquarters of the city." More hostages would be taken, promised the notice, if the administration's orders were not obeyed. It is worth noting that the sixty Jewish hostages were chosen randomly, from various groups of the population. Among those taken out of their beds by force in the middle of the night were many ordinary people, workers and employees who had no special involvement in communal life.

On July 4,1941, another notice was issued by the city committee of Vilna. It ordered all Jews, irrespective of age, to wear prominently displayed on the chest and on the back, a badge that was a ten-centimeter square, white cloth with a yellow circle in the middle. In the center of the yellow circle the letter *J* had to be clearly marked. A sample of the design was displayed at the police stations. The notice also stated that all Jews were to be permitted to be on the streets only between 6:00 a.m. and 6:00 p.m.

Our home immediately became the manufacturing center of the yellow badge for all the neighbors in the building. We produced the "royal decor" from our yellow window curtains. With the required decoration on my summer suit I ventured out during the legal Jewish hours to the pharmacy on Niemiecka Street (the pharmacy had previously been the property of the Szpar family) to visit my non-Jewish colleagues.

My Polish colleagues comforted me that having to wear such a rag should not be considered an embarrassment. "Let those who have invented the sign be the ones to be embarrassed but not the ones who are forced to wear it."

Jews adhered strictly to the order, but nevertheless many fell victim to it. They were arrested under many pretexts: the white piece has not been attached properly; the badge was not clean; its size did not conform to the specifications of the decree, etc. A considerable number of Jews paid with their lives for "disobeying the instructions."

Within a short time the order for the Jew-badge became the source of all misery for Jews under Hitler that lasted till the very end, until the German defeat. The original decree was modified a few times in various places and ways before it became finally set in its unified appearance. But the German intention was always the same – to torment the Jews; to torture them mentally as well as physically.

The original order for the Jews of Vilna lasted only a few days. The new German Commander Zehnpfenning ordered all Jews to wear a white band with the yellow Star of David on their left arm. Jews interpreted the new order as a sign of improvement – making the Jew-badge more liberal. The eternal Jewish faith and hope remained stronger than all anti-Jewish experiences. The "liberalization" and "improvement" didn't last long. In a matter of days there was a third order: to remove the armbands and go back to the old system but with a new design. A ten-centimeter yellow Star of David was to be worn by Jews on the breast and on the back. The latest modification eventually became the standard model that lasted until the final collapse of the Germans. It lasted in Vilna until the final destruction of the ghetto at the end of 1943.

There was no longer any doubt that the constant change of orders in general and the endless daily change of the anti-Jewish laws in particular were meant to disorient its victims. With changes in orders coming so fast it was easy to find Jews continuously "breaking the command." For this "crime" the most often applied penalty was death. This was of course the original intention of the Germans and the main reason for inventing their orders in the first place.

But while we were only beginning to get used to the German methods and to learn how to survive them, the Germans had already some years of experience and were well trained in their sadistic methods on how to pull the noose around the Jewish neck still tighter and tighter. From individuals who managed to escape from other places we heard details of a murderous pogrom on Jews in Novogrod and an even more vicious one in little Sznipeszok. In Sznipeszok the Germans had torched the main synagogue with the holy Torah scrolls in them and rejoiced vastly over the suffering of the local Jews.

Kidnapping Jews off the streets and making them disappear had become a daily feature that frightened us not less than a helpless dog feared the dogcatcher. Jewish males went out of their homes and never returned; they disappeared into thin air... Lithuanian sources informed us that they were being sent as "laborers" to the new occupied parts of the Soviet Union. This, together with the bewilderingly fast victories of the German forces, added to our misery and fear for the future.

A new Lithuanian daily, similar to the infamous German newspaper *Der Stuermer* appeared in the streets. Its contents were mainly, if not exclusively, devoted to incriminating Jews in the most hideous crimes. Everything of this kind of material that we might have read in the past paled against the sins we were supposed to have committed according to the Lithuanian press.

In one issue the Lithuanian daily described in detail how in the township of Poniewierz Jews slaughtered the entire Gentile medical staff and all the patients at the local hospital. Jewish Communists purportedly tortured and raped Lithuanian nurses. The details, given over two pages, were illustrated with "authentic" pictures. A short time after this "revelation" the same paper published an order of the local authorities in Kovno: Jews in Kovno had been ordered to leave the town within a month and settle in Slobodka – in a ghetto.

Each day the noose around the Jewish neck was tightening a little more. Regardless of the fear of being taken off the street, never to be heard of again, I could not remain in the house. Risking my life, I ventured out almost daily to visit Professor Noah Prylucki and Dr. Wygocki.

We had set a daily routine for our existence. Early in the morning my mother would venture out into the street to find out what had happened during the night. She was the most unobtrusive one among us so she became our scout. On the basis of her information we made our plans for the day. One morning she came back pale and slightly disoriented with deadly news. During the night the Germans had closed off a number of houses in Sovitsher Street and forced all Jewish tenants out of their beds half-naked into the yards. They separated the adult males from the rest, beat up the women and children, closed the dwellings and warned the women and children in most vile words not to dare to return to their homes. Leaving the distraught and helpless group standing half-naked in the yard they ordered the men to march out under guard to an unknown fate.

Any thoughts we might have had that that was an isolated incident quickly proved to be wrong. The same spectacle turned into a cruel routine that made us all feel totally helpless. It repeated itself nearly nightly for weeks. We feared not only for our own fate but for those who were left in the yards during the night – with their menfolk taken away, their homes shuttered and their families torn apart, they became immediately destitute. To this day it remains impossible to describe their situation in words. Within hours, hundreds of families ceased to exist as families, and the broken parts that remained were left in the nightshirts or pajamas they had been wearing when they had been driven out of their beds. They were left in the dark without a roof over their head, without food or shelter and without the menfolk, about whose fate they did not know. Their misery was beyond description.

The nightly scenes did not move any human element of those who performed the ghastly acts. The screams, the cries, the pleas of women and children, the tears of the final goodbyes from the men went on during the hours of darkness. They were happenings known only to those involved. The details of each incident became common knowledge each dawn when the desperate victims dared appear in the streets. The victims of the closed dwellings had nowhere to turn for immediate help. The daring ones opened their dwellings to save whatever they could, while others left everything they had ever possessed to the looting of the Lithuanians who came during the daylight hours to haul away whatever they wished.

Morning after morning we received these deadly reports from my mother and the Christian neighbors who were subletting my sister's apartment.

During those weeks I visited both Prylucki and Dr. Wygocki. Together we sought ways to establish contact with the Lithuanian authorities. After a few meetings we decided that Dr. Wygocki, a former minister in the Lithuanian government, should compose a letter to the Lithuanian Committee. In that letter he should request the Lithuanian Committee to act vigorously to alleviate the fate of the Lithuanian Jews, to enable them to survive this difficult period with the least number of victims. In his letter, Dr. Wygocki proposed to arrange a mutual conference to lay the foundation for cooperative work between the two peoples.

I was delegated to hand over the letter to the Lithuanian Committee on a particular day. Due to the fact that according to our "scout" report, being in the street on the arranged day was particularly dangerous, the letter was handed in to the Lithuanian Committee through Mr. Eliahu Flaks, the director of the Jewish cemetery who lived close to the offices of the Lithuanian Committee.

We waited for a reply but none was received. However, on July 4, 1941, two German officers who came to the synagogue ordered the beadle, Haim-Meir Gordon to establish, within twenty-four hours, a Jewish representative body. This order was later confirmed by the Lithuanian Vilna Committee. That was not an easy task. During the time of the Soviet occupation the Jewish communal authority had ceased to function. To revive Jewish activity we needed to contact many individuals. This was extremely dangerous. Nonetheless, within twenty-four hours a committee of ten well-known personalities was established and by order of the Germans it was later expanded to twenty-four. The body included: Dr. Wygocki (who at first declined to join but later consented), Rabbi Yosef Szuv, Eliezer Kruk, Abraham Zajdsznur, Pinhas Konn, Shaul Trotzki, Anatol Fried, Roza Shabad-Gavronska, E. Sadlis, Yosef Shabad, Israel Verblinski, Shabtai Milkonowicki, Grisha Jaszunski, Joel Fiszman, Shaul Petuchovski, Leon Katzenelson, Shaul Hoffman, Abraham Zalkind, Lyuba Cholem, Nahum

Sofer, Yosef Shkolnitzki, Rabbi Katz, Boris Parnass, Rabinowicz. It should be noted that all members of the committee were well-known activists of the Vilna Jewish community representing most of the political parties and communal organizations.

The Jewish Committee took over a house that had once been the property of the organization *Tzedakah Gedolah* (the Great Charity) and was later transferred to the community. The address of the established body immediately became the address of all the Jewish misery, trouble and pain. In spite of the great danger, people risked their lives and came from all parts of the city seeking help, protection and advice. Many individuals, believing they would find help and save the members of their families through the help of the committee, put themselves in danger of being taken off the street and ending up in the world of ghosts. Many Jews never made it to the desired address. They were simply trodden down on the way like ants squashed under a human shoe.

The members of the committee, all respected for the many years of their communal activities, devoted their energy to the task of dealing with daily problems. They worked with total dedication and during all hours – but it was a futile exercise. They could achieve very little, as the Germans had already secretly decreed to destroy the Jewish people without exception. No woman and no child, no deserving person, not even the most worthy and needed Jew was to be spared from the German death industry.

But at the time we did not know about the German master plan and so we tried and tried again and again to help. The Jewish Committee tried to save whomever the members believed was possible to save. Our attempts led us to the Germans and more so – to the Lithuanians.

For the moment the most significant help came from a single individual, Dr. Lyuba Cholem. On her own initiative she made contact with Dr. Zelech, the German head of the military medical establishment. It was rumored that in earlier years she had studied together with the German doctor. From him she received "iron letters" for all Jewish doctors. The letters ordered the various authorities not to take physicians off the street for "labor" (as we learned at a later time, "labor" meant instant death at the infamous Ponary). In addition, the German letters also prohibited anyone from entering the homes of Jewish doctors or to remove any of their belongings. At the time it meant being saved from death. All Jewish doctors eventually survived the pre-ghetto period and found themselves in the ghetto when it was finally established. It was an incredible achievement of Dr. Lyuba Cholem.

Having been informed about her success I met with Dr. Cholem and requested that she should try to get the same documents for the Jewish pharmacists. She promised to do everything possible. She added that she would try to get the same assurances for all medical personnel. I handed over a prepared list of names of all Jewish pharmacists but nothing came of it. The result was tragic; two thirds of the Jewish pharmacists were snatched off the streets by the Lithuanians during the first two months of German occupation.

When nothing resulted of my attempt to save the pharmacists I decided to try a different approach and turned to the chairman of the Union of Pharmacists, Roman Gonczarenko.

I was well acquainted with Gonczarenko and knew him to be a very decent man. I had no doubt he would do whatever possible to help his Jewish colleagues in such a difficult moment. Through some of my Christian friends I let him know that I would like to meet with him. One late afternoon, knowing how life threatening it was for me to appear in the street, Gonczarenko came to my home, though this was no small danger for him either. I told him about the disaster that had taken the lives of most Jewish pharmacists; he already knew about it. Whatever name I mentioned he knew the answer: "They have gone, disappeared," he said straight out. "They were grabbed by special 'catchers.'"

We decided to go together to the director of the Department of the Medical Pharmacy to beg him to help save whomever was left. The only time to undertake such a visit was in the early morning hours, which unfortunately was also the most dangerous time since the Lithuanian catchers were most active at that time. It addition it was impossible for us to walk together. Knowing the risk and not without fear I went, realizing the importance of the meeting. I made it to the appropriate office in the center of Vilna – in the building that once belonged to a Jewish family named Zalkind. The director, Mr. Garbut, gave us a cold reception and looked at me askance. Although he did not say anything negative it was obvious that he could not understand how we dared to approach him – especially how I, a Jewish pharmacist, had the audacity to appear in his office.

Together we made our request. In a chilling manner he informed us that he could not employ any Jews. As for the certificates of protection we requested, he said he was not entitled to issue such documents. The whole matter, he said, was out of his jurisdiction and he could not do anything. Turning to Goncza-renko in a demonstrative way he promised to speak to the chief doctor of the Department of Health.

We waited some days and after more than a week we decided to visit Gar-but once more. The second meeting was much shorter than the first one and we left empty-handed. While I suffered little for my "audacity" in facing Garbut twice in his office on a Jewish matter, Gonczarenko paid for his human kind-ness dearly. Garbut revoked Gonczarenko's right to be head of the pharmacy where he worked. Moreover, Garbut warned the fine man that at the next simi-lar intervention he would deal with Gonczarenko in a much harsher fashion.

Words are often insufficient to present reality. Our situation changed with a rapidity that is difficult to convey. Day by day it became more and more desperate.

As Jews avoided walking out into the street unless absolutely necessary, the Lithuanian human-catchers began entering Jewish homes and seizing their male victims. In this way my colleague Miron disappeared. A day after his disappearance, on a beautiful summer night of July 11, 1941, the Lithuanian Militia, the human-catchers, surrounded the building where he lived and took away all Jewish males; the "catch" of that night was sixty people.

Miron had been a pharmacist for more than thirty years. He had worked for three decades in the same pharmacy, remaining there even when the own-ers of the place changed. He was an unusually fine man, and a good friend. We worked together in the professional societies of pharmacists for a considerable number of years. He was loved and respected by all who came into contact with him, Jews and non-Jews alike. Many people came to his pharmacy to ask his opinion and advice regarding aspects of their illnesses. During heated professional and political debates between Jewish and Polish or Lithuanian pharmacists, Miron always remained calm. His calmness and his balanced opinions during such moments reduced the heat of our debates and his words were listened to with respect. When I became director of the pharmacy in Antakalia he came to work with me. It was a great sacrifice on his part, giving up for me his place of work where he had toiled for thirty years, all to be with me.

The news that Miron has disappeared shocked me deeply. But at the time Vilna was in a lawless state and the living had to carry on living. For this they had to earn an income. Very few Jews had food reserves in their homes. Every day they were forced to risk their lives in desperate attempts to get some food. It was a vicious and very dangerous circle in which the Jews of Vilna had to maneuver. This was the atmosphere of Vilna during the first six weeks of German occupation. The Jewish population paid for that period with rivers of blood.

While it should be clear that the Germans ruled the city, the execution of their sadistic and murderous orders was performed by Lithuanian hands under the leadership of the Lithuanian Committee. The executors of the orders of their new overlords did their work with great precision and even greater enthusiasm. One aspect of their morbid work haunts me day and night like a dark ghost and will probably haunt me for the rest of my life. How could normal people who had families, parents, wives and children, turn into carnivorous beasts over the course of a single day? How could they become professional cold-blooded and heartless murderers, slaughtering masses of other human beings on a daily basis? Did the tears and cries of children, even if they were Jews, standing in front of them not touch their stony hearts? How did it happen that tens of thousands of good people turned in the span of a few hours into professional mass executioners of an unimaginable number of innocent people, slaughterers of their own species? But it happened. Overnight they became voluntary killers. They underwent a metamorphosis that should have frightened them. But it didn't. The opposite happened – they enjoyed their work.

I am not speaking about the lawless looting, robbing the deserted houses that Jews were forced to abandon without taking anything with them. I am not questioning their taking Jews to useless "work" or lampooning of Jewish misery and helplessness. I am trying to understand how thousands and thousands of ordinary Lithuanians became professional workers in human slaughterhouses. I often ask the same question without ever hoping for an answer...

CHAPTER 3

The Advent of the
German Civilian Administration

The Arrival of Kommissar Hans Hingst

The end of July brought about a radical change in the life of Vilna. The joint German Military-Lithuanian Administration was replaced by a German civilian administration. Hans Hingst replaced the military governor Zehnpfenning as the Gebietskommissar of Vilna and Hingst's assistant F. Murer was placed in charge of Jewish affairs. In time, that changeover would prove that we had been very naïve in thinking that what we had experienced up until then was the extreme limit of men's bestiality.

With the arrival of the German civilian administration, order in the city was established. Lawlessness came to an end and the rules became strict, which in simple language meant that the situation became worse. While until now Jews were exposed to "primitive" Lithuanian executioners, their fate was now in the hands of SS and Gestapo units that arrived with the express purpose of implementing Hitler's directives concerning the occupied territories in general and the Jewish population in particular.

Soon after their arrival, on August 6, 1941, Murer commanded the Lithuanian official in charge of Jewish affairs, Petras Buragas, to order members of the Jewish Committee to appear before him. A. Zajdsznur, E. Kruk and S. Petuchovski went to the meeting. He met them in a side street near his office and informed them that by the next day the Jewish Committee would have to deliver five million rubles. He demanded two million to be in his hands by 9:00 the next morning, the rest by the end of the day. If the money was not received by 10:00 all members of the Jewish Committee would have to appear to receive the bodies of their colleagues. Stunned by the request, the three committee members informed the Jewish Committee of the German's demand, causing an immediate panic. How could they collect so much money in such a short time? Jews were only permitted in the streets until 6:00 p.m. and many streets were out of bounds to the Jews. Organizing a collection would be almost impossible! It was Dr. Wygocki who brought everyone to face reality. Rather than panic, he said, collection must start immediately. By 9:00 the next morning a substantial sum of money, gold, diamonds and jewelry were collected and delivered to Murer. Seeing that the total was short of the two million rubles that he demanded, Murer ordered all members of the Jewish Committee to report to him immediately. At the request of the committee, Dr. Wygocki, who was not a member, also went to the meeting.

Throughout the meeting Murer kept waving his spiral whip in front of the Jews. "You Jews have started the war, now you have to pay for it. Jews have to surrender anything of value: diamonds, gold rings, watches…anything of value." Dr. Wygocki started to say: "As the elder of Vilna Jewry – " He did not finish what he was going to say. Murer interrupted him angrily. "Shut your mouth, you old, filthy Jew." Dr. Cholem, also present at the meeting, tried to explain: "You are giving us little time – " Murer interrupted her even more forcefully: "You whore, shut your mouth before I lose my patience!" Murer took Rabbi Szuv and another member of the committee hostage until the demanded "contribution" would be paid. "If not," he finished his lecture, "you will all be shot like dogs!"

I visited Dr. Wygocki a few hours after that incident. He was still visibly trembling and stammered as he tried hard to recount details of the meeting. "You know," he said, "I am not a man who gets easily frightened, I know the Germans not just from today. But what my eyes saw at the meeting and what my ears heard I could never have imagined. To speak to a lady, a woman doctor, with such vile expressions; his turning to me with his filthy and arrogant language and his waving the whip before my eyes, all that spells a tragic future. There is nothing to expect from those two. The money has to be collected. We may only hope that the money will calm the beast…at least temporarily." This was the first and last time the doctor met the Germans as a representative of Vilna Jewry.

Late afternoon on August 24, I went to visit Dr. Wygocki and was met by his wife Helena. Frightened and with tears in her eyes she told me that earlier in the day several Lithuanians came into the house and after a thorough and brutal search they arrested Dr. Wygocki and took him away to the Lukishki prison. The efforts of the Jewish Committee, my efforts and those of many other individuals to secure his release were unsuccessful. Dr. Wygocki died several days later at the age of eighty-six. With the death of Dr. Wygocki the Jewish community lost its most respected and beloved leader and I lost a dear friend who had guided me since my early student days and who was an inspiration throughout my public life.

The Jewish Center was now in the building that had once belonged to the Jewish community. It was not far from another formerly Jewish building, the home of Mefitzei Haskalah. On top of all other endless troubles, a new worry came to that address: the "contribution" demanded by the German Gebietskommissar for the District of Vilna.

The disastrous news spread throughout the Jewish community and the response came quickly. Jews began to donate money, golden chains, watches, rings with precious stones. Treasures collected over generations. Pieces of jewelry Jewish women used to wear during the Sabbath and Jewish holidays. Jewelry that had been handed down from mothers to daughters and from grandmothers to granddaughters. Jewelry that adorned Jewish women at family weddings and other joyous occasions, all this was now handed over to the Jewish Committee to be devoured by Satan's beasts. It was all thrown into the boxes standing on the tables in the office of the Jewish Committee.

Due to the danger of being grabbed off the street, a decision was made to ask the Lithuanian official Petras Buragas for more German certificates in order to enable individuals to go around and collect the demanded "contribution"; a few certificates were given.

Jews offered their treasured possessions. What other choice did they have? Eighty Jews were hostages in local prisons; another two Jews were taken hostage at the first meeting with the new German Kommissar and the remaining members of the Jewish Committee were threatened with being executed like dogs. What other choice did the Jewish community have? We hoped that the money would replace the human sacrifices that Jews had been giving since the first day of the German attack.

Jews had an additional cause for cautious optimism. They made themselves believe that after paying the "contribution" they would at last receive some information about their loved ones who had been taken away. The collection took some days. In the end, the collected treasure of gold, jewelry and money was handed over to the Germans in a large crate.

It was not the whole sum required, but Hingst took it all just the same. He demanded that the cash be parceled, counted and sorted like in a bank.

It should be noted here for the sake of history that Gentiles, true, righteous people, came forward and out of their own conviction brought to the Jewish Committee donations and offerings. They helped not only with money but in some cases also by donating precious jewelry. The number of such Christians remains unknown. There may not have been many – but they were there in our time of great need and their saintly acts should be recorded.

No member of the committee suffered any consequences as a result of the shortage that remained after the collection ended. The two members of the committee that Murer took hostage remained in his cellars for a few more days and were released after the first part of the "contribution" was made. My family contributed all we could from what we had.

During the time the "contribution" was being collected I was asked to appear before the committee in order to help. Unfortunately I could not fulfill the committee's request. A personal disaster befell my own family.

During the first days after his arrival in Vilna, Hingst sent an order to the Jewish Committee that forbade Jews from entering certain central streets or from walking on the sidewalk. Jews were ordered to keep to the road. The order reached the committee in the middle of the day and Jews were not informed about it quickly enough. Only a small number of individuals had been contacted about it on the day the order was given; the rest of the community knew nothing about it. Of course, every anti-Jewish order was given to bring new Jewish victims; this one was no exception.

The greatest number of victims of the new order this time were women. Men avoided the streets as much as possible and matters that had to be dealt with outside the home were generally handled by the women.

My wife had left home to visit a Christian friend and was informed by the friend about the new order. On her way home she walked in the middle of the road in accordance with the new rule. Passing the Zelazny Most (Iron Bridge), a column of military trucks blocked her way. For a second she stopped helpless. Seeing that the column was not stopping and she was about to be killed by the trucks she jumped out of their way onto the sidewalk to save herself. At that precise moment a Lithuanian policeman appeared as if out of the ground and arrested her. He wouldn't take any notice of her plea that she would have been flattened to death by the military trucks and she was forced to step out of their way. He wouldn't accept her protestations that she had walked in the middle of the road until the last second in accordance with the new law. He arrested her and took her to the police station at Ostra Brama. There she met many other women, already victims of the same law. After some hours they were all sent under guard to the well-known Lukishki prison. But that prison was already full of Jewish males arrested for similar "crimes" and there was no place for women. The arrested women were sent away from Lukishki prison to the women's prison. Some hours later we received notice of the calamity.

I was helpless. How was I to reach the police station when Jews were forbidden to pass through the streets leading toward the police station? There was no other way to reach the station and the children were crying helplessly in fear. I had two choices: to jump into the fire or to fry in the frying pan. To run to the police station was running to death and leaving the children without both their parents. Not to run meant to sacrifice the life of their mother and my wife. If that was not enough, the curfew hour for Jews to remain locked in their home was fast approaching.

I took leave of the children and of my mother and probably also of my senses and went out, hoping for God's assistance. My troubled mind diminished my awareness of the danger involved…and I reached the police station. My luck was holding! The police officer on duty was one of my Lithuanian friends. When

I told him that my wife had been brought to the station he became seriously distressed. "Why did she not say that she is your wife – I would have released her immediately. Now it is too late to do anything. I could not keep the large number of women here and sent them all to another prison."

I proposed to pay a large fine so that he should give me a notice to the prison to release my wife. His helplessness was noticeable even in my own distress: "This is now impossible; the penalty must be decided by the city commandant. The penalty might be any amount between three thousand to fifteen thousand rubles." I became momentarily paralyzed – such a stiff penalty! At that time a kilo of bread was a single ruble on the black market; the sums that the police officer had mentioned were not a fine but a demand for a forced "contribution." Seeing my reaction he showed me the secret order the police had received before the order was handed in to the Jewish Committee. Time was running out. The police clock was showing less than a quarter to five in the afternoon.

The whole building knew already of my distress and believed that I was already in the hands of the Lithuanian human-catchers. No one believed that, having irrationally decided to run through streets forbidden to Jews, probably on the sidewalk and close to the police hour, I would not fall into the hands of the Lithuanians. Coming home at the last moment I was greeted by all neighbors; they had come to our apartment to comfort my mother and the children; and suddenly I appeared, an apparition from another world. The pain visible on my mother's face and the children's crying tore at my heart. A feeling of helplessness came over me but I could not succumb to it. Come morning I had to find a way of saving my wife. The next day I began my attempt with a visit to Professor Birzyszko. Very humbly I requested from him a letter to the Lithuanian commandant as the case was now in his hands. I have to admit that for once the professor greeted me in a friendly way and immediately gave me a strong letter of recommendation to the commandant. Full of hope I ran to the city commandant, who now occupied the home of the Vilna banker and active social welfare activist, Israel Bunimowicz. I noticed that the house had been taken over by its new resident and workers were renovating much of the building – a sign that the commandant was planning an extended stay.

When I handed the letter to the commandant he expressed his regret that it was already too late; he had already signed the fine for "only" three thousand rubles. He added: "I signed for the smallest penalty myself. The crime had already been recorded and could not be changed." I felt that he was telling the truth and I would not get anything more from him. I thanked him and went home.

Three thousand rubles was a large sum of money, much more than we had in cash. But the change on my children's faces when they understood that I had achieved something positive was all the encouragement I needed to raise the money. Things that we could sell fetched at that time less than half their real value. It was a buyers market for Jewish possessions and we had to hurry. It took two days to put together the required sum. This alone was not enough. I now had to bank the three thousand rubles and get a receipt for the money. From there I had to reach the office of the city commandant to get the confirmation that I had paid the fine and to receive from the office the required note for the release of my wife. It took a whole day and an unimaginable amount of luck to be in the streets so much and fulfill all the requirements, all the while evading the human-catchers.

It is very difficult to describe in words how much anxiety, fear, patience, hope and despair those two days exacted. Not only we who were directly involved in the calamity but also our neighbors and friends all paid the mental "contribution" to see the "happy end" to the life-threatening danger.

Having the release form was still not enough. I had to go to the police station and ask the police officer to accompany me to the prison. I was afraid to reach the gate of the prison on my own and was also advised not to go alone. The police officer agreed to come with me. He was riding on his bicycle and I had to follow him in the middle of the road like a prisoner being taken to prison. Only the Lithuanian policeman entered the prison. I waited in the yard. But my wife was not immediately released. She had to stay in prison until the next day for the release document to be processed.

The anxiety continued. In those days one could not count on what might happen during the next hour, let alone overnight. From early the next morning we did not leave the window, waiting for the happy moment when we would see my wife coming home. All of us broke out crying when we saw her crossing the street. The room became crowded with neighbors, including the family of the poor tailor whose wife was among the almost one thousand Jewish women who had been arrested during the first hours of the new order. For her release the commandant asked fifteen thousand rubles. The tailor sold everything he owned and brought his wife home to two empty rooms, counting his luck at having her home again – alive.

From my wife, we learned about the conditions in prison. The prisoners received 120 grams of bread as their daily ration and some dark water called "coffee." They were forbidden to receive food or clothing or visits from the family. The prison cells were overcrowded and the filth was overwhelming. Each night a group of prisoners was taken out of their cell to disappear into thin air. The ones who were not taken away during the night sometimes spent weeks waiting for something to happen. Any prisoner who spent more than a few days there had to have great luck to come out alive. During the next few days a very small number of women prisoners were released. The vast majority became ghosts of the unknown. Only at a later stage did we learn that all those who had disappeared were taken to Ponary, shot down in groups and buried there.

Once the "contribution" was out of the way, the Jewish Committee had to try to regulate the question of work. Seizing Jews off the streets had become a veritable plague. It was no longer possible for Jewish males to count on ten minutes of luck outside the house. Hundreds of Jews disappeared daily; like stones thrown into lakes, there was no sign of them. The "good" Lithuanians said that they had been transported to Russia, Minsk or Vitebsk, Gomel, Smolensk and other places as laborers. When taking people out of their homes the instruction was always the same: to take only a towel and a bar of soap. "There is no need for anything else. You will be given everything you'll need where you will be sent." It turned out to be the only true sentence the murderers spoke to their victims; the victims didn't need anything once they reached their destination. They were given a free bullet and a free burial.

Work became an acute problem. People had no financial means to buy even the minimum food requirements; in many homes bread was rationed for lack of money. Hundreds had to risk their lives daily to find work that would allow them to buy food for the next meal. A few people managed to find work for themselves with Germans or Lithuanians but it was a very small minority. Even the "lucky" ones who found work risked their lives daily in reaching work in the morning and coming back home in the evening. A greater number of Jews obtained work through the Jewish Committee, which had received a concession through the mediation of the middleman Buragas to provide daily large numbers of workers for Germans and Lithuanians. At dawn thousands of Jews arrived at the Jewish Committee and were dispatched in groups to their working places. The groups were supposed to provide insurance against being taken away – and disappearing. The insurance lasted only a few days. It happened more than once that a whole group on its way to work was taken by the human-catchers and that was the last time they were seen.

The working groups were coordinated by a Jew named A. Langbard, who was not a member of the Jewish Committee. Before the war he was a director of an old, established Jewish bank and a prominent member of the Jewish Democratic Party. He later disappeared with one of the working groups.

Together with the operation of the committee in Vilna, requests for Jewish workers began to arrive from the surrounding areas, including Kena, Zatrocze, Czarna Gora and Biala Waka. Jews were employed at those places cutting peat. For the first few weeks they had reasonable working conditions, though the workload was very heavy. Young Jews, city youth, who had never in their life seen turf eagerly accepted the work to earn a living and at the same time escape the torture of the big city. They didn't reject the work even when they found out that the hard labor had to be performed half-naked in swamps and the working time was from sunrise to sunset. Women also accepted the very difficult jobs. One had to admire the perseverance of these young men and women. In a very short time they became specialists in their work. Believing that it would eventually lead to a better future, they adjusted to the devilish pace of the hard labor and continued.

Work in the provinces had its advantages. One could obtain food products in the smaller towns much more easily than in Vilna by buying directly from the local population. Of course this was illegal and many a young Jew paid for it with his life, but the business continued – there was little other choice. Dealing with the locals meant assuring food not only for oneself but also for the folks back in the city. Again, those who worked for the Lithuanians, or better yet for the Germans, received work passes confirming that they were employed by this or that institution. The passes were supposed to be security against being taken away. At the beginning, every working place handed out its own pass with its own rubberstamp. After the human-chasers began ignoring such documents, the passes began to be confirmed with the rubberstamp of Lithuanian or German official bodies. When this too lost its recognition, at least as far as the catchers were concerned, the security documents bore the official stamp of the Lithuanian authorities: the emblem of a horse. But this stamp was also ignored and people began chasing the "iron document," the one typed in German with the swastika stamp.

For a few weeks people were driven out of their minds trying to obtain this note or that note, or another kind of "safe" document, with the "safe" stamp. Nothing helped. The Lithuanians seized people with the stamps issued by their employers, with the stamps of institutions, with notes bearing the Lithuanian horse and even the German swastika. The catchers just tore up the documents and took their owners away. The one-time owners of the "safe" document simply disappeared…

During those days, I was not working – I did not want to work for the Germans. I helped out at the Jewish Committee when needed, which was often enough. I could not become a permanent member of that body because the committee had no "security" document for me. And according to A. Langbard, to remain in the committee without a document was far too dangerous and he would not let me take such a risk. So I remained at home for a number of days. But sitting at home had also become dangerous, not much less than being in the street.

The situation was becoming unbearable. The committee members applied themselves to their task with urgency and dedication, working to alleviate people's suffering. But what could they do when the secret plan of the Germans to totally destroy the Jewish nation had already been finalized in Berlin and actions in that direction had already begun, even if we were not aware of that decision at the time.

During one of my visits to the offices of the Jewish Committee I met the lawyer Pinhas Konn, an old friend from my university days. While talking about the hopelessness of our situation, which had become even more evident after the meeting between the committee members and Hingst, we heard loud voices coming from the street. Somebody came running and told us that the human-catchers had grabbed the venerable Rabbi Szuv just outside the office. We ran out and saw a Lithuanian trying to take the rabbi away. We offered him money asking how much he wanted to let the rabbi free. We might as well have spoken to the wall. In the usual cold-blooded way of his kind, he refused to accept money, or the gold watch someone in the crowd offered him. He took away the rabbi, the man who had been a pillar of the Jewish Committee and who was on his way to the office. The rabbi disappeared the same way all his predecessors had disappeared – to die at Ponary. No sooner had the news spread throughout the community than a similar report came about another rabbi suffering the same fate. The venerable and beloved Rabbi Fried had been taken out of his home in the usual manner by the Lithuanians. He was sick and could not walk. Friends who had come to visit and help him had to carry him. They carried him and disappeared together with the rabbi. All interventions for the two rabbis ended fruitlessly.

Rabbi Fried had been the Lithuanian military rabbi in Vilna. He officiated at the swearing in of Jewish recruits to the army. He was a most respected scholar and the symbol of the older generation that justified calling Vilna "Lithuanian Jerusalem."

During the early period of occupation, Jews had direct contact with Lithuanians and Germans. When I visited the Lithuanian Committee with regard to my wife's arrest I met two Jewish personalities there – Eliezer Kruk, the leader of the trade workers, and Pinhas Konn. They were at the office of the Lithuanian Committee in the matter of the contribution payments that was going on at the time. To my question as to how they saw the situation developing with the new Kommissar, Hingst, in charge, both responded the same way: "Very, very bad, desperate."

I told them about my own calamity and they informed me that any direct contact between Jews and Lithuanian or German officials had been prohibited. From that day on everything had to go through the mediation of Mr. Petras Buragas, who now had the final say in all Jewish matters. Their information was an additional nail in our coffin. The Jewish community had friendly contacts in many Lithuanian offices and until the new order had been issued some personal difficulties could be resolved through them. Now another door had been closed.

The Need to Find Work

In late August the Germans embarked on yet another repressive tactic: anti-Jewish rallies. On Sunday, August 24, at midday a large public gathering took place near the building of the former Russian theater. It was an anti-Jewish meeting at which vituperative Lithuanian speakers incited their listeners against Jews by telling the most atrocious lies. We stood hidden in corners fearing for our lives, understanding that such meetings did not take place spontaneously. Our Polish subtenants came back every few minutes with new and frightening details.

With our hearts pumping wildly we awaited the end of the meeting, fearing the consequences. From the pages of our long history we knew that after the hatred expressed in such speeches we could expect a pogrom. In spite of our dark expectations the public dispersed without any outward reaction. We slowly gained our equilibrium, remaining deeply troubled by the eternal Jewish question – whatever have we done to deserve such a pain-filled fate?

It was a beautiful Sunday. The streets were lively with throngs of people walking along while we had to be locked up inside the walls of our insecure homes, being afraid to stick our noses outside the door; simply afraid to show ourselves. Why? Now we understood that such an ordinary thing as freely walking in the street is not something to be taken for granted. Is there anything more painful for a human being than to be caged like an animal? Are the people who are free to move around outside in God's world on a sunny Sunday any better or more worthy than we are? What have we done to deserve such a merciless verdict of destruction? What?

As if in a state of hallucination the same thoughts kept turning and turning in our minds without even seeking an answer. This was reality, the very, very sad reality. The scum rules over you; he speaks and you must grit your teeth and take it.

It was painful to see the sad faces of the children who knew it was summer. They well remembered past summers, with happy vacation days spent away from school. But now they understood they had to stay inside. The children did not complain; they did not ask any questions or demand an explanation. The opposite happened – they protected and guarded us, the grown-ups. They did not let us take a single superflous step. We were not to take risks. Often when I felt like going out to meet friends and temporarily escape from the torment of imprisonment the children were the ones to stop me. Many times I had to give up my desire to leave the house. Their begging forced me to stay: "Papa, don't leave! The human-catchers are outside. Don't go out – stay at home." When I decided not to take notice of them they sometimes cried or returned sulking to their corners.

I remained at home without working. Nearly everybody else was already "employed." The Jews of Vilna were working for Germans or for Lithuanians. They received food and the certificates that were a form of life security. One's whole life turned around the word "certificate" – even though it did not always mean security. The Lithuanians, the human-catchers, often joked when shown such a piece of paper: "Oh, yes," they would say, looking with a satisfied smile right at the victim, "does it tear like this?" They would tear the document to pieces and turn to the victim. "Now you no longer have any document, so come with me." And having such a piece of paper was what our existence revolved around. One early morning my mother went out as usual to find out what had happened during the night. We were still in our beds when we heard the first noises in the yard and soon after that my mother came running in, pale and shocked. "They have surrounded our block of houses and are going from apartment to apartment looking for something."

We hurriedly began to dress but before we could finish we heard a series of sharp knocks at the door. My mother went to open the door and, perhaps because she was frightened, the key jammed in the lock and it took a minute or two before she managed to unlock and open the door. The murderers waiting for us to open must have considered such a crime unforgivable. A German and two Lithuanians with guns at the ready barged into the room. Screaming in German one of the Lithuanians asked my mother why she had not opened the door immediately. She tried to say that the key jammed in the lock but the visitors did not wait for the answer. They strode across the room and barged into the room of our Polish subtenants.

The young Polish woman had presence of mind and said she was Lithuanian. They left the room immediately, returning to us. By then we were dressed, or nearly so. The children were in bed. Another German, an elderly one, came in accompanied by a Lithuanian official. "Who are you?" the German asked calmly. "I am a pharmacist," I replied. "Are you a Bolshevik?" he asked in the same calm way. "No, I am a pharmacist," I replied. "Have you any arms in the house?" "No." "Where do you work?" For a moment I was lost for an answer but regained my calm: "At the hospital." "Who are they?" he asked, pointing in the direction of the children in bed. "They are our two children," I replied, now a little more calm. "All right then," he said and turned toward the door.

We felt an unimaginable sense of relief in having them on the other side of the door. Such a measure of good fortune was very unusual. On the spot I realized that that I could no longer be without work. I had to find work somewhere, simply as a means of self-protection.

Soon after, we lived through another fearful and dangerous situation. Early one morning the caretaker of our house knocked on our door and when we opened he entered with a Lithuanian policeman. The policeman asked for my passport, confiscated it and asked me to report immediately to the police station.

I washed, dressed and as soon as the children woke up I took leave of my mother, wife and children and without breakfast went to the police station. My heart was beating with fear and I had to stop before I entered the station; but nobody was there except a lonely officer on duty. I asked him if Officer Shlisim (the cashier in the pharmacy who resigned on the first day the Germans entered Vilna) was available. The policeman was neutral, neither harsh nor friendly: "No, he is not on duty at the moment. Why do you ask for him?" "Because Shlisim knows me – he worked in my pharmacy. My passport has been taken from me and I was asked to report for work." Without saying anything the policeman asked my name and checked the large pack of passports in front of him. He found mine and handed it to me: "Take your passport and go home; we will do without your work." I thanked him and made my way home, like a thief who fears being caught.

Having escaped twice from close calls I decided to find work – whatever kind I could find. It had already become normal for Jews to work for "good" Germans in "good" units. Those working for such units were treated decently, even humanely. They received food and often did business with their "good" employers. But the greatest advantage of having such employment was the German document with the swastika that went with "good" jobs. The papers with the seal of the horse, or even with the large word *craftsman*, had lost their value during the last few days as far as the human-catchers were concerned. They no longer honored documents, certificates or work confirmation letters. All who had managed to get a job with "good" Germans did their utmost to get a German document with the swastika – and the word *craftsman*.

On Monday morning, August 25, after the frightening anti-Jewish demonstration of the day before, I presented myself at the Jewish Committee in order to obtain work.

Langbard, the man who was organizing the working parties and sending them in columns to their daily tasks, was doing his duty. He was my colleague and friend; we belonged to the same political party. Langbard explained that he could not put me in with an old established group, because the Jewish workers who had passed the test with their German or Lithuanian employers would not accept anyone who did not already belong to their group. They would be afraid it might be dangerous for them. He suggested that I should seek out a group waiting to be employed and then he would be able to confirm me with the group. For me this was no solution. I had to come home with working papers. The only way out of my predicament was to wait in the yard of the Jewish Committee until a German or a Lithuanian would appear and ask for workers.

Waiting was also a dangerous step. Many times Germans came and asked for Jews, supposedly for work, without having any work for them. Such Germans asked for Jews in order to play out their own sadistic instincts. Those who fell into the hands of such Germans finished up as miserable, helpless and tragic victims. Often they ended the day as invalids. They were beaten, pushed around from pillar to post and treated like helpless domestic animals in the hands of sadists. Many never came home as they were simply beaten to death.

Some Germans had already been noted for their cruelty and when one of their kind came to ask for workers nobody was willing to go with them. When this happened the Germans took whomever was available at the moment. Waiting in the yard meant that such a fate could befall me.

When the first German arrived to ask for workers, a member of the committee and Langbard asked in a very cautious way what kind of work was involved and if the German would provide "his" workers with a document. The German answered the questions politely and actually made a good impression. As I had little choice and nothing to lose, I went together with a few others with the German, hoping to come home safe with the desired life-saving document, as the German had promised.

He led us to a large building site and a house erected shortly before the war. It was a very modern building, only partially finished, but it was already considered to be one of the finest buildings in Vilna. We found two other groups of Jews already working there. The first group included the past owner of the building – a man named Salamianski and a lawyer named Teitelbaum. Two other men I knew were working with the second group. A man by the name Abrasha Kranik had already managed to become the headman of all and had become the contact man with the Germans. I remembered him from my earliest childhood days at the heder. Now in different times we were half strangers to each other; he was the chief and I had come a nameless Indian. The people working at the place were acquainted with the Germans. They had given them valuable gifts and did good business with them – quite profitable for both sides. As a result of these exchanges they had reasonably good incomes and, what was most important – they had all been given the coveted German documents with the swastika.

Considering the prevailing situation, the location was excellent. It was in the center of the city, affording me an opportunity to meet with non-Jewish friends and acquaintances. All in all I could not have made a better decision.

It was no wonder that those already at the place before us did not accept us very well; they were concerned for their own security, which might have become endangered by our arrival. They were working on the section of the building that was still unfinished – putting in windows, glassing, finishing the floors. Jewish women worked there too – laundering for the Germans, cleaning the rooms already occupied by Germans, darning their socks and performing many similar duties.

When I approached Kranik to obtain for us the desired document without which we could not go home, he found excuses: "There is not enough work continuously for so many people," he said. When I mentioned that we came because the Germans believed that there were too few workers, he had another excuse: "We may become too noticeable. They might get rid of us all." I understood his position; it was not just him but all the others as well. To some extent they were right to protect themselves. But on the other hand we also had homes with families who were waiting for the piece of paper as if it were the Messiah himself. We too wanted to save ourselves and our families; we too had the right to fight for it! The excuse that there were too many of us was unfounded because the Germans cared little how many Jews were employed at the building.

Seeing that with Kranik we would not achieve anything, we became desperate at the very thought that we might lose such an exceptional opportunity and might have to leave without the life-and-death deciding certificate.

We turned directly to the German officer, requesting in a most humble way that he accept us, the new group, as permanent workers at the site, and provide us with the necessary documents. The German officer did not directly respond to our request. He asked his adjutant to call Kranik. When Kranik came, the officer ordered him to make out the list of the new group and send it to the office to obtain the blessed documents. The officer gave specific instruction to his soldier-adjutant how to go about fulfilling our request.

Some hours later we had the "winning" life tickets. Kosher ones! Made out by our German employer, in true German language and sealed with the real swastika seal. It was hard not to be deeply moved as we realized that this was the lifeline for us and our families. When I came home and produced the note, my wife and the children fell over me kissing and hugging me again and again. What an achievement! In one stroke I had legalized the existence of the whole family. From that day onward I went to work every day and after two days the new group became accommodated with the others.

The fear of "too many workers" in our place was a matter for the Gestapo and the human-catchers. At short intervals people were taken away with the best documents, mostly at nighttime when work certificates were ignored but also in daytime. But what more could we have asked for? Our work was to bring the huge building to completion in order to establish it as a home-away-from-home for the German female telegraphic personnel. They were expected to call the building "home" with all amenities required, including a reading room.

In order to make the forty-room house a home for German "ladies" we had to bring forty sets of furniture of the best quality from the city. After all, this was to be home for young Germans and they had already been brought up to obtain the best from the inferior races. And the new tenants of our building had been specially trained for their jobs. It was a serious matter that had to be attended to with German precision.

Every day for several weeks we traveled with the German officer inspecting the empty homes of rich Jews who had earlier been removed, and taking away every piece of valuable furniture. The pieces we brought back every day were installed in the finished rooms as the work progressed. Later, when we were herded into the ghetto, we also found fully outfitted homes of Jewish families that had been taken away earlier. Of course lighter items, such as clothing, underwear, silver cutlery, Jewish silver candelabras used for the Sabbath and holidays, all had been taken beforehand by Lithuanian robbers. Many places had been left without curtains and even without bedding. But in the Jewish houses that we inspected everything was in its place.

That is how we furnished all the rooms for the German "ladies" with the best that Vilna could offer, free of charge. When we did not go to the city for one reason or another, we were occupied finishing the individual rooms. Some needed the final floor work done; others needed to have the doors adjusted; windows had to be cleaned – we had no lack of work.

We had a few tradespeople who knew how to go about the work still to be done. But most of us were business people, academics, people who had worked in the free professions – all men who had never before had any experience working with their hands in the building trade. However, the Jewish proverb was confirmed: "Necessity breaks iron." We had to fit in with the new conditions. A qualified carpenter would show us how things should be done and we followed his instructions while he went to help out others.

And so we became painters, electricians, carpenters and whatever trade was needed. I became a carpenter; not quite a real one but all the same – a carpenter. I would give the real carpenter the board he asked for, or put in the nails as he instructed. I learned how to use a handsaw to cut the board, but not quite perfectly. The main thing was to pass the day. We didn't ask for more than that. When the Germans were not around we allowed ourselves to discuss our situation. Our main worry was the question of what happened to the people who disappeared. What became of them? What is being done with them?

This was a riddle that never completely went out of our minds. There was also another daily worry: where to obtain saleable items, where to buy a little food for our basic sustenance. Living off the work we did was out of the question. We worked not to earn a living but to stay alive. Everything that could be sold had to be sold. It was painful but unavoidable and slowly we became used to it. Vilna became a market for Jewish possessions. The best underwear, shirts, dressing gowns, suits and coats were all given away for a loaf of bread. It was a new time: we sold what we had accumulated over years and our non-Jewish neighbors bought it for less-than-bargain prices.

Every day new German curses fell on our heads. More and more horrific rumors began circling around and what was rumored yesterday was confirmed today. Did the Germans listen to our dark prophecies and fulfill them? Who knows...

The latest rumor was that the Germans were preparing a ghetto for the Jews of Vilna. Where the ghetto was to be, or when we would have to move into it – no one knew. Coming to work in the morning, we used to share our news about the happenings of the night. Each section of Vilna had its own nightly story to tell and seldom was there a peaceful night. The main motif of our nightly news was "taken away," "taken away."

It was always "taken away in the street," "taken away at work," "taken away from the house," all gone into thin air.

When I started to work I lost my contact with the Jewish Committee, with friends and with people in general. I used to arrive home minutes before the curfew hour. This made it impossible for me to go anywhere, let alone to take the risk of being seen at the forbidden time in the street. Arriving from work we used to hear from our neighbors and from other workers in our yard what had taken place in the last few hours in other parts of the city. Wherever Jews worked there was a "good" German who would bring the latest news; usually it was "good news"...

Those who stayed at home, mainly women, got together at one of the neighbors and listened to the German radio news, followed by the news from the front broadcast by the German okw, the headquarters of the German army.

This invariably brought us deep depression, pain and endless pessimism. My wife used to collect the radio news, note it down and relate it to us during the evening gatherings. Occasionally one of my Polish colleagues would secretly appear and tell us what was going on in town. The victories of the Germans were, to our chagrin, great and their boasts even greater. With deep pain we read the German, Lithuanian and Polish papers. Except for the news of German victories the papers were full of poisonous hate and agitation against the Jews.

When one of our old Polish friends, Tatiana Elert, came secretly to visit us, I showed her the Polish newspaper and said: "Look, what your paper writes about us! Aren't the Poles ashamed to besmirch us with such vile lies?"

She was astonished by my outburst: "What are you talking about, my colleague and friend?" she said with obvious surprise. "This is not a Polish paper. This is a filthy German publication, printed in the Polish language. One day it is against Jews; the next day it can be in the Lithuanian paper against the Poles. We have learned to understand the devilish German game. We cannot do much about it except try to educate each other. But we must survive. What is happening now is not our last word…"

The Second Rally

On Sunday, August 31, we were all at home. Remembering the previous Sunday and the meeting that had taken place in the city hall square, we awaited with trepidation what the next few hours would bring. We expected the worst and the worst happened.

In the early morning hours, German soldiers entered Szklanna Street, one of the predominantly Jewish streets. One of the soldiers fired a shot for no reason. Immediately the others started to yell: "Jews have shot at us from their windows!" Following the wild shouts the soldiers started shooting at the windows. The Jews living in Szklanna Street hid themselves in every possible nook and cranny, in mortal fear for their lives. A riot broke out in the street. Within minutes military and police units arrived in a show of strength and spread out in every direction. Immediately "eyewitnesses" turned up, they had seen "with their own eyes" Jews shooting out of the windows. A huge crowd gathered. It flowed over from the street of the alleged shooting to the square near city hall.

Similar to the previous Sunday the gathering turned into a public meeting; speakers appeared from nowhere. Watching through our windows we could not hear what they said but from the facial expressions of the speakers and body language of the crowd that intensified with every minute, we could easily understand that ugly Jew-baiting agitation was taking place. The crowd was restless; the tension kept rising. We stood in our corner, lost and resigned, awaiting the worst. We understood that the meeting this time would not end as peacefully as that of the previous week.

The first piece of bad news came to us through our friendly neighbor, the young Polish woman. She ran into our room like a fireball, began wringing her hands and screaming: "Oh, Jesus, sweet Jesus, what a calamity… What a calamity. I saw with my own eyes what your Jews can do… I saw it."

"What did you see?" we all asked in one voice. "I saw with my own eyes your Jews shooting dead a German… What a horrible thing… Oh, Jesus, what a calamity… What is going to happen now?" We tried to find out details about what went on but the woman just kept screaming: "I saw it with my own eyes!" She spoke incoherently in half words, and it was impossible to understand her. She ran out once more and we were left paralyzed with fear. We no longer had any doubt that we were faced with a prearranged provocation. A few minutes later an older woman came in. She was the mother of the younger one who had just run out. She repeated the same words: "Jews shot a German." She did not say that she saw it, but the blood was running cold in our veins all the same. What a dangerous provocation. Only God in Heaven knew how this was going to end… While we were frozen in fear, the meeting came to an end and slowly the crowd dispersed. Some turned back in the direction from where they had come. A few minutes later we saw people running. We held our breath, waiting for what would happen next.

We waited for a while before we ventured out into the courtyard to find out what had happened. Needless to say, no German soldier had been killed but as a result of the provocation many Jews had already been arrested.

We spent the rest of the day trying to disappear into our own shadows, not exchanging a single sentence. The children understood the horror of the situation and kept out of our way. Only at intervals our son like a little kitten came close to me or to his mother to find unspoken security.

We spent the whole evening in the yard discussing our fears with our neighbors and reliving the monstrous day. We all knew, of course, that arresting some Jews would not end the provocation and we prepared ourselves for the worst. But as hours went by and nothing happened, we returned to our apartment, exhausted by the events.

On Monday morning I left the house as usual on my way to work. Passing the streets I took every day, my eyes caught a row of very large red posters adorned with large swastikas. I first noticed the signature; the posters were signed by the German District Kommissar, Hingst. Under his signature came the date, September 1, 1941. The text was the same in all three languages: German, Lithuanian and Polish. The announcement stated:

> Yesterday, Sunday afternoon, shots were directed from an ambush at German soldiers in Vilna. Two of these cowardly bandits were identified – they were Jews. The attackers paid with their lives for their act – they were shot on the spot. To avoid such hostile acts in the future, new and severe deterrent measures have been taken. The responsibility lies with the entire Jewish community.
>
> All Jews, men and women, are forbidden to leave their homes from today at 3:00 in the afternoon until 10:00 the following morning. Exempt from this order are Jews who have valid working papers. This order is for the security of the population and to protect the lives of the inhabitants. It is the duty of every honest citizen to cooperate in preserving quiet and order.

It is not hard to imagine in what a state of mind I reached work. But no matter how bad I felt already, I was to be much more troubled by what my coworkers had to say. During the night a number of streets in the mainly Jewish area had been surrounded by Germans and Lithuanians and the whole Jewish population living in those streets, some four thousand human beings, had been taken away. Not a single exemption had been made. The whole Jewish population of the quarter was gone – young and old, sick and healthy. The infirm had been taken from their beds. All were allowed to take only whatever they could carry.

Many in our group did not come to work that morning and those who were present had little ability to concentrate. Each of us had lost direct family members, relatives or friends. Not a single person from the group at our workplace had remained untouched. Appeals to the "good" Germans began. They were promised gold, jewelry and diamonds for bringing our nearest and dearest out of the prison to which the victims had been taken, before it became too late. Our Germans would not intervene for any price.

Coming home from work, I learned more disastrous news. My mother was totally distraught. She kept walking restlessly from one end of the room to the other, wringing her hands and hardly understanding what was said to her. When she comprehended anything spoken to her, her own reaction was not coherent. "They have taken Moshe Aaron Bershtel" (our neighbor from the house behind our street), she kept repeating, "and his family." From our own family we had lost all the relatives of my brother-in-law Rachmilewicz together with their families. All gone, together with numerous friends and people we knew and had been living with for generations.

But this was not to be the end of the Sunday provocation. The next morning I learned more of the same. During the night the bloody spectacle had been repeated! This time the murderers surrounded the remaining streets in the same area and arrested anyone not taken the night before. It was something we could not fully grasp: the heart of Jewish Vilna had been destroyed in two nights! Just as on the previous day we started running to "good" Germans, offering them whatever they would ask for rescuing our dear ones from the Lukishki prison and the other places where they were held. At other working places it worked – but not at ours. Crafty Jews managed to become middlemen between the pleading Jews and the "good" Germans, advising the Germans to stand up for the prisoners and demand the release of "their" Jews. It was all done for very large payments to the Germans and not much less to the middlemen. But of the many thousands that had been packed into the prisons only a few individuals returned. They told stories about the conditions in the prisons that made us age years in the space of hours. Not only were the cells of the prison overcrowded to the point of standing room only but the prison yards were in the same condition – literally, standing room only...

Soon after the victims arrived to whatever location they had been taken, the Lithuanians took everything they had brought. This was accompanied by murderous beatings. When this came to an end the passive hell began. The Lithuanians did not provide a single drop of water or a single crust of bread. Physiological needs had to be taken care of wherever one was standing. It was not difficult to understand what conditions had become within just hours and what they were like after a day or two.

Within days we received information from non-Jewish sources. We were informed that each morning before dawn large groups of Jews were taken from the prisons and driven in the direction of Landwarovo. In the reports about the transports the name Ponary began to appear more often but, tragically, we still failed to understand its significance.

But we did begin to understand the diabolic German plan that began with the Sunday provocation. It had been criminally planned and meticulously executed. The actions of the past two nights were undertaken to clear the area for the coming ghetto, which now became a priority in the German plans. Although during the months of July and August thousands of Jews were taken from the streets and from their homes and we had no knowledge as to their whereabouts, we believed that that was a result of Lithuanian cruelty and lawlessness, instigated by the Lithuanian Committee and inspired by the Germans and their need for labor. The fact that most of the Jews taken were males, fully capable of work, allowed us to accept the thought that they were sent to labor camps. The "cleansings" following the Sunday provocation were different. They were not limited to males alone; this time whole families – men, women and children – were driven out of their homes and taken to Lukishki prison in order to make room for thousands of Jews in the new ghetto. It was clear therefore, that the German plan for the approximately forty thousand Vilna Jews was to concentrate them behind the walls of a ghetto. Perhaps that, we thought, would bring to an end the dangers of the Lithuanian human-catchers. But neither the unknown fate of the thousands of Jews taken over the previous two nights as "retaliation" for the "shooting at German soldiers" nor the imminent formation of the ghetto led us to understand, or even suspect, the true criminality and bestiality of the German plans – the total destruction of Vilna Jewry. That was precisely the aim of German duplicity. And it worked.

During the days following the provocation we talked to "our" Germans, trying to find out something about the situation. They refused to answer our questions: "You are here to work and be protected," was all they would say. One elderly Austrian let fall a very meaningful sentence: "Yes, yes, the Gestapo is doing it…"

The dwellings from which the Jews had been taken during the past two days remained ownerless. The ones taken away were ordered to leave their dwellings open and to leave the keys with the non-Jewish caretakers. This gave the caretakers a marvelous opportunity to become wealthy in no time. Whatever was of any value was immediately removed for themselves. The best clothes, furs, linen goods and underwear were gone in hours. After that came the best dinner sets, silver cutlery, crystal shared with neighbors and friends. The only things the human vultures did not immediately tear from the Jewish body were the items that Jews had themselves handed over to their non-Jewish friends as gifts, or for safekeeping until better times would arrive. Many Polish and Lithuanian neighbors felt our tragedy deeply and were, like ourselves, helpless about it other than to be with us in our hour of great need, to keep in close contact with us as much possible and encourage us to keep up our hopes.

All that had been toiled for, earned, collected and assembled over generations in thousands of Jewish homes was gone in the two months and a few days that passed since the German attack on the Soviet Union. And gone were the thousands of Jews who had been snatched away. Gone – as if they had never existed.

Many members of the Jewish Committee fell victim to the latest German "cleansings." Jewish life had become entirely paralyzed. In the first days during the provocation and after it, the Jewish Committee did not function as an active body. Near the end of the week a few of the members who escaped the raids came together at the office and took up their "normal" work. In a resigned way they did their work, asking mutely, "What next?"

We carried on with our work and tried to get information from the Germans and the Lithuanians at our workplace. But our minds were burning with thoughts of our perilous situation.

A new rumor started circulating. It said that the only way to save ourselves was to have a working document with the large seal of the Arbeitsamt, the German employment office, saying *craftsman*. Once more the vicious circle of running to the German employers to change our certificates began and spread like wildfire. Some of our workers received the stamp. Many others, myself among them, failed. Once more we came to work with fear in our hearts. As before, we got together after work to hear and debate the radio news, which depressed us daily. The German official position was that they would go only as far as Moscow and that Bolshevism would be, as they expressed it, "kaput"! We trembled at the thought of this being the end of the war, knowing what this would mean for our fate.

But political discussions were of secondary importance during those days. A rumor suddenly spread that the ghetto was about to be established. We knew that when the ghetto in Kovno was created the Jews were given a month to move. We considered a month to be a considerable amount of time in our situation. In a month we might be saved. The situation might change; our tormentors might fall prey to the Red Army... The eternal rumors suggested that the ghetto would be in Novogrod, because it was outside the city proper and a poor area. The reasoning was that the Germans would not make the ghetto in the center of Vilna and leave the Jews in good buildings with all amenities. But what about the areas that were cleared after the provocation?

Nothing was clear; nothing was certain. At work we could not learn anything. The "good" Germans knew nothing.

My restlessness did not let me sit and wait for the next disaster, I had to find out what the Jewish Committee was doing or planning to do; if anything at all. I was not quite sure if the committee members knew anything more than we, the ordinary Jews, knew; I but hoped they did.

I took the risk and went out even though it was not absolutely necessary. My nerves were close to breaking point and so was my mind. I cautiously reached the building of the Jewish Committee and went inside – and I froze. All the rooms were empty; the place was desolated and destroyed. The rooms had obviously been deliberately wrecked. The furniture, office tables and chairs had been turned upside down; some chairs had been broken; documents were strewn all over the floor – wrecked was the only word to describe it.

On the upper floor of the building I met three committee members who emerged from a small closet to meet me. For a moment we looked at each other in a state of disorientation. I learned from them what had happened.

On September 1, Gestapo Officer Horst Schweinenberger arrived at the office and ordered the committee to supply ten carts and horses by 9:00 the next morning. On September 2 at 10:00 he returned to the committee and demanded to know why the carts and horses were not delivered. The chairman, Engineer S. Trocki explained: "Sir, you know that all means of transport including carts have been forbidden to Jews and our horses have been taken away. We ordered ten Gentiles with their carts for you. I am sure they will soon arrive at the right place." Schweinenberger became violent. He arrested everyone he found in the building, including people who did not belong to the committee. Sixteen of them, including Chairman Trocki, were taken to Lukishki. Six others were released, including committee members A. Fried, A. Zajdsznur, G. Jaszunski and J. Fiszman. The offices were vandalized and the committee ceased to exist.

On the day that I went to the Jewish Committee scores of Jewish activists who had given a lifetime of service to the Jewish community were taken away all over Vilna. Nothing was known except that in the near future there would be a ghetto for us like in Kovno. Nobody knew anything more than that. It was clear that our cup of savagery had not yet been filled. There was more to come. How much more, how many laws against Jews were still to be formulated, how many thousands had still to disappear and how many Jews had yet to die by other means of the German sadistic mind was known only to the Germans – and to God.

We did not know that this was our last week of freedom. We did not know how much longer we would be permitted to stay where we were. But at least we were in our own homes, with Gentile neighbors who sometimes stretched out their friendly hands as much as they could to comfort help us, often taking risks to do so. We had the freedom to spend time with them, to speak with them. More than once they helped out by providing food and other things we could not obtain in the open. Of course we paid, but only for what they had spent for us. They never asked for any reward for their help and felt insulted when we offered to pay for their deeds. We had to be grateful for this kind of freedom.

On Friday I came home from work a little earlier than usual. In the evening we discussed as usual the news of the day. Someone mentioned that our house, at 50 Wielka Street, had been very, very lucky. We didn't know who should be thanked for that luck but it was a fact that we had so far avoided the calamities that had befallen the buildings on both sides of us and directly behind us. All Jewish dwellers in the building behind ours had been arrested on Sunday night. But all the raids against the Jews in our building had passed relatively "peacefully," without a single victim. We were five Jewish families in the building, besides the Gentile ones. One of the Gentile neighbors was a veritable angel: the elderly Mrs. Zosia Kozlowska and her niece.

For almost fifty years Mrs. Zosia Kozlowska kept a small shop selling – of all things – soda water. Before World War I there was a Jewish tradition to go to her small shop on Friday night and Saturday to drink soda water. It was said that Trampczynski's soda water at Zosia's place was the best in all Vilna. She was an unusually good and honest soul. We lived next door to each other. When our family arrived from Lodz at the beginning of the war, during the winter of 1939 we often spent time with her. She felt particularly close to my sisters. When one of them was taken away by the Soviet Militia and deported to the far east, Zosia Kozlowska cried together with us.

With the arrival of the Germans Zosia Kozlowska was happy to be able to extend her help to the Jewish neighbors and her many Jewish friends. The neighbors filled her small room with the dearest and most expensive things without having to say if it was for her or only to keep the items for the time being. Later when we were in the ghetto the saintly woman sent over the things we asked for to enable us to sell them. Many times she literally risked her life to help one Jew or another. During the two Sundays when the anti-Jewish provocation meetings went on and we feared for our lives, expecting any moment the outbreak of a pogrom, she had kept her door open, prepared to hide the Jewish children of her neighbors. She was a veritable angel of God's earth.

All this came to a sudden end the next day. The Jewish Sabbath on September 6, 1941, was destined to become the Black Sabbath of Jewish Vilna. On that day the Germans, with the help of the Lithuanian police, herded the whole Jewish population of Vilna into two ghettos. They had planned their criminal act over some weeks but prepared its implementation for a single day: Saturday, September 6, 1941.

◆

PART TWO
In the Small Ghetto

CHAPTER 4

The Ghetto Becomes Reality

Entering the Small Ghetto

On Saturday morning we rose earlier than usual. A restless feeling didn't let us stay in our beds. As always the first thing was to look out the window – but nothing unusual was going on in the street and we remained calm. As usual, my mother went to scout out the situation and was quickly back saying she was not allowed out of the building and the street was surrounded by soldiers. Though by that stage we had become used to bad news, her information scared us. We returned to the window carefully and looked out in the three directions we could see from our room. Only then did we notice that at the gate of each house stood an armed German soldier guarding the entrance. At the same instant we saw a large cart loaded with white boards being driven into a nearby yard. We sadly concluded that the process of driving the Jews to the ghetto must have started. We had of course expected it for some while but we had counted on having sufficient time to prepare ourselves. We had not known how much time that would be, but if the transfer in Kovno took a full month we had thought we would have at least two weeks. This had been our calculation. Obviously we had not taken into account how cruel the other side could be – and how well they had prepared their plans.

From other windows our neighbors were also looking out, seeing the same things we did, but we could not make out what was actually happening.

A few hours later we noticed groups of Jews walking with packs on their backs, women and children walking with them, and Lithuanian guards surrounded them all. Now we no longer needed additional information; this was the dreaded day. The caretaker came to fill us in with details that we might not have known for ourselves: those in the streets were being ordered to the ghetto while the wooden fence around it was still being put up. Panic broke out among the neighbors and each of us started preparing packs and suitcases, to take as much as we would be able to carry.

Many things we had kept for ourselves were immediately handed over to our Gentile neighbors. In our house we packed everything with a system, according to what we considered each of us could carry. We decided that each of us, including the children, should be prepared to act alone and be independent in any eventuality. First of all the children were given their underwear, some clothes and some food, a pillow and a blanket. After that we made similar bundles for each of the grown-ups, putting on ourselves as many clothes as we believed we could wear. When the packs were ready we sadly noticed that we were leaving our home untouched. All that we had packed to take away was actually of very little value compared to what we were going to leave behind. Everything we had collected ourselves during our lifetime, plus what had been in the house for two or thee generations before us would be left behind. In addition, we were going to leave what we had taken in lately – the household goods of our sisters, our mother's possessions and what we had brought from Lodz. We were to leave behind goods that would have allowed us to live in some economic security for years if we had had the time to take them with us.

We didn't know what was going on in town until the administrator of the building, a Lithuanian, came to our rescue. I took him up to our home and offered him a pair of trousers I had worn only once since I bought them. He sat down at the table and as we all stood around he told us: "A ghetto has been established in Vilna. All Jews must immediately move to the ghetto. Jews are permitted to take as much as they can wear and carry. Your building had long since been marked to have its Jews evacuated but I intervened against it. Now, in the ghetto made for you, you will be safe and have complete peace. Nobody will bother you, nobody will disturb you or touch you and nobody will have any business with you. I want you to know that the Jewish tenants in this building have been spared because of my intervention. I did it for you because I know who you are. Until today I guarded you and I will do the same in the future."

We were touched by his assurance, his goodness. I didn't know the Lithuanian; I was seeing him for the first time in my life. But there was not much time to consider anything. I thanked him in the name of all the Jewish tenants and asked him what we had to do right then. "You don't have to do anything. In the evening I'll come with a cart and take you with your belongings to the ghetto where I will see to it that you get a nice apartment. It will all be in order; you need not worry."

Hearing how much our administrator had done for us already and was going to do, the neighbors and I relaxed somewhat. During the previous few hours we had seen groups of Jews walking by carrying packs and suitcases guarded by Lithuanians armed to the hilt. We noticed that that the Jews could hardly walk. It was obvious that they made a superhuman effort…while we would have a cart at our disposal.

The hours went by as we kept packing and repacking what we had not given away already. My mother had already taken a considerable part of our household and given it to relatives, friends and as donations to the Jewish Committee. We had been sure that the Germans would start with the rich Jewish families; there they would have valuables worth stealing. Time had shown that we had been wrong. The first to suffer had been the Jews of the poor streets. Their homes had been cleared for the ghetto and they were gone, disappeared. Now we saw the result of our miscalculations; the things we had taken out of the house were lost.

But what was still to be left was more than enough to break our hearts. One last time, probably for the tenth time that day, I looked around over everything within the walls I had always called home. Why was I punishing myself? I don't know but again I went over the inventory that we had accumulated. The hard work that both my father and my mother had invested in making this home what it was now, plus the things that had come in from our relatives over the last months. It was all going to the Devil. Everything was now falling into the hands of our blood enemies as a reward for what they were doing to us. How many decades of toil and sweat it had taken us to build our home…

No! I didn't want to go on torturing myself over and over! In a few hours, in minutes, all this would be finished, dismantled, destroyed, wrecked. And the same was now going on in hundreds of other Jewish homes. Physical destruction performed by murderers was taking place, and we were waiting our turn in line.

Once more I went next door to our neighbor, Zosia Kozlowska. People had brought her a colossal amount of items. They had turned the small room into a great storehouse packed to the ceiling. We personally handed over many things to the caretaker. Others had hidden possessions wherever they could: in the attics, buried in cellars; they hid jewelry in the ground and marked the place where they hid it – at the headstone of the grave of a relative at the cemetery or at the foot of a near one's grave. It was all the same. Only the wise ones had kept such items on themselves. I came back to look at my mother's Sabbath candlesticks. Simple ones made of brass but how much grace was in them now! How much joy and sorrow those candlesticks had served in our family. Since childhood I used to watch my mother as she lit the Sabbath candles every Friday at sunset. As the candles flickered, she covered her face with her hands and said her silent prayers. I saw the tears on her gentle face when she removed her hands. The same candleholders were part of our joy at weddings and holidays. In times of sorrow they stood at the head of the departed in the family, lit with mourning candles. For fifty years the silent friends had served us – and now we were to abandon them to the filthy hands of robbers!

I noticed my mother moving around touching and caressing the pots on the shelves, each one separately. She stopped somewhat longer at the samovar. She was engrossed in her action without noticing that her son was weeping together with her. Saying farewell to it in his own way; everything in the room was dying alone as we were leaving. How can one explain in words how the dead items came to life in those last moments, to take leave of us in their silent way. No matter what people might say I shall insist that I heard them take leave of us the way I was taking leave of them… and so our Jewish home was dying.

Unable to watch the pain of my mother, my wife, and my children, I went into the yard to the neighbors. All were preparing for the move. Restless and impatient we waited for the moment when the bandits would arrive in our yard. I still had some hope about the administrator – he had promised! Perhaps he would come to help us. I called the neighbors to our room for a last tea and a bite. I boiled the water, made the tea and offered the neighbors bread and honey.

It was a last meal of the condemned before they were taken to the gallows.

We had just finished our meal when we heard a noise in the yard and within seconds the noise turned into a veritable battle cry of a large crowd. The door to our room was torn open and the room was filled with Lithuanian military and civilians and their wild screaming. Putting his hand on the man standing nearest to the door a uniformed Lithuanian pushed him out of the room screaming in Lithuanian, "Quick! Quick!" The bandit had no time to be a little human. Of course not – we were apparently not the last ones and they wanted to finish their job and go back to their normal weekend enjoyment.

Immediately the house was full of people crying. My mother embraced her old friend Zosia Kozlowska and kissed her, tears streaming down their faces. The Lithuanian messengers of Satan could not leave the two elderly women alone, not one but two of the hooligans tore them apart. We quickly gathered our bundles as there was no sign of the administrator. Possibly he was not allowed to interfere in the orderly work of those destroyers. More likely, the story he told us in the morning was nothing more than taking advantage of our misfortune. He would come, tell us how much he had done, and would do for us and profit in this way from our misery. I was not the only one who had handed him a gift while he was in our home.

In the middle of the turmoil I managed to ask the civilian Lithuanian – the only one who stood around patiently, as if he were only observing what was going on: "What will happen with all the things we are leaving here now?" His answer was calm, completely detached from what was going on around him: "I am here to seal the room and nobody will touch anything. The keys will be at the police station and the seal will stay on until it will be decided what to do." After his pronunciation the bandits stopped pushing us around and I began helping the others put the packs on their backs and take the suitcases as we had prepared them. I picked up my own pack and an electric kettle, thinking that such a thing might come in very handy; it might provide a warm drink on the road. I put the kettle down for a moment to help somebody and when I turned back the kettle had disappeared. The whole thing took no more than a fraction of a minute. No strangers were present in the house by this point, only the young subtenant from the next room. I asked her, "Where has the kettle disappeared to?" "I didn't see any kettle," she answered calmly. For a moment I lost my mind despite the dramatic situation. The kettle appeared to me for some reason to be of great importance and come what may I had to get it back. I asked again about the kettle, the Lithuanians screamed to get moving: "Quick, Quick." and I, having lost my sense of proportion, had to find out what had happened to the kettle.

I dropped the pack and ran in to her room. The kettle was standing on the edge of the table. She hadn't even bothered to hide it!

Grabbing the kettle and putting the pack back on I let myself go: "We leave you more than enough to steal. I never thought that you would be able to be so disgusting. In a moment like this, instead of helping your neighbors you are trying to steal the little we might need to survive..." I was pushed out of the room by one of the "nice boys" and went slowly down the staircase. The older woman came running after me: "I swear by Jesus that I did not take it. She, the young one, has done it. May Jesus pay her for it. Please forgive, please." At the gate my mother was already waiting impatiently for me. My wife, the children and the other families began to take leave of each other. We didn't know if we would be separated from each other. We had to be harder than iron not to collapse on the spot. Something must have touched even the stony heart of the Lithuanians, if they had such a thing as a heart. They stood silently waiting for the few minutes without interfering. They let us embrace and kiss our other neighbors and after those few minutes it was all over.

Already in the street, I turned my face back to the three windows of our room. I spoke to them in the same way the mute things had earlier spoken to me: "We will probably come back to you but you keep looking out, to be the first to see us if we should ever return."

Banishing Jews from their homes and forcing them into the ghettos had begun early in the morning all over Vilna. Most people, however, did not receive the humane treatment that we had experienced. In many streets the executioners did not allow their victims to take anything. The Jews in those areas were chased out of their homes with no belongings at all. Whatever they held in their hands they had to drop and go. Beating was the norm in those places and victims received it in abundance. In the more distant areas there was no such prohibition and people took as much as they believed they would be able to carry. The result was that many tired to the point of exhaustion along the way and had to leave their packs on the road. Many threw off some of the layers of clothing they had put on in the hope of taking a little more with them.

The huge mass of people was herded like cattle in several directions. One stream was driven in the direction of Rudnicka Street, where one ghetto had been marked out, the other stream was directed toward Gaon Street into another ghetto. There was a third direction of which we were not aware at the time – to Ponary, to the slaughterhouse for Jews. Those who lived close to the Lukishki prison and the nearby areas were taken in that direction. That group, we found out a little later, was driven into a small side alley, taken to Lukishki prison and from there they were sent to their death in the killing fields of Ponary.

From all directions columns of Jews were walking in the middle of the road, some with heavy bundles and packages, others without, some under Lithuanian guards that were relatively passive, others with guards who kept screaming, pushing and beating men, women and children with their rubber truncheons. The black parade of Jews being herded had taken the whole day before it had reached us.

When we arranged our individual packs for the road, we had put them on to see how much each of us would be able to carry. It seemed that we could carry the finished bundles all the way. However when we were already on the road we found that we had no energy to carry the loads we had packed. Later, recalling how we had managed to come into the ghetto we marveled that none of us, neither the children nor the adults, wanted to leave the packs each one was carrying. We went in pain and cried a little but we persevered, knowing how much each item would mean in terms of a piece of bread. The women and children went in front and the men followed close behind. Every few minutes somebody stopped. When this happened, I immediately ran forward to help lift the packs back on the back of the carriers. But my energy was also fading. By the time we reached some two-thirds of the way I had to stop and throw off the two packs I was carrying. During those fleeting moments my childhood passed through my mind. We were on Sovitscher Lane, where I went to my first heder, and here also was the first elementary school I attended. I had spent the happiest years of my childhood there, and now I was standing in the same street, the last remnant of the last of the many branches that comprised our family…and they were chasing me like a dog. Not only me, but also the whole Jewish world of Lithuania.

The Lithuanian guard had stopped with me and let me rest for a few minutes. But when I tried to lift the large packs I found I had no energy – my situation was hopeless. As I was still bending and trying once more to lift the bundle, a Christian man stepped off the sidewalk and threw the bundle on my shoulders. The whole exercise took seconds but it saved me. I felt momentarily refreshed, revived. I started to go forward with a faster step and caught up with the family. I was thinking about the exceptional act of the stranger who risked his life to help another human being – a Jew – in spite of the fact that rumors were circulating (which were later confirmed to be true) that the authorities had issued a strict order to the non-Jewish population not to help us in any way.

When we passed Szklanna Street, the street that had been emptied out the previous Sunday night, we saw a high wall closing off the street from the nearby alley. At the entrance to the street we saw a large contingent of police and soldiers. The street was closed off. We halted for a moment and had a chance to catch our breath while others entered. When we had to move, I helped the others lift their packs once more. Again the same thing happened – I could not lift my own packs. Again a young Gentile ran off the sidewalk, threw the two packs on me and took hold of one of the two suitcases I was carrying. At first glance I could not believe my luck, but immediately I noticed that my helper was not following me with the suitcase he had taken. He had started to walk the other way with the suitcase that had the most valuable things we had managed to take with us. I stopped and began screaming: "Stop him! Stop that man! He's taken my suitcase with my possessions – stop him!" Among the people on the sidewalk some noticed my predicament and reacted. The policeman guarding us stopped the man, took the suitcase and handed it back to me without arresting the thief.

In those few moments I was shaking with rage but at the same time regretted the commotion I had started. I could have drawn attention to myself and the guards could have taken the lot away from me. With my last ounce of energy I entered the alley and rejoined my family. They had already stopped and thrown off the heavy loads while they anxiously waited for me. The two minutes I had stopped had badly affected my family. They were able to stop and wait only because the queue in front of them had stopped for some reason. Here we relaxed a little longer.

While we rested a man near us spoke to me. "You are a risky gambler," he said. "Let them go to hell with the suitcases. Oh, Lord of the Universe, help us to reach the ghetto!"

Somebody on the other side had a different view: "But at moments like this we see what kind of people surround us. To try to steal the last things we have – " The first speaker didn't let him finish the sentence: "Are you surprised? They are in a hurry. They cannot wait for the moment when they will be allowed to inherit what we have left behind."

In this way we passed the minutes of relaxation, not knowing what we were waiting for, or where we were going. It turned out that we were standing near the ghetto gate. We had been forced to stop and wait because there was a holdup at the entrance. The Lithuanian guards had gone forward to clear a path for us. But when the time came for us to move forward, the same thing happened; we had no energy to lift the packs. We were helpless.

At that moment some young Jewish men came forward: "Let us help you, we will lead you in to the ghetto." To tell the truth after the last experience, none of us was willing to trust strangers with the last crust of bread that the packs represented... Sure, they were Jews but who were they? We had dragged ourselves so far and this was all that stood between us and total destitution. We didn't want to lose it now.

Two young men approached me: "Mr. Balberyszski, we know you. Let us have your things; don't be afraid. We will hand everything back to you the way we took it. We'll take full responsibility for your things." Their words calmed me: "Thank you, children, from the bottom of my heart for your kindness. Here are our things."

With renewed energy (from what sources we had the energy, we would never know; life has its own will and its own ways) we lifted our packs and within minutes we stood at the new, white timber gate of the ghetto. The pile-up was endless; we couldn't move an inch forward. Our helpers forced a way forward and minutes later we had passed the gate and stood on the other side – in the ghetto.

It may be difficult to comprehend, but the moment we passed through the gate a sudden great sense of relief filled our hearts. *Oh, thank You Almighty! Thank You. At last we are on our own. Let it be in the ghetto, as long as we will be free from the city, its robbers and murderers. There are no Lithuanians in the ghetto, no Germans. Just Jews among themselves. No matter how difficult living conditions in the ghetto may be, Jews should be safe behind the locked ghetto gate.*

With a sudden burst of energy we made our way through the crowds jamming the area around the ghetto gate to a building on the corner of Szklanna and Gaon streets. All packs we had entrusted into the hands of the wonderful young men had been returned to us. We put them all in one place and made our "lodgings" inside the gate of the building. After a few minutes of the first unhurried relaxation since we had been driven out of our home we began taking notice of where we were and what was happening around us.

I knew the inner court of the building from way back. For decades a man named Gurewicz had his paint shop here. During my childhood a man named Shimon, known as "the nose," had his shoe-leather workshop here too. My father, of blessed memory, and Shimon were the *gabais* (honorary administrators) of the prayerhouse where we prayed; we grew up and studied together in the same high school. Now we were standing at the gate like beggars, homeless...

I left my wife to guard our possessions with the children and together with my mother went out to see, to listen and to gather some news. The inner court was full of people, friends and others we knew from various places. It was the first free gathering of so many Jews since the Germans had entered Vilna. To all questions about this one or that one, the reply was mostly: "taken." No longer did anyone add where, when or under what circumstances the individuals had been "taken." However we heard at intervals also a sudden scream: "Oh, thank God you are here. Thank God."

The place was bubbling like a boiling kettle. From the court I went out into the street and began walking the old lanes of Vilna that I knew so well. It was a short walk. I went over to Zydowska Street and after a few paces realized that I had reached the boundary of the ghetto. At the house of Nahum the beadle a fence had been erected indicating the border. Crossing to the other side of the lane I began searching for a place to spend the night but I saw nobody that I could ask. It was already dusk and all of us were mentally only half functioning. I turned back to our lodgings at the gate.

During the short time that I had been wandering on my own my mother had managed to achieve more than I did. She had met an old friend who had been living here since before the war and she immediately invited my mother to her house. Every one of the friend's family had been "taken away" on the provocation night. Hiding under the bed, she had managed not to be noticed and remained in the house; now she was alone. She had already given shelter to others and she took all of us in to spend the first night in the ghetto at her place.

We climbed up to the second floor of the house and found a little place for our packs. The children immediately fell down on them. My mother and my wife found accommodation in the corner near the packs and another man and I bedded down for the night on the table.

The noise reaching us from the court was endless. As darkness fell on the nice summer evening we heard a constant cry: "Cover the light, cover the light." The windows in all houses were open and the people that kept arriving had a need to accommodate themselves somehow. They switched on the light for a moment without covering the windows and the shouts immediately went up. The Lithuanians threatened to shoot into the windows if the lights were switched on, thereby "giving signs to the Russians."

The stream of arrivals went on until late in the night. The noise was like in a beehive. Those who had arrived earlier had grabbed the better apartments. As time went on the situation became more acute and the pressure for accommodation became greater. In some cases the people who had managed to get hold of the better rooms would not let anybody join them. The stronger late arrivals forced themselves into rooms wherever they could against the resistance of others.

Exhausted and depressed we all dropped onto our beds, falling or not falling asleep, everyone with his and her own thoughts about what had happened during the day. In a single day, tens of thousands of people had been brutally torn out of their homes where they had spent a lifetime. Lying in the dark we related to each other details of how the day had passed for each of us. We mostly knew each other, veteran Jewish residents of Vilna.

The sum total of our conversation was that there was not a single house that has not lost some of its people and that some large groups had not been brought into the ghetto but had been led away somewhere else… The separated families comforted themselves with the thought that those missing might have been sent to the other ghetto. "We will meet up with them," they reassured themselves.

Slowly nature overtook our worries and we fell into short slumbers. At first daylight we went down to the water pump and after washing ourselves as best we could we went out, this time to scout for ourselves and see how the new life was starting. Not everyone had such great luck as we had had the previous night. We were indeed "lucky." We had some place to put our heads down to sleep. Many people had nowhere to spend the night. Not for the first night and not for many later nights. They slept in the streets or at best on the steps inside the buildings wherever they could.

In my exploration of the ghetto over the coming days I saw how terribly the Germans had destroyed the buildings that we held dear. They had shown their special interest in the many religious buildings Jewish Vilna had erected over generations. They were particularly interested in the old city synagogue, known as the Great Synagogue.

Demanding the keys from Mr. Gordon, the synagogue beadle, the Germans entered the synagogue and stood astonished by the beauty and richness of the building. They then immediately began to despoil it. They vandalized the beautiful holy ark and took out a larger number of holy scrolls that the synagogue had accumulated over three hundred years. Some of the scrolls were unique items in the Jewish world, known everywhere to academics of Jewish studies. They plundered and took away the silver ornaments, the "dresses" or "coats" of the holy scrolls: the crowns, the breastplates, the silver pointers in the delicate form of a tiny hand with the pointing finger... The hands had been used for generations by the reader of the weekly portions of the Torah during services. With the pointer he guided the individual who had been honored to see the position where the reader was reading. They took away all the copper and brass lights and fittings as well as many other items.

In later days, local boot makers used the parchments of the scrolls on which the five books of Moses, the Torah, had been handwritten by trained scribes, to make linings for boots and slippers for the "higher German Aryan race." The makers of balalaikas made back covers for their instruments out of the same parchment. All desecrated the scrolls with the Ten Commandments without removing the holy text.

It would appear that Mr. Gordon the beadle, foreseeing the danger, hid many antiques in secret places within the synagogue. At a later time when we entered the vandalized synagogue we found a secret place behind a wall, secured with a heavy iron gate which had been forced – and everything the beadle might have hidden there had been removed. Still later we found that the Germans had vandalized another hiding place in the study house of the *Hevrah Kadishah* (Burial Fraternity) in a similar manner.

Adjusting to Ghetto Life

On my first day in the ghetto I came across my friend, Haim Remigalski. I had met Remigalski for the first time before the outbreak of the First World War. He worked at that time in the large pharmacy of I.B. Segal. Later I worked with him in the Professional Union of Pharmacy Employees. In 1918

Remigalski was elected as an independent, with no party affiliation, to the first Jewish Community Administration (Kehillah), the authorized Jewish representatives to the Polish government. He later went to Palestine and came back to Poland to the free city of Danzig. In the end he left the pharmacy and worked as a permanent member of YIVO. We used to meet in his house in Vilna, and then later in Lodz. When we encountered each other in the ghetto we embraced and kissed one another, both of us happy and deeply moved to see each other alive.

He came into the ghetto with his wife and his son, a medical doctor. After the second day in the ghetto we went together to visit the new chairman of the Jewish advisory board (Judenrat), I. Lejbowicz, whom we both knew well from before the war. Lejbowicz was pleased to see us and was eager to tell us about the curious incident that led to his being chairman of the Judenrat. Lejbowicz lived on the street from which all Jews were removed during the second night of "cleansings" after the provocation on August 31. His family managed to escape the German raid. On Saturday morning, seeing that a wall and a gate were being erected in the court across from their home, Lejbowicz quickly moved his family to the other side and took over one of the empty apartments. Thus his family became the first citizens of the ghetto.

Gestapo Officer Schweinenberger and District Kommissar Hingst directed the operation in which the Jews of Vilna were herded into the ghetto. They came early Saturday morning to see how the construction of the wall was progressing. Meeting Lejbowicz, Schweinenberger commanded him in his usual loud and arrogant voice: "You will be the leader of the Jews. Understand?" In the same manner the Gestapo officer stopped several other Jews and nominated them as members of the ghetto Judenrat. They were Nahum Lewit, Zelig Levin, Feldman, Szneiderowicz and Jacob Zyrowski, who became the Judenrat secretary.

"What can we do now?" Lejbowicz asked. "We have no guidelines, no instructions and no money. Conditions are catastrophic; alleviating the shortage of dwellings and space is beyond our means; people are living in the streets, in yards, on the steps in houses. How do we begin?" Lejbowicz asked in despair.

"We cannot go out into the town. The German who appointed us as Jewish leaders does not allow us to talk to him, or ask anything. All we can do right now is to wait to see what the day brings…"

The whole of Sunday, the first day in the ghetto, was taken up with searching for accommodation. People who had been pushed into the ghetto early Saturday morning were happy. They immediately took over the best dwellings left by the families who had been taken away during the two "cleansing" nights. (All non-Jewish residents, including caretakers, had been removed from the streets designated for the ghetto during the week.) In many apartments the new "owners" found a considerable quantity of household articles that the non-Jewish neighbors had not had time to remove during the few days at their disposal. Some families had stored wood for the winter, coal, potatoes and dried foods. Many apartment houses that had not been looted by non-Jewish neighbors had complete sets of linen, underwear, dresses and suits, crockery and cutlery. Those who came to the ghetto early Saturday morning were able to occupy those houses and take possession of those items and immediately became wealthy by ghetto standards.

Already on the first day it was obvious that even in the cataclysm that engulfed us all some were luckier than others. Many had managed to find good accommodation, others had not done too badly either, at least sufficiently well to continue, while a great number of families had nowhere to lay their heads down and lived on the streets – totally destitute.

There had been a very large and noticeable difference in the ways people came to the ghetto. We, for example, had brought with us quite a few things – a little of everything. Many others had not been allowed to take anything. Others, coming from far away, had thrown away the heavy packs they had prepared or had them confiscated on the way to the ghetto.

The main, immediate and very acute problem was food. Some people had brought small amounts of food with them, while others found a few items in the homes that had been cleansed during the two nights at the beginning of the week. But the majority had absolutely no food at all. Not a single morsel of anything.

Masses of people walked around as if in a trance; nothing interested them. They wandered around seeking relatives. When the Jews were being herded into the ghetto, many families had been torn apart, some members had been driven to the ghetto while other family members were sent directly to the Lukishki prison. Members of such families (and they were in the thousands) walked around like mental patients who had taken leave of their minds. To them, the need for shelter, furniture, bedding and food had no meaning at all.

It was natural that in the given situation the group known as *Die Shtarke* (the Tough Ones) used their physical force to get hold of the wealthy, well-equipped homes. That group consisted of underworld types. Against them, the great majority of ordinary people were helpless. Right from the start, the most helpless ones were the people with higher education, the professionals. Within the first few hours of their arrival in the ghetto those who had been used to wealthy surroundings with all comforts became destitute and powerless. People of completely different backgrounds and education, cultural upbringings and habits, often more than ten people, were shoved together in one apartment or even into a single, large room. They were a non-segregated mix of men, women, and children, old and young. Some knew each other, but others were complete strangers who had been thrown together by circumstances.

However, necessity has always been the mother of invention and a majority discovered their own abilities and found a way to accommodate themselves. On Sunday, the Lithuanians brought additional groups of Jews into the ghetto who had managed to avoid the murderers on Saturday, when the whips of the herdsmen led the pack of Jews in the first drive to the ghetto.

The Lithuanians packed more than nine thousand Jews into the small ghetto, which consisted of a few poor, small and dirty lanes. On the first day, when I became acquainted with the borders of our "kingdom," I understood only too well our situation. Perhaps I should describe in detail the map of the new "kingdom" by naming those few lanes and stating which part of each of them was in the ghetto and what remained outside. But this would be meaningless to the stranger who doesn't know Vilna. A clearer description of the ghetto is provided by the fact that on average eight to ten people had to live in a single room, some not much bigger than a large cupboard.

The Germans closed off the ghetto with a thirty-foot-high timber fence. At the single entrance to the small ghetto they constructed two gates: a narrow opening at the side for individuals passing in and out and, in the center, a large gate with two wings leading out to the road. The wings opened for the traffic of horse carts and German autos, but mainly, as we found out later, the gates were there to enable the quick removal of thousands of Jews to Ponary.

Ghetto planners deliberately converted the streets of the ghetto into a twisted labyrinth by making sections of the streets outside the ghetto boundaries. It made it more difficult for people to move around and initially created a lot of confusion. Many of the large inner courts that had been built in earlier times to allow passage from one lane to the next had been cut, part in and part out of the ghetto. The Great Synagogue court, which had been the nerve center of Jewish Vilna, was divided with what may only be described as deliberate sadism. Many old institutions that made up the synagogue court had been deliberately left outside the ghetto. The communal latrines of the synagogue court had been left inside the ghetto and now bordered with the wall of the ghetto. The synagogue court had been treated the same way as Vilna Jewry. The broken Jewish community and the destroyed synagogue court complimented each other in more than a symbolic way.

After a few days in the ghetto we learned about a gruesome tragedy that occurred while Jews were being herded in. About two thousand Jews had been separated from the stream and directed into Lidski Lane and not into any ghetto. That happened because the Lithuanians had pushed such great numbers of people into the large ghetto in Rudnicka Street that it was no longer physically possible to squeeze in any more. A large number of Jews had remained at the gate outside the ghetto. The Germans decided on the spot to force the overflow into Lidski Lane. When this was accomplished they simply closed off the street from both sides and left them under the night sky. From there they were then sent to Lukishki prison, and on to Ponary. While in Lukishki, the Lithuanian guards subjected them to the cruelest savagery, beating the victims – men and children – and laughing merrily when the poor Jews cried out in pain. Thousands of Jews, totally destitute, torn from their families, famished, tired and injured languished in the Lukishki prison, many wishing for the end to come soon. After suffering under indescribable conditions for days, they were relieved; they were driven one final time – to Ponary.

However, even in the Lukishki prison, some Jews had contacts with "good" Germans. During the first days these Jewish middlemen managed through their "good" Germans to bring individuals out from the prison to the ghetto. This was as usual accomplished with very large gifts and payments to the Germans and to the middlemen. But this time the outcome was tragic. The names of those who were supposed to be given the freedom to join their near ones in the ghetto were called out in the corridors leading to the cells. Sometime the persons whose names were called out did not answer, as they were afraid that they might be called to die. At the same time, there were others who also believed the names called meant being called to death but they wanted death to come quickly and replied to their names. To their unimaginable surprise they were released in place of the ones for whom large sums had been paid. In this way a small number of Jews were saved.

Prominent among the Jewish middlemen in the trade for prisoner release were Weisskopf from the large ghetto, his colleague Azierjanski and the head of the sanitary department, Voronov. They all became very rich from the trade, especially at a later stage when the ability to procure a yellow pass meant the difference between life and death. The trade was ugly but it did save a number of Jews from death.

Settling In

The first Sunday in the ghetto was taken up with trying to accommodate ourselves. My mother went through the lanes of the ghetto looking for relatives and friends. In one of the courts that led from one lane to the next we had relatives who had lived there all their lives. The head of one family was the locksmith, Moshe Aaron Bershtel. During the time between the beginning of the German occupation and the establishment of the ghetto my mother had entrusted to him costly furs, dresses, linen and other valuables. When my mother came to his place on Sunday, the dwelling had already been taken over by others. She went to the address of another relative and found the door locked with a padlock. The family of that relative had a small child and when they were taken away they must have hoped to return home and put on a padlock. Without any hesitation, my mother forced the outside lock and went into the room.

The apartment was a single room on the fourth floor. Under the circumstances it was a virtual palace of an apartment. The two windows looked out to the roof of the building. A cupboard divided the room in two, with the dining room on one side and the bedroom on the other. The dining-room area was about thirteen feet long and six feet wide, with a low ceiling and a large oven at the entrance. The whole room was full of furniture: a large bed, a sofa, the cupboard, a table and some wooden chairs. On a shelf near the oven was a collection of pots and in one corner of the room stood a small, well-kept bed for a child. Everything had been left untouched. In the cupboard the family had left pots and jars with preserved foods prepared for the winter.

We decided to take the place immediately. When I pointed out that we should not take it without confirming it with the Jewish advisory board my mother retorted: "Don't you see what is going on? If we don't take over the room right now others will do it and we will be left to roam the streets."

In this way we had found an untouched home. True it was a very humble place, the home of poor people. But who else but the poor would have lived in this district? In addition I liked the strategic value of the room. It was in the attic with windows looking out to the roof. For ghetto conditions it was a place of great value. We would have paid for it with gold and diamonds. In times of searches and raids it could be turned into a marvelous hideout…as it proved to be later on.

In the large oven we found a considerable quantity of locksmith and electrician's supplies apparently readied for the war situation. We also discovered a small storage room stocked with wood for the winter. The dwelling had been well prepared for the approaching winter but the owners were no longer around to make use of it.

The beautiful but empty child's bed made a painful impression on my mother and me. Everything had been left untouched. The bandits had left everything as it was but had taken the poor parents and their child. Now we had a fully furnished home because its rightful owners had been taken to the abyss of Ponary.

The dwelling had an additional advantage: the only way to reach it was through a dark and twisted old, wooden staircase. People standing at the bottom of the staircase got the impression that the staircase led to the roof.

The room had no toilet or other facilities. Water had to be carried from the courtyard pump and filled buckets had to be carried down. Inside the street level entrance there were two storage rooms and an opening that led to a cellar. The cellar could be turned into a hideout – and so could "our" fourth-floor room which we had all to ourselves – no one else but us, the whole family together.

We took a deep breath, a breath of freedom, like everyone else who had been forced into the ghetto. Logic dictated that. What more could those villains want of us? They had already murdered close to half the Jewish population. They squeezed us into the dark cage of the ghetto; what else could they do to us? Now that they had banished us, surely they would let us live in peace...and we Jews are used to living under any kind of conditions. Those who had been taken could not be brought back; fate had intervened. But those who stayed and persevered would remain, so we told ourselves. They would not destroy us all! They needed Jews for all kinds of work in, or for, the city. The assurance for this had been given by "good" Germans: "Now you will have peace," they had promised us. Even the friendly Lithuanians and Poles had comforted us: "What happened, happened; now a new time is beginning for Jews."

The half of the Vilna Jewish community that was still alive settled into the two ghettos as well as was possible. Nobody questioned the German reason for making two ghettos, assuming that that was done to prevent the overcrowding of a single ghetto. The future would reveal to us that the creation of two ghettos was part of a well-prepared master plan by the German administration that would confuse the Jews and ultimately make it easier to destroy them. But the future was still to come and for the moment we did not care if they made one ghetto or two.

A new way of life began. At dawn every morning, groups of Jewish men and women went out under guard to their work places for the duration of the day. They returned to the ghetto somewhere between four and five in the evening. At first, Germans guarded the groups. Later, when there was only one ghetto, the position of a Jewish brigadier was created and they took over the role of the German guards.

Women and children, the old and the sick remained in the ghetto when the men went out to work. In time, the ghetto administration began to function and those employed by the Jewish Council (Judenrat) also remained in the ghetto. Every day for the first few weeks, the women and children used to wait impatiently for the return of their men who had gone to work in the city. Thousands of people congregated near the gate. During the first days, meeting a near and dear one coming back was an occasion to embrace and kiss, as if the one who had left the ghetto was coming back from another world. Those who had remained inside feared for our fate while we, outside the ghetto, worked in constant deadly fear for what might happen to those we left behind.

Before we were forced into the ghettos, the city authorities had established large production plants for the fur trade company, known as "Kailis." Hundreds of Jewish tradesmen found work in those places, manufacturing fur coats, gloves and similar items. On the day the ghettos were established, the Kailis workers were taken to two large buildings located near the workshops which were designated as their living quarters. They were separated from the ghettos, as if forming a little ghetto of their own.

My work outside the ghetto remained the same as before, finishing the large building for the German women who were to come and work as telephone and telegraph operators for the Germans. Their homes had to be furnished for them.

The looting of Jewish homes that had started on the first day that the German army entered Vilna became a major industry after the Black Sabbath.

After we came into the ghetto the Germans began using a considerable number of trucks to collect stolen Jewish furniture and other goods from the many thousands of homes we had been forced to leave. Now it had become a complicated matter, no longer as simple as before. Earlier, when we had started emptying the better Jewish homes it was a matter of trial and error. We were driven to a section of town, the German who took us, usually a military officer, decided with a yes or no if anything we found was worth taking away. Now it had become a planned industry, with prepared lists of where we had to go and what we were expected to find and bring back to the Germans. Obviously inspectors had gone before us.

We now brought back the best and the most beautiful furniture from Jewish homes whose owners had already been relocated to the ravines of Ponary. How we felt facing the empty homes of another family, of murdered Jews, remains indescribable in print. We worked as slowly as was possible. During the hours of work, we had to run up staircases of two, three and even four floors carrying down, again and again, heavy pieces of solid timber furniture to load it on to the truck. During the first days I returned home totally exhausted and fell on my bed half-dead. In my weary state my mind continued to do the work that my body did not do. It went on carrying cupboards, beds, mattresses, tables, chairs and sofas while every bone in my body, every muscle, was screaming in pain. But I got used to it. After a short while, the heavy load became no more than routine. Within twelve weeks we had deposited in the store of our working place a huge amount of expensive furniture.

On occasion, the Germans did not take us to individual Jewish homes. They took us instead to a place where they stored all kinds of goods stolen from Jewish homes. For years the place had been a Talmudic study house in the Novogrod district. At our first encounter with the two warehouses there we realized how puny the store at our working place was. Two large buildings had been filled with the loot the Germans had collected thus far by robbing thousands of deserted Jewish homes. It became clear to us that the Germans had taken everything that our neighbors, the Lithuanians and others had not managed to clear out in time and had brought the goods here, to what we thought must be the central collection point for the plundered goods.

The truck that brought us to the place for the first time was driven into a large yard with a two-floor storage building. The ground floor, which took up about a thousand square feet, was filled with all kinds of furniture, most of it not less valuable and some of it more valuable than the furniture we had collected. On the first floor were stolen household goods: elegant decorated boxes with sets of silver cutlery, full sets of crockery, beautiful coffee sets of expensive porcelain, clothing, pictures, samovars and expensive light fixtures. With the robbed goods of this store alone a complete housing district could have been fitted out quite comfortably.

We found everything here stored in an orderly way on shelves and in cupboards, ready to be sent away for the use of the Germans. On the first floor between the cupboards and shelves, was the "garbage." It consisted of prayer shawls, phylacteries, silver candlesticks, hats and shoes. One had to step on them to get from one place to the next.

I managed for a moment to walk over to a corner where large paintings had been stored. One portrait drew my attention. It was of a famous Russian singer and had a handwritten dedication of gratitude: "To Dr. Levande, for healing me from a very difficult throat inflammation." From the way the paintings around this one had been stored, I concluded that they all belonged to the same household. Dr. Levande no longer had any need for the valuable paintings.

Together with Teitelbaum, the lawyer, I stood for a moment and took in the cataclysmic size of our destruction. Teitelbaum remarked: "Titus could not have done as well when he sacked Jerusalem." I didn't answer. The other workers who had been brought here with us kept filling their pockets with whatever they could hide. A young man, the leader, came over to us and explained: "Here one is allowed to take whatever one can. These are our own goods and it is preferable that we take it than leave it for the Germans. It may become useful for us and for our families in the ghetto. You know, bread… We should not be embarrassed about it and play false sentiments." Neither Teitelbaum nor I made any remark. Perhaps the man was right but neither of us touched a single thing. We had some strange feeling about the things that we found there.

On another occasion while we were on our way out of the huge store, we met up with a large, horse-driven cart that was coming in with a load of robbed goods. A Polish worker jumped off the cart and stumbled. A drawer full of small items fell down from a desk and spread its contents. I picked up a few photos and, for a moment, became confused. My eyes failed to focus for some seconds. I was holding the family photo of my cousin Arkadi Yadlovker. Arcadi was a talented violinist. During the years 1919–20 he was a student of the virtuoso Malkin. Malkin and his wife lived with Yadlovker when they came from Russia. I too lived with the family for a short while. Several years after the First World War, Malkin was brought to the United States by his former student, Yasha Heifetz.

Yadlovker had been a soloist in the Vilna Symphony Orchestra. He was also often engaged to play in Polish theaters. His wife was from a well-known family. Her brother, M. Zabludowski, owned a renowned candy factory. When I came home that day, I learned that Arkadi had been taken from his home by the human-catchers. Later, other members of the family died in the ghetto.

During the period that the Soviets ruled Vilna, Arkadi bought a small violin for our son and introduced him to its music. After the first lessons he said that our son had a good ear for music. Coming face-to-face with the family picture disturbed me for the rest of the day.

I had a similar experience the first time I came to the second building of the huge store where our murderers collected Jewish goods. The synagogue and the yeshiva in the building lay in ruins. The bima (raised platform in the center of the synagogue from which the Torah is read) had been vandalized. The holy ark stood open; its beautiful curtain had been taken away together with the holy scrolls. The benches that had not been destroyed were dirty and covered in dust. The whole building, including the synagogue and the other study rooms, had been turned into storage rooms. Just like the first building, here too the goods robbed from Jewish homes were collected and stored. In this second building I saw Germans coming and shamelessly taking tablecloths and tableware, crystal glassware and other home wares for themselves.

We constantly walked over stacks of things that Jews had collected with blood and sweat over the course of generations. It lay around here valueless – except to Jews. I felt as if the goods here were proclaiming to the robbers, "Come and take whatever you want. Come – it is free. Now is your opportunity!" The visits we made to those stores were tragically painful. But we had no choice. Our masters ordered us to come and we had to obey if we were to survive.

One day while sorting things at the store I came across a large container full of silver goblets, the kind over which we recited the benediction on Friday nights. I could not resist the temptation any longer. I took a large goblet, one that was similar to my father's goblet at home. I went over to the officer who was in charge of our work and asked him to permit me to take the goblet as a memory of my father. The man was a "good" German. He permitted me to take it but warned me to be very careful, saying that I should know that if I were found with it, it might cost me my life. Jews were not permitted to have silver goods. I took the gift and gave it to a German woman at work to hide for me. In the end I never managed to bring the precious goblet to the ghetto.

Our working team, consisting of three groups, worked at the building designed for the German switchboard operators through the month of September and half of October. We survived – but not the easy way. The work finished halfway through October, precisely at the time when life in the small ghetto underwent a complete change for which we, experienced as we were, were not prepared.

CHAPTER 5
The Judenrat of the Small Ghetto

The Judenrat Refuses to Deliver Jews

On Monday, the second day after our transfer to the small ghetto, the Judenrat opened its office in Yatkowa Street. Immediately people appeared with all sort of questions, receiving little help. The next day, the city administration sent in a cartload of bread. It was sold at five rubles for a two-kilogram loaf. Although the price was double the black market outside, the cartload was sold out within less than a quarter of an hour. There was no other food available. People who worked outside the ghetto brought some products daily for themselves and also to sell, but this was a huge risk to the individuals who dared do it and therefore was not nearly sufficient to satisfy the hunger in the ghetto. This went on for five days, from Monday, September 8, until Friday, September 12.

On Friday before noon a young Lithuanian officer entered the ghetto and went straight to the office of the Judenrat, where he met two members of the council: Lewit and Levin. Waving his whip he ordered: "I want you to prepare for me five hundred Jews for Monday morning!" When he was asked why he needed the five hundred people, he answered arrogantly: "That is none of your business!" Lewit tried to find out a little more: "What kind of people do you need for your work? Workers? Young ones? Would elderly do? We need to know what kind of people to prepare for you..." The Lithuanian refused to give a reasonable answer and became hostile: "You heard me! Five hundred Jews. You can choose whomever you want," he said, giving Lewit a heavy kick in the leg. As Lewit fell, the officer left the office.

A short while later the arrogant scoundrel was back, but this time not alone. He came accompanied by a German army officer whose position at that time was unknown. The officer had visited the previous Jewish Council in Vilna and the workers of the pre-ghetto office knew his name – Schweinenberger, but the people of that office were not active in the ghetto Judenrat, which he had established the previous Saturday morning. Coming into the office he started by slapping Judenrat member Levin. This was followed by a harsh and arrogant shout: "For Monday morning you have to prepare one thousand, five hundred Jews. I repeat – one thousand, five hundred Jews!" And with this he left together with the Lithuanian.

The people in the office became very agitated. "Why would the Germans and Lithuanians need fifteen hundred people?!" It didn't take long before the whole ghetto knew about the order and the calm that had started to settle over the people turned to fear. Speculation began to fly left and right. The members of the Judenrat did not panic and decided on a course of action. A delegation was immediately sent to the German Department of Labor. For the price of a very expensive leather overcoat the delegation obtained a letter in the form of an order to the ghetto. The letter, signed by District Kommissar Hingst, stated that no one was permitted to take Jews from the ghetto to work without an order from the Department of Labor. The delegation came back to the office elated. "The arrogant scoundrel can drop dead with his order." The Judenrat had obtained a release order signed no less than by the District Kommissar! No Jews would be taken out of the ghetto on Monday. The ghetto calmed down.

On Monday morning, September 15, Schweinenberger came to the ghetto, went straight to the office of the Judenrat and asked about the fifteen hundred Jews he had ordered. This time the chairman of the Judenrat, Lejbowicz, was there expecting him. He calmly showed him the letter signed by Hingst.

Schweinenberger became enraged: "What is this?! You *Scheisse juden* (shitty Jews) will tell me what I have to do? The Department of Labor is *Scheisse*! And so is the District Kommissar, all *Scheisse*! I give the orders here, Gestapo!" He banged his fist hard on the table and went out more enraged than when he came in. But no Jews were taken from the small ghetto on that day. Tragically, though, Jews were taken – from the large ghetto. The next day, when we arrived at our work place, we learned that on the same Monday, September 15, 1941, Germans had ordered the Judenrat of the large ghetto "to transfer all people without work permits to the small ghetto." The ghetto police immediately went into action and posted notices ordering anyone without a permit to assemble before evening at the ghetto gate. Over two thousand people arrived and were marched out in the direction of the small ghetto. A small number of them arrived; the rest were taken directly to Lukishki prison – and death.

Events depressed us and we became despondent. The naiveté of the Judenrat, to believe that Hingst was the man in charge and his signature had any meaning, was incredible. The illusion to which we clung for a week – that the ghetto provided security for the Jews who had the "good fortune" to enter it – blew up in our faces. Nothing, absolutely nothing was left to hope for now that the "taking" of Jews was continuing in the ghetto. And yet, we still lived in denial. We refused to accept the thought that all those who had been "taken" had been sent to their deaths. We tried to kill the thought itself, but how? We reasoned that if those taken had been taken to work, why did they also "take" women, children, the old and the weak? They would not send such people to Minsk or Smolensk. On the other hand, if they wanted people for slaughter, why would they take young, healthy men and women, craftsmen and strong workers? These thoughts tortured us, but we had no answer to the riddle. The Germans we met at our working places "didn't know" what was going on. Even the "good" Germans couldn't say anything more than "we know as much as you Jews know."

We came home from work more depressed that when we left, and we left the next morning dreading what we would learn at work. How was it possible that we, hardened by all that we had gone through over the past three months, were shocked day in and day out by new German atrocities? It was impossible to explain.

The Judenrat Creates an Official Advisory Board

Coming home from work one day I was told that somebody from the Judenrat was looking for me and that I should report to Dr. Vladimir Poczter. I tried to contact him the same evening but had no luck. I met him very early the next morning, before leaving with the group on my way to work.

I had been given his address: 10 Zydowska Street. When I arrived before dawn the room was packed with people. The whole floor was one big bedroom and I found Dr. Poczter in his bed on the floor. Dr. Poczter informed me that the previous day the Judenrat had a meeting to which it had invited people in the ghetto who were known for their communal work before the war. The meeting discussed ways to begin an organized, methodical way of work. The members of the Judenrat realized that they were unable to do the necessary work by themselves. Therefore, they asked that the internal administration of the ghetto be managed by people who knew how to organize communal work and the Judenrat would remain the official representative of the ghetto vis-à-vis the Germans.

While still in bed, Dr. Poczter told me that the housing department – the most crucial department at the moment – had been reserved for me. In the evening, the first meeting of all heads of the departments was to take place and I should immediately start to organize my department. I could not start immediately as I was hurrying to my job, but I told Poczter that I agreed to take on the position and would begin to work for the housing department as soon as I returned.

I came back to the ghetto earlier than usual and started in the housing department. I asked the Bender brothers, two very gifted people, to become my assistants. They were originally from Kovno but had settled in Vilna. During the period when Lithuania was independent one had been a journalist and the other had held a secretarial position. Within days we managed to draw on the help of a few others who became house administrators and caretakers.

Our first task was to find out what resources we had in the form of dwelling places in the ghetto – not a simple task but one that had to be done. We could not work in the dark; after all, we had recently become the "owners" of the ghetto. We had to know what we had at our disposal. At the same time we needed to make a precise list of ghetto residents. This was an extremely difficult task. In the end we realized that for a variety of reasons it was impossible to prepare an accurate accounting of the ghetto population. People kept changing their "residence" from one place to another. Mostly it was on the basis of an understanding between the parties. But sometimes it was because of quarrels between strangers thrown together, and even between family members. Others changed their residence because they could not accept the place they had been given in the mixed households; others were simply trying to move to better accommodations. The situation during those days was quite chaotic.

At the same time, we had to pay close attention to the sanitary state of individual apartments and houses as well as to communal institutions. Here I feel it my duty to state that during the fifty years that I had lived in Vilna before the German period, I had never experienced the level of cleanliness I saw during the days in the ghetto. Something made people realize that without keeping every corner clean, not just from time to time but always – we would all succumb to the first epidemic that would engulf the ghetto. At the first ray of dawn, caretakers of buildings were already at work, cleaning the sidewalks, washing toilets, and attending to remove whatever refuse was collected over-night and was lying around. Jews who had never held a broom in their hand and had never cleaned the boards of a public toilet became the most efficient house caretakers, well beyond our expectations.

The caretakers were prewar business people, craftsmen and intellectuals. Even academics who could not or did not want to work for the Germans had accepted jobs as caretakers for the Judenrat. The Judenrat gave them confirma-tion letters that they were employed as caretakers, but the certificates of the Judenrat were useless at German or Lithuanian "cleansing" times.

The housing department also had the task of finding accommodation for people who came from the large ghetto. We used to accommodate the newcom-ers in dwellings that were already full, disregarding the sharp protests of the "old" residents. In many cases we had to use the power of the police. We did it in cases where we considered the protest of the "old" residents to be unfounded. The work was nerve-racking. We had to act as mediators between parties who were in constant disagreement. Often we settled quarrels by threatening one side or both, that we might throw them out of the house and leave them in the street. The difficulty was the constant yelling – when strangers had different needs and different ways to solve their problems and often simply because their nerves failed them and they had to find an outlet for their feelings.

Looking after the elderly and the sick, those who were lonely and had
no family to look after them, also fell under the jurisdiction of the housing
department, although we were not really the right address for such an activity. However we did not shirk our duties. We found shelter for them in a few
former study houses, known as the "Kloiz."

One of our main duties was to find appropriate buildings for various ghetto
institutions, such as the orphanage, schools and infirmaries. We opened the
first school in the Burial Society Synagogue, at the cost of moving out people
who had made the synagogue their home. Thanks to the great dedication of a
number of teachers the school was brought into existence in a very short time.
The driving force behind this effort was a teacher named Shaye Gesundheit.
We also converted the Straszun Library into an infirmary. When we first inspected the place we were disheartened. It had been completely wrecked. The
heavy iron office cupboards, which once held the most precious manuscripts,
had been broken apart. Their contents – that is, whatever remained after the
Germans had plundered them – were strewn all over the place. We found precious material among the papers and documents that had been overlooked by
the German vandals who didn't know its historical value. Books, deliberately
torn, were strewn about all over the building. It was then that we decided that
this reading hall would house the infirmary we were planning on opening. We
made that decision for two reasons: the hall was the only large and bright place
in the whole ghetto and we wanted to protect the valuable treasures that had
escaped the tragic destruction.

The housing department managed to find craftsmen who did some res-
toration work to bring the building up to the state that we needed. The same
people also managed to do minor repair work on the apartments that stood
empty because of their state of disrepair. In addition, in some cases the housing department helped people find relatives they were looking for. Finally, the
house administrators and the caretakers were used to distribute food products.
In sum total, the housing department was a vital nerve of the ghetto.

My friend Haim Remigalski was the head of the food-provision department. His office and the food store were located on the premises of a former

bakery in Zydowska Street, in the immediate vicinity of the ghetto fence. All dried food products that came into the ghetto were distributed at that address. Working together we soon noticed that thousands of workers were leaving the ghetto at dawn to their various working places without having a warm drink before leaving. Within four days we established what we called a "tea house." Early in the morning anyone who wanted could get hot, boiled water for a very small fee. Under the conditions of our existence the tea house was a very important instrument in making life a little less difficult, especially at the start of the day. The mornings had begun to be cold and windy, and a warm drink at the start of the day helped keep up the spirit for the first hour or two.

The food department took the first steps to build a large communal soup kitchen but the project was never realized. The main difficulty was where to obtain a large enough kettle. By the time a realistic possibility emerged, the conditions in the ghetto had changed to a degree that made the kitchen project useless, just as many other projects became useless as time went on.

In time we received bread and other products from the city administration, but the amounts they allowed for the ghetto were ridiculous and even cynical – less than starvation rations. The workers who left the ghetto in the mornings, were for the time being, the main providers of food for the ghetto. Individually they could smuggle only small amounts, but as they numbered in the thousands, the food that they brought back was many times the official amount we received.

During the first period, bringing in a few kilos of beans, flour, bread or potatoes was not difficult. This depended, of course, on the Lithuanian who guarded the entrance. More expensive items, such as fish, butter, meat, eggs or fruit were nearly always confiscated by the guards. When a worker was asked to open his food container and it was found that he or she had received a quality soup from a humane employer some guards would let it pass while others would pour it out at the gate into a large drum that stood there for just that purpose.

Dr. Poczter was the head of the health department. He had his surgery at the infirmary in the large hall of the Straszun Library. The hall had been partitioned with light, timber walls to provide medical cubicles, and each cubicle had its own specialist. In cases where the required specialist was not available in our small ghetto, we collected the sick people and took them in groups under police guard to the large ghetto, known as the first ghetto. There they had a large, well-equipped hospital with X-ray machines and other facilities. Nearly all doctors had brought to the ghetto some of their own instruments. We also collected some medications from various people and received some more from our friends in the pharmacies outside. Under the circumstances, we managed to provide good quality medical first aid. Shenker, a qualified pharmacist, installed his pharmacy in the infirmary.

The second important work of the health department was organizing the sanitary-epidemiological department. The narrow lanes of the ghetto had always been the darkest and dirtiest section of Vilna. With thousands more Jews squeezed into the tight confines, the fear of a catastrophic epidemic was at its highest. Physicians would go from house to house and appeal to people to maintain cleanliness as a protection for their own health and the health of others. They explained the need to keep not only the body and premises clean but also the yards and the floors in the passages and the staircases. Two physicians, Dr. Lewinson and Dr. David Elterman, performed miracles. The ghetto was kept clean to an unimaginable degree of communal hygiene. The old mikvah (Jewish ritual bath) established many years earlier in the large synagogue court was very useful in this respect. It remained just inside the ghetto fence.

At the head of the works department was another friend of mine, Jakobson. He was in charge of the daily dispatch of many thousands of workers to various places, as demanded by German or Lithuanian institutions.

His work brought him into permanent contact with Germans and his reward for it was frequent painful beatings. But he was very dedicated to his task and to the people he dispatched daily at dawn. He continuously asked for good work certificates for the people he sent out and in many cases he obtained such documents for them. Such certificates had enormous power if they were sealed with the right stamp. The documents were not always honored but in the majority of cases they proved decisive. The works department also registered the professional qualifications of individuals for the Germans and Lithuanians and made use of this knowledge for internal ghetto needs as well.

I hardly knew the head of the school division, Shaye Gesundheit, but he was a very experienced teacher who had a major role in organizing the ghetto school. I noticed his enthusiasm when we handed over the Burial Society Synagogue to be turned into a school. He went into a state of euphoria when the Housing Committee showed him the desolate and vandalized place and told him that with a little work it could be turned into a school. Immediately he began to collect children of all school ages, teachers and any resources that were obtainable in the ghetto. With the assistance of some teachers, the building became a children's center. Many of the children needed special care as they were already orphans, having lost one or both parents.

As soon as orphaned children came into the care of the children's division (some had gone on fending for themselves on their own) we had to provide them with a sleeping place, food and clothing. After the initial period, bathing and clothing was not a great problem as the household goods of the thousands that went to the slaughter were left behind. The stores of the Judenrat became "rich" with household goods. Unfortunately in one of the "cleansing" raids, that wonderful man Shaye Gesundheit was taken away. Chairman Lejbowicz and I immediately intervened with the Lithuanians to release him, as he was in the hands of the Lithuanian Gestapo. Sadly, our intervention was unsuccessful.

The Office of Personal Registration and Addresses was another major department. A man named Sackheim, a former employee of the Jewish People's Bank (a prewar Jewish cooperative credit society), was the head of the office, while Miss Gurewicz, also a former employee of the bank, worked with him. During the first days a third man, named Emes, worked with them but he left after a few days. The Office of Registration and Addresses was at that time very important; for some individuals it was the heartbeat of the ghetto. The ghetto contained thousands of families that had been torn apart and the family members knew nothing about the whereabouts of the others. Thousands of letters arrived daily from the large ghetto asking for information about family members, relatives and friends. In many cases the office was able to help by contacting the individuals and sending letters in return. As part of the housing department we tried to make a list of all inhabitants in the ghetto, but with the continuous German and Lithuanian raids that kept removing thousands of Jews, our register became useless and we decided not to go on with the work.

A lawyer named Pawirski, Chairman Lejbowicz's brother-in-law, was the head of the police in the small ghetto. At the outset, it should be noted that the police in the small ghetto was totally different from the police in the large ghetto. The police force of the small ghetto was limited in number and staffed by individuals known for their good character. The police force had many difficult tasks on its hands. Keeping order and peace in a community where everyone lived under constant tension and unrelenting strain was not an easy task, but it managed to reduce tensions and break up fights in what has to be considered a peaceful way.

A more difficult task was attending to duties at the ghetto gate, together with the Lithuanian guard. At the gate the ghetto police assisted in bringing in food and wood delivered to the ghetto. It also had to greet the Germans and Lithuanians who entered the ghetto and to be at their disposal.

When required, the police of the small ghetto took groups of people over to the large ghetto for medical reasons and other needs; they also helped the sanitary workers in their fight to keep the ghetto clean and tidy.

It should be underscored that quite unlike the police force of the large ghetto, the police in the small ghetto never cooperated with the Germans and Lithuanians and never participated actively in the "cleansings." It never had Jewish blood on its hands – the opposite was true. During the later days when the raids of the Lithuanians and Germans were at their height the police did everything that was possible to save people, sometimes risking their own lives. When Jewish policemen had to accompany Lithuanians on a raid they used the situation, whenever possible, to help the Jews. The Jewish police never deceived Jews by spreading false information that would assist the Germans in attaining their objectives.

This behavior of the police in the small ghetto was a result of the spirit that imbued the ghetto administration. Everyone in the Judenrat, from Chairman

Lejbowicz down to the caretakers and administrators of the various departments and their helpers, understood the enormity of their task. There was not
a single case in which the Judenrat of the small ghetto caused the death of a
single Jew by handing someone over to the Lithuanians or the Germans. The
Germans and Lithuanians did not receive Jewish help when they raided the
small ghetto and took away thousands of Jews. We were helpless, totally helpless – but no Jew in the small ghetto decided who would live and who would die.

Precisely because the Judenrat in the small ghetto was made up of ordinary,
good, simple people who never had high aspirations or political pretensions,
it used a humane Jewish approach steeped in Jewish tradition and morality
when dealing with the great tragedy that had befallen us. The members of the
Judenrat viewed their task as making life bearable under ghetto conditions and
saving Jews whenever possible, and they did so until the very end.

These were the departments of the small ghetto and the people who ad-
ministered them during the six weeks that the ghetto existed. The difficulties
of the administration, real as they were, were really minor in comparison to
the difficulties of the Judenrat who represented us. Lejbowicz and his Judenrat
members faced off against the lions in the arena on a daily basis. According to
their own rules, neither the Germans nor the Lithuanians should have had any
contact with us; District Kommissar Hingst had ruled that all Jewish matters
were to be brought to the Lithuanian contact man, Buragas. But German rules
and laws regarding the lesser beings – Jews – were applicable only when it suited
them. Thus the Judenrat had daily contact with Germans, who never stopped
coming to the ghetto. The Jewish representatives had to face them, speak with
them and somehow deal with them. The dealing was the worst part – because
how were Jews to "deal" with Germans? Often it was by receiving slaps on
their faces or kicks to their shins or even a fist to their stomach. But usually it
finished with the Judenrat bribing their "guests." And that too proved very risky.

The Judenrat was also in constant contact with the municipal authorities
regarding food deliveries, sanitation, rent and other day-to-day matters.

The whole administration had been put together in a matter of days and
soon after we met one evening and held our first meeting in a former study

house on Dominikanska Street. Each department head gave a short report about his work and we resolved to create a general secretariat with a legal department. We also resolved to invite Advocate Smilag as head of the new secretariat and legal department. I do not know how a rumor started that Advocate Smilag had converted to Christianity – but we decided to invite him and offer him to lead that department. As it turned out, he worked diligently in his position to the last day of the existence of the small ghetto. At the same meeting we also decided to invite a past director of the Bunimowicz Bank, named Kaszuk, to take over the financial department.

Ponary – The Third Ghetto?

All the while that we were making plans we could not hide our real feelings – that the sword of Damocles was dangling over all our heads. We could not ignore the question of what was happening to the Jews who had been taken away. It needed only one of those present at the meeting to say something and the subject was burst open. Everyone insisted on finding a way to figure out from the Germans what happened to the people taken out of the ghetto. We spent the next three evenings debating the subject.

It is interesting to note the words of Lejbowicz, the chairman of the Judenrat in the small ghetto. He was probably the first man in Vilna to speak the words that we all knew but that no one had dared to pronounce before. "In the early days," he said, "the human-catchers took away from our court two brothers who were known for their strength and their courage. They were resourceful and feared nothing. I believe that if they were alive they would find a way of contacting us. And yet we have heard nothing. That can only mean that they are dead. And if the Germans are sending strong, young and healthy people to their death than, clearly that is what is happening to the old, to the women, to the sick. In other words, we are all being systematically exterminated in a methodical, German way."

These were the words of the chairman of the Judenrat. How prophetically true they turned out to be.

But at the time when the chairman spoke his mind we did not want to believe that this was really so. At that stage it was impossible for us to accept the truth that the German plan demanded the total slaughter of the Jewish people. But it is very likely that the chairman's beliefs contributed to the Judenrat's decision to hold back from taking an active part in the raids. After the three evenings of discussion the meeting accepted my proposal to contact the Judenrat of the large ghetto in order to consider a united stand to the tormenting question. I was of the opinion that it made no difference to us if a Jew was in our ghetto or the other one. To us all Jews had to be equal. Therefore we had to act united. We had to consider the situation together and arrive at the best possible way to save ourselves. I said: "The ghetto walls that divide us might have meaning for the Germans but we Jews are not allowed to consider ourselves divided and different because the German put up walls. There is no difference between Jews of this street and the Jews of the other street."

Lejbowicz and Dr. Poczter were authorized to make contact with the large ghetto and I was authorized to try to find out from my Gentile friends the destination of the Jews taken out of the ghetto. Inside the ghetto and outside it, all sorts of odd rumors were circulating. "Odd" was definitely the word for the rumors…

From Polish sources we were told that Ponary was the third Jewish ghetto. They even knew that city authorities provided Ponary with bread every day. Others told us that those taken away were sent to the newly conquered Russian territories to work. But we questioned what happened to the old, the sick and the children who were not able to work? And there were those among us who spoke without hesitation: "The Germans are taking the people and killing them. None of those who have been taken away are still alive."

It is curious that of all the rumors that circulated, the German murder plan was the least believable. It was lacking a basic rationality. How was it possible in wartime to take young people, the most important available working element, craftsmen who were needed to fill in for the soldiers – and kill them?! No matter how strong Germany might be it surely needed working hands; this was our compelling logic.

We racked our brains, but the fact remained that those taken had disappeared like pebbles into deep waters. Not a single one had returned, we had not heard a single word about them and not a single letter from them had reached us. We had not received the slightest sign that anyone of those taken away was still alive.

Finally, I made contact with a few friendly Polish Christians and put at their disposal any sum of money they might need to bribe some Lithuanians or Germans connected with transporting people out of the ghetto. We had to find out what happened to them.

The only thing we learned was that all parties were transported on the road leading to Landwarovo. The parties were halted at the junction leading to Ponary. But it was impossible to get any further than that because the whole road to Ponary was heavily guarded. Gentiles living close to the place told us that each time after people were brought to Ponary they heard the rattle of machine guns. They also said that groups of drunken Lithuanian police very often appeared on trucks going to Ponary and back. They were usually singing happy songs as they were driven along but they also appeared to be under the weather.

It is – once more – interesting to note the psychological condition of those of us who were still alive. On a few occasions wounded individuals survived by some miracle and returned to Vilna to the ghetto. They told us what was going on at Ponary, but seldom did anybody believe them. Much later I witnessed a case in which a wounded woman who had been taken away came back and managed to reach the ghetto hospital. She gave precise details of how the Lithuanians police shot a large group of people in front of her eyes. She had also been shot and thrown into the pit while still alive. She waited until nightfall when the murderers left and managed to get herself out of the half-covered pit and returned to Vilna. The doctors who listened to her story made silent signs pointing to the head, meaning the woman was not of sound mind. It is impossible now to understand, but the truth was that we didn't want to believe the most tragic and dreadful information. Like little children we accepted any good news that allowed us a shred of hope.

In a depressed state of mind the Judenrate of both ghettos came together on Sunday, September 21, at around seven o'clock. We made our way to the large ghetto as if we were a group of workers returning home from outside. For the first time I passed through the gate of the large ghetto on Rudnicka Street. At the gate a Lithuanian policeman was on guard. A metal board attached to the ghetto wall informed: "Attention! Typhoid danger! Jewish quarter. Entrance is strictly forbidden for military personnel and non-Jews."

After passing through the narrow gate the Jewish police of the large ghetto took charge of us. We found ourselves in a veritable human beehive; it was all sky and people without an inch of ground to be seen underfoot. It was Sunday night when everybody in the ghetto was out on the street. We went straight to the Judenrat building at 6 Rudnicka Street, where the Jewish High School had been before the war; it had a large yard. The yard was a sea of people and the humming noise was like in a hive. The large steps and wide corridors leading to the office of the Judenrat were packed full of people. Each one of our delegation met friends as we passed through, but we didn't stop. Our top priority was to finalize the matter that had brought us here.

A policeman stood guard at the door of the chairman of the Judenrat. He informed the chairman of our arrival and we were immediately invited in. Our delegation consisted of our chairman and the heads of the departments we had created. On the side of the Judenrat of the large ghetto the representation was similar. The Chairman, Engineer Fried, opened the first and last meeting we ever held together and the general secretary of the large ghetto recorded the proceedings. Two members of the Judenrat of the large ghetto kept coming in and out but they did not take part in the meeting. Fried asked formally who we were and Chairman Lejbowicz presented us and stated the reason for our coming.

Fried began with a monologue that made the situation clear: "We have no contact with the Germans. Everything goes through the Lithuanian middleman, Buragas. When the Germans come and demand people from us, we are forced to give them the required number in order to save the others. If we would not hand over the required number they would still take as many as they would want and whomever they would want and it would be worse for the remainder. It is useless to intervene with the Germans or to try to bribe them. Soon they will have more Jews than we have. We tried once to intervene with Murer and Schweinenberger about the crowded conditions and lack of accommodations in the ghetto and the answer was: 'Crowded conditions are no problem.' They took away two thousand people and said that that should solve the problem. We learned our lesson. With interventions we will not reach far."

Fried continued: "As for contact between both ghettos I have nothing against it, but we cannot consider any combined action because that will only damage our own position. Our ghetto is a productive one, established by the Germans for the working element while your ghetto is only for the old and sick people who are not able to work."

He went on this way and told us how he was planning to organize the inner life of the ghetto. His exposé depressed us. Our representatives, Remigalski and Poczter, managed to say a few words but they did not succeed in making the chairman reconsider anything. In the end I spoke my mind: "Mr. Fried, we cannot and should not let ourselves be slaughtered like cattle. Please see for yourself – they demanded fifteen hundred Jews from us and our Judenrat did not oblige; the end was that they did not take anyone from our ghetto. They came to you and took two thousand people because you produced them. So what is 'special' about the large ghetto? Besides, what is the difference for us Jews if we are in Rudnicka Street or in Zydowska Street? We are all one people – Jews. We should act as one people. We should be able to say to future generations the biblical words: 'Our hands have not spilled this blood!'"

Fried became enraged and another member of the Judenrat quickly intervened and requested Lejbowicz to recount in detail what took place in our ghetto during the demand for fifteen hundred people. Lejbowicz told them and underscored the fact that after the screams and the threats of the Lithuanian scoundrel and Gestapo Officer Schweinenberger, fifteen hundred people that the Lithuanians and the Germans demanded were not handed over. Fried excused himself for a moment and left. The general secretary of the large ghetto who recorded the proceedings turned to me: "Mr. Balberyszski, I noted down your words exactly as they were spoken."

The meeting lasted quite a long time. Only Fried spoke for the large ghetto and this left our delegation with the impression that all the other members of the Judenrat in the large ghetto were afraid to speak up. The representatives at the meeting, well-known prewar activists from the Bund and Zionist organizations, did not say anything. When the meeting was over and we left, it was clear to us that no matter what we would have done and said the end result would have been the same. We knew however, that we would be able to say: "Our hands have not spilled this blood!" Could the members of the Judenrat of the large ghetto say the same?

We left the meeting devastated and dispirited. We felt that the members of the large ghetto Judenrat knew something; some tragic secret that we did not know. The secret was inadvertently hinted at in the words Fried had uttered: "We are a working ghetto and your ghetto is for people not capable of work." His words penetrated our minds. In spite of it we said that the facts spoke for themselves. The first two thousand Jews the Germans took out of the ghetto were taken from the "secure" working ghetto and not from ours.

In the end we were shocked by the passivity of the Judenrat members of the large ghetto. Disappointed, we returned to our ghetto under Lithuanian police guard.

When we met the next day, one thing was clear to us all: The Judenrat of the large ghetto has already disposed of the ten thousand Jews of the small ghetto in their belief that by giving the Germans what they demanded they were condemning us and saving themselves. They had already given up on us and therefore they were forbidden to go together with us or take any common action with us. They were – so they believed – the "privileged Jews," the entitled ones, the kosher ones. This made taking any common action with us impossible.

They had fallen into the German trap, designed to methodically create divisions among Jews. This was the German plan and the Judenrat of the large ghetto responded to the German bait exactly as the Germans had planned. Most probably the Judenrat of the large ghetto had already been given to understand that only one ghetto would remain and that in the end our ghetto was to be totally liquidated. This was the reason that they distanced themselves from us in good time. Future events confirmed our fears.

I could never free myself from thinking about it. These thoughts haunted me in the ghetto and they haunted me in the concentration camps. Later when I had already survived and regained my freedom I was still haunted by them. And to this day I consider the indifference of Jewish leaders to the fate of a third of the ghettos' Jewish population as a moral crime. They had fallen into the German mire and kept sinking deeper and deeper into it. As our sages had foretold, one sin attracts the next one.

Our visit to the Judenrat of the large ghetto made clear to us that if we were still able to do anything to save ourselves we would have to rely on our own capabilities.

CHAPTER 6
The Black Yom Kippur of 5602

Yom Kippur in the Small Ghetto

A new rumor started circulating inside both ghettos: all the work documents given out until now were no longer valid; new documents with the imprint *craftsman* were now required. In conjunction with this rumor we also heard that all craftsmen would end up living in the large ghetto. These rumors further confirmed our suspicions that the creation of two ghettos did not happen accidentally.

We, the ones who worked for Germans, asked our employers to obtain the desired rubber stamp on our documents. Only a few received the craftsman stamp – the majority remained without it. The killers had created a new situation to divide us and a new despair began eating our hearts; we were suspended once more, hanging by the thread between life and death.

Life in the ghetto did not settle down though we had created all the necessary departments and had a large number of people working with great dedication to mitigate the situation. We lived on the edge of a volcano. The worst conditions were in the housing department, with hundreds of people wandering daily from one ghetto to the other.

The frequent visits of the police from the large ghetto worried us, particularly the visits of the soon-to-be infamous Jewish policeman Bernstein. (After the liberation, former partisans got hold of him and he was executed.) Every few days Bernstein came and delivered groups of sick, old and weak people to the ghetto. He always brought his unfortunate group with a detailed list and I had to give him my signature when I took charge of them.

Soon it was Rosh Hashanah, the Jewish New Year of 5602 – our first inside the ghetto. The New Year passed uneventfully and Yom Kippur, the Jewish Day of Atonement, approached. That year Yom Kippur fell on Wednesday,

October 1, 1941. The small ghetto had many synagogues, prayer houses and study buildings. In the large synagogue court only two places were functioning – the famed Gaon of Vilna's study house and the upper women's section in the Great Synagogue. It was on the eve of Yom Kippur that I went up to the women's section.

Through the large windows with the heavy iron bars I looked down into the lower male interior. The emptiness made a devastating, painful impression. How desolate the glorious, old synagogue was now when seen from above. Master of the World! Why, oh why did the Great Synagogue, the meeting place between You and us have to be so shamed?

On Yom Kippur of years past the Great Synagogue of Vilna was magnificent. The splendid holy ark with its gold and white curtain; the *ammud* (cantor's lectern) at which the greatest, world-renowned cantors led us in our prayers. Which of them had not considered it the greatest honor to represent and pray for us on Yom Kippur at the lectern of the Great Synagogue? Sirota, Steinberg, Roitman, Hershman, Kussevitsky…the world had embraced all of them after they presented us and our prayers before the Master of the Universe from this very spot. Soaring choirs graced the services on Yom Kippur. In the center stood the raised pulpit with the four pillars, where the most impressive Torah readers in the whole of Lithuania and Poland read from the holy scrolls. At the eastern wall, the symbolic place of honor in our holy places, sat the rabbis, leaders of the community and honorary administrators of the synagogue, surrounded by the thousands of ordinary Jews who came here to pray and listen to the greatest religious orators and preachers. All this was once the glory of the Great Synagogue on Yom Kippur.

And here on the eve of the most sacred day, the synagogue was empty. All her greatness had been plundered, raped, shamed to the utmost – gone forever. Not only the Great Synagogue but also the court around the synagogue stood orphaned and degraded.

Once upon a time, long before our cataclysm began, the eve of Yom Kippur in the synagogue court of Vilna was the center of our being. The many prayer houses here were packed with Jews. Charity plates were spread out

to be filled for many and various institutions; close to prayer time everyone
had eaten their last meal before commencing the twenty-five-hour fast. With
large, thick, white candles in their hands they clogged the streets, streaming
like a river to their prayer houses, synagogues and study houses to place the
lit candles in sand-filled holders. And now I stood in the empty section of an
empty synagogue in a corner – and numbly took it all in.

I was scared about the Yom Kippur day. My heart prophesized that the
day would not pass without some provocation and I found myself conversing
with God. About what? About the golden past or about the black present. Was
I asking for God's intervention?

It was getting close to prayer time and I left the Great Synagogue. I went
over to the Gaon's study house; it was already full, packed to the doors. I went
to another place close by and arrived as the Kol Nidrei (the prayer that ush-
ers in the Yom Kippur holiday) was already being sung. When the Kol Nidrei
was finished an elderly man came and took hold of me: "Come, Balberyszski;
take your father's seat." I was astonished! I didn't know the man. It turned out
he was *Gabai* Abraham Hofstein. For many years my father used to pray here.
Before the First World War he had been *gabai* in this synagogue.

I didn't know the old man but he had recognized me. With great respect
I accepted the honor and took my place at the eastern wall. But it was not the
study place that I knew when I was growing up. The study hall of my younger
days had burned down and the one that replaced it was modern and impressive, richly furnished.

The Kol Nidrei evening passed without incident.

The next morning we did not go to work; we had bribed our supervisor
and he had given us the day off. Once again I went to the same study house
and remained until Torah-reading time. I was given the honor to be called
up to the reader's lectern. When the blessing in my honor was recited I asked
that my name not be mentioned, but instead the blessing should mention "all
the Jews in the ghetto." After that I put down my prayer shawl and went out. I
met up with Chairman Lejbowicz. He proposed that we go to the large ghetto
and I agreed. As the chairman of the ghetto he had an ironclad document that

exempted him from any "cleansing" that might take place and he could take his secretary with him. We used the occasion and went to the first ghetto. We arranged where we would meet and each went our own way.

I knew the address of Paulina Prylucki and went to see her. She burst into a spasmodic cry that tore at my heart. We exchanged our not very happy news about the days since we had become separated. She was in a very difficult situation, close to starvation. Often, she told me, she had only one small meal a day – and it showed. Leaving her some money, I went out to look around for other friends I knew.

In the street I was stopped by a member of the Judenrat named Joel Fiszman: "You are here, and in your ghetto something is going on." I asked him what was going on but he didn't reply and left me with a worried expression on his face. I became restless and looked for Lejbowicz. I found him and told him what Fiszman had said: He gave a sharp and quick answer: "We have to go home. God knows what kind of a Yom Kippur they have prepared for us."

We came to the gate half-dead. A policeman stopped us: "Where to?" "To the other ghetto," Lejbowicz replied. The policeman explained: "You cannot go there; the place is not quiet." Lejbowicz was in command: "That is precisely why we are going there!" And with this we left.

We reached the small ghetto on the run. We passed the gate and found masses of men, women and children collected in Gaona Street. Seeing us they began screaming: "Save us, save us!"

The first "cleansing" in our ghetto was taking place. Along Gaona Street a few hundred people stood in rows guarded by Lithuanians with their guns at the ready. Lejbowicz immediately approached the German who was leading the "cleansing." I did not have any valid document. At the same time a frightful thought hit me: What is going on in my house? Four souls are there in God's care.

As if by some miracle I managed to reach home. I burst into the room and all four attacked me – "Where have you been? The Lithuanians had been here but the Jewish policeman who came with them said you were at work, working for the Germans and that you are also active in the Jewish advisory board. Luckily another member of the board was with them and confirmed the policeman's words." The Lithuanians had left the room. My family had been saved from a certain death.

The "cleansing" went on for two hours. When the group had been collected they were taken out of the ghetto under heavy guard. We were relieved that the "cleansing" was over.

But it was not over. Within an hour or so, the demons were back and the "cleansing" continued. Now, collecting hundreds of people was not as simple as the first time. The first "collection" had been easy. The Lithuanians had taken Jews out from the prayer houses, in their prayer shawls. Now everybody was in hiding. But what was the kind of hiding that we had prepared worth? Nothing. There was nowhere to hide in the ghetto. They dragged people out of the houses until they had again collected five hundred people.

We listened through the window to the screams, the heartrending supplications to God that remained without answer. Suddenly we heard heavy boots walking up our steps and we froze.

The door was torn open. Two armed Lithuanians came in accompanied by a Jewish policeman who knew me well. The policeman made light of the situation: "Well, Apothecary, have you some real, apothecary spirit?" I was quick as lightning: "Of course I have; the best – real Pesachovka."

I went over to the cabinet and took out a 90-percent-proof spirit still with the Hebrew label, "kosher for the most exacting." It was a bottle the previous owners of the place had left behind. I poured two large doses for the two Lithuanians and my mother handed them some hallah; they drank. "May I also have a drink?" the Jewish policeman asked. I handed him a glass: "Drink in good health." The policeman drank and when they all were satisfied he said to the Lithuanians: "Well, we may as well leave now. You can see that he is one of us." And with this they left.

How can one describe what we went through in the few minutes of the visit of our uninvited guests? This is one of the experiences that remain with you for the rest of your life. It would be hard for us to explain where we took the strength to remain outwardly calm in such moments.

Minutes after they left our room we heard the heartrending screams of our neighbors. They were a large family. We froze in a delayed reaction but my mother collapsed. "Oh my God! They are taking them away." It was as if my mother and all of us had already forgotten that a minute or two before, we had all experienced the same danger. Listening to the screams behind our wall I could no longer take it and became irrational. I ran into the room and saw the Lithuanians driving out a large number of people. I screamed at the Jewish policeman: "My sister, my sister, let my sister go!" "Which one is your sister?" one of the Lithuanians asked.

Before me stood a number of women whom I hardly knew, all wanted me to help them. The Lithuanian murderer pushed them brutally away and asked once more: "Which one is your sister?" I pointed to the one who looked the youngest: "This one!" The Lithuanian grabbed her and screamed: "Get out of here!" I grabbed the woman by the arm and ran out with her to our room.

The young woman stood for a few seconds with us in our room, disoriented, and began to scream: "Let me go to my mother and my sister! I don't want to be left alive alone! Where are you? Let me go." I felt my heart was stopping. I had brought the calamity on all of us with my own hands.

"Be quiet," I said to her. "The murderers are still here; in a single moment they could take us all. Have compassion on the children, on us all." My wife and mother fell on her pleading, crying and kissing her, begging her to be silent but she didn't want to calm down. I spoke to her again: "A moment ago I saved you from certain death and you want to pay us all back by bringing the Lithuanians to take us all away. Be quiet until they are gone."

She calmed down. The noise passed and outside it became completely quiet. The bandits led away their victims.

The second "cleansing" raid also lasted some hours. The murderers collected more than they had planned. Gestapo Officer Schweinenberger counted the rows and when he came to five hundred he chased the others away: "Off with them. Away with the cursed!"

The ones in the last rows ran away in all directions, saving themselves from certain death. Among them was my cousin Sonia Kulbis, her husband Volodia and their daughter Shoshana. For them it was the second time they had escaped death in one day. During the first raid Lejbowicz took them out from the column just as we arrived from the large ghetto. This time the archangel of death, Schweinenberger himself, pushed them aside. All the others were driven out of the ghetto.

The ghetto became empty and quiet.

We believed that we had been freed for the day. The groups of Jews had already been taken away, we had prayed and received a marvelous verdict from above, all signed for the year… But no! The day had not yet finished for us. Soon after, we again heard alarming screams through the open window. It had started once more.

We held our breath, listening for any noise on our staircase.

It was already Neilah time, the concluding prayer of Yom Kippur when God's judgment for the year is sealed. The time when we used to fill the synagogues and pray: "The gates of the Heavens open up for us"…

We stood nailed to our places ready for any eventuality, our heads pounding.

The heavy sound of boots reached our staircase. I awakened out of my synagogue dream. "Mother, Lisa, children – they are coming close."

Someone was already trying to open the door. I ran over and pushed against the pressure from outside so as not to let the intruders in. At the same time I removed my expensive watch and, putting my hand outside the narrow opening, I pushed the watch into the Lithuanian's hand. I felt him finding my hand and taking the watch. The pressure on the door let up… The sound of the steps were moving away. At that moment I fell into the arms of my wife, I embraced my mother and the children and hot tears streamed down my face.

They didn't know what had happened a few seconds ago; they hadn't noticed anything. All they saw was that the door began to open and the Prophet Elijah (who comes to the rescue in times of urgency) held the door back from opening. At that moment my watch had been the Prophet Elijah.

When we regained our senses somewhat we began wondering if this was the end.

It took some time before we heard that the third "cleansing" had ended. We understood that this was probably the final raid for the day. We knew from our experience that the Germans worked according to a very disciplined plan. They had to take a certain number of people and they would not take a single person over the planned total. Their raids began at a set time and they came to an end at a set time. Everything in their demonic plan had to be carried out with Germanic precision. Murderers with a system. When we calmed down we remembered that we hadn't eaten since midday the day before. We put the kettle on to boil, ate whatever was at hand and fell on our beds in the clothes we were wearing, exhausted. That was the way that Yom Kippur, the holiest day of the year 5602, passed over us.

The night passed peacefully. We woke up early and the first steps we took outside our room told us of the disaster. Fifteen hundred people had been taken away. Many rooms and apartments remained open, ownerless and abandoned.

But some people had already forgotten what had happened less than twelve hours earlier. They had already started to make themselves more comfortable by moving into better rooms, or taking whatever they wanted or needed from rooms that stood open. Some workers of the housing department had already started to go around and to mercilessly seal the rooms of the people who had fallen victim to the Yom Kippur raid.

In the narrow, dark lanes of the ghetto, lonely people who had lost their families walked around like ghosts. Not all had sufficiently recovered to know what to do and whom to approach to try to save their near and dear ones. A few among them had not completely lost their basic instincts. Gold and diamonds were the currency they were prepared to pay for the redemption of their near ones. Before they went to sleep they had already approached the middlemen who had their "good" Germans. But for the moment the ghetto looked as if the Heavens had closed the gates of mercy.

The only thing that filled the air was death. Death spoke out of every corner of the ghetto with a strength that made fear and death the only fragrance of the ghetto. The mood of death now ruled the ghetto.

In such a state of mind I had to join my group at the gate in order to go to work.

Yom Kippur in the Large Ghetto

The workers in our team who resided in the large ghetto told us about Yom Kippur in their place. In the early hours of Yom Kippur, their ghetto was calm. The restlessness started when it became known that something was going on in our ghetto. Many families had been torn apart during the drive into the ghetto and they had members in both ghettos. Hearing that the Germans were raiding the small ghetto caused them to panic. Of course they were taking people "only" in the small ghetto, but the people the Germans and Lithuanians were taking were their own flesh and blood.

There were others – more than a few – who comforted themselves with the unspoken thought, "They will not take any people from this ghetto. We are the working ghetto with 'ironclad' documents." They were proven wrong. At Neilah time Schweinenberger entered the ghetto with a large group of armed Lithuanians. They began catching people off the street, but they had a very lean harvest. People ran in all directions and disappeared… They had not forgotten the September 15 raid.

Schweinenberger then changed his tactics and went to the office of the Judenrat, demanding that two thousand Jews be delivered to the gate. The Judenrat of the large ghetto obliged and ordered the police to deliver the two thousand people that the German murderer demanded. The Jewish police had no better luck than the Lithuanian henchmen; remembering September 15, people went into hiding – the population had vanished.

Schweinenberger was becoming impatient. He threatened the Judenrat and the police – and then somebody found a quick solution for which Schweinenberger became willing to wait a little longer. The police went from house to house and courtyard to courtyard calling to the invisible people: "Jews, all those who have craftsmen documents are asked to report to the gate of the ghetto where the certificates will be confirmed and registered. You'll all be free." All true and good craftsmen came out of their hiding places with the documents in their hands. They went to the gate, certain that nothing would happen to them. When they assembled at the gate they were surrounded by the Lithuanian murderers and taken away.

At the end of the most holy day in the Jewish calendar, the Day of Atonement, the large ghetto buried its best craftsmen. It was done with the help of the Judenrat and the Jewish police in order to pacify the Gestapo Officer Schweinenberger. The people of the large ghetto could not calm themselves. The few who had "good" certificates and had come to work kept muttering over and over, "I don't know what made me remain in hiding. A miracle…only a miracle must have saved my life." They just couldn't understand how the Jewish leadership, the Judenrat and the ghetto police could deceive the Jews with such a perfidious provocation. Throughout the day bitter curses were directed toward the Judenrat and the police.

All workers from the large ghetto walked around, unable to do much work. We of the small ghetto did most of their work for them, which was not easy. We had the same curse of our own but without the treachery that they had experienced.

We tried to intervene with our "good" Germans about taking people out of the prisons. Naturally, we offered large bribes for their favors. At our place, no German was ready to help at any price but, as we learned later, the Jewish middlemen had their own "good" Germans who were ready to do favors to their workers for "small" gifts, such as diamonds, gold and a few large banknotes. In exchange for such gifts a few people were rescued from the Lukishki prison – and from Ponary.

In the days that followed, individuals who managed to return to the ghetto told us of the terrible conditions at Lukishki. One woman who had been released from Lukishki prison by sheer accident told us the bizarre way in which she had returned to the ghetto. She had been taken to the prison with many hundreds of other women. The cells were overcrowded, conditions unbearable to the point that she and many others were praying for a quick death.

Unexpectedly the cell was opened and the name of a woman was called. Noticing that nobody answered to that name she exploited the moment and pushing herself through to the door she said: "I am here!" She was immediately taken out the cell and together with a few others she came back to the ghetto.

When we investigated why the woman with the right name had not answered, we found that the women were convinced that the names called out were of people who were to be killed. The woman with the right name was in the cell but did not answer. But she, the woman who was brought back to the living, wanted to end everything quickly. She didn't think she was going to live, that was the reason she volunteered. "I had nothing to lose, nothing to live for. Why wait for death when I had the opportunity to get it over with?" Simple! Gruesome, but simple.

I was told another, similarly "simple" story: A German came to the prison with a list of "his Jews." He went along the cells, called the names and collected his people. Of course such moments always had their tragedies and this time was no different. The tragedy of this case happened before the people who had been called managed to leave the prison. At the gate of the prison, the "good" German counted "his Jews" and noticed that he had one more than the list showed. He asked that one of the Jews, anyone, go back. Nobody answered. The "good" German took out his revolver and shot one of the Jews already waiting at the gate. He explained his position. "I must have only 'my Jews,' only as many as there are on my list. Swindles are not allowed. Now let's get going!" The dead body was left where it fell as he brought "his Jews" back to the ghetto.

When I returned home, my family already knew about the disaster that had taken place in the other ghetto. It was hard for them to understand how the raid there had happened. Like everybody else, my family knew that the other ghetto was supposed to be "protected." It was a riddle they could not solve: If the craftsmen with the crafsmen documents living in the "protected" ghetto could be taken away just like the others, what was their "protection" worth? Why move over there, where many are living without a roof over their heads? Here, at least, one had a place to put one's head down. That was the way we went around debating and discussing, all the time filled with thoughts that kept changing from one extreme to the other, without knowing what to do. Large ghetto, small ghetto – try to guess where death is lying in wait for you.

We lost many members of our Judenrat on Yom Kippur, taken in the three different raids that day. Among the victims was the very dedicated and experienced head of the Department of Children's Culture and Education, Shaye Gesundheit. The Judenrat decided to intervene with the Lithuanians for his release. Together with Lejbowicz, I went to the Lithuanian Gestapo head office located at 12 Vilna Street.

We were received by the head of the "Ifatinga," the Lithuanian Gestapo, a man around thirty years old, with dark hair and bloodshot eyes. When we entered his cubicle he took off the revolver he carried. From a side pocket he brought out a second one and put them both on the desk. Speaking Lithuanian he asked what we wanted. Lejbowicz replied in Russian. The Lithuanian promised to free Gesundheit – if it was not too late. We did not leave the office – we flew out as if on wings. "We should thank the Almighty," Lejbowicz said, "that we came out alive from that murderous man's office. It must have been sheer madness to do what we did. Fancy putting our heads between the teeth of such an animal." Of course nothing happened as a result of our intervention.

We no longer had any illusion about the ghetto. Up until the time they drove us into the ghetto they were catching Jews in a kind of "retail" way, taking them off the streets or having to collect them from their homes individually. It must have taken a relatively long time to collect a sufficient number of Jews that way. Now that we were in the ghetto, the murderers could take many thousands of Jews in a matter of hours. By concentrating the whole Jewish population in one place they made their work of destroying the Jewish people easier.

On October 3 and 4 the small ghetto was once more disturbed. Lithuanians came and once again took Jews off the streets. Less than a full month had passed since we were closed off in the ghetto and they had already managed to destroy half of the ghetto population, some four to five thousand Jews. At that rate it would not take them long to finish their work, we reasoned to ourselves without sharing the thought.

For a few days we were left to ourselves to stew in our fear and uncertainty, and work went on as "normal." Every day I went to work in the city and each day we managed to bring some food through the gate.

Every day we met in the office of the Judenrat. Apart from the daily agenda that had to be discussed and acted upon, the question "What next?" always came up. How long could we continue before the end would come? Levin, a member of the Judenrat, a simple Jew, once spoke his mind: "If they will come to take people once more, we should go out on the balcony of the square (where four streets came together) and call out to the people. "Fellow Jews, they are leading you to the slaughter. Don't go! It means death! Let it happen here on the spot!"

This instinct of the ordinary, simple people brought about the first mass resistance of a group of Jews that had been taken out of the ghetto in the "cleansing" of October 4. Passing through the town they realized that they were being taken in the direction of Lukishki prison. At that point they refused to continue and lay down in the middle of the road in front of passersby. They refused the orders of the Lithuanians and Germans to get up off the ground. It didn't take the trained murderers much to overcome the revolt. They opened a volley of bullets, killing a large number but many of the young people in the group escaped.

Within days the situation in our ghetto became easier. Every day many people left our ghetto and went to live in the large ghetto, believing that it was safer there. Many came to ask for my advice. To all of them I said the same thing: "Do as you understand. How can anybody give any advice? I decided to stay. We will see what will happen."

It didn't take long before we knew "what would happen."

CHAPTER 7

The End of the Small Ghetto

The Ghetto Is Dying

At one of the daily meetings of the heads of the various departments, the Juden-rat dealt with the question of how to obtain good work documents for the employees of the internal ghetto administration, which would protect them from being taken away during "cleansing" raids. We had already lost a considerable number of good workers, among them people who held important positions. In addition to the ones taken by Schweinenberger's henchmen, we had become further impoverished by workers moving to the large ghetto. One of the first to leave was the member of the Bund Gutgestalt. He had worked during the first days in the housing department while his wife had begun working as a teacher.

On Sunday, October 12 (the Jewish holiday of Hoshana Rabba), a few of us met at the apartment of Shlomo Gordon, Lejbowicz's father-in-law. Gordon was a wealthy man and through his caretaker he had a permanent contact in the city. He had lived at the same address before the war and his home was well supplied with a variety of food. Although the place was not very large, all the guests were accommodated around a table that had been laid out for the holiday meal with the lavishness of past years. We wished each other a peaceful year. But in the ghetto where we couldn't be sure of a peaceful day, the wish for a peaceful year was not taken seriously by anyone.

On October 14 and 15 (the final days of the holidays) our ghetto experienced additional "cleansing" raids and lost a large number of Jews. The destruction was now much more noticeable. More than half of the ghetto population had gone and whoever had a chance ran away to the other ghetto, which had been quiet since the treacherous raid of Yom Kippur. It was no longer possible to hide the truth. The ghetto was dying in front of our eyes like the flame of a burned-out candle. We started to prepare for the end but we did not think that the end would come as suddenly as it did.

Young people left the ghetto in droves, moving to the other ghetto or leaving the two ghettos altogether. One of the first to leave was the son of my friend, the young Dr. Remigalski. His father told me in confidence: "I did not discourage him. He is young, speaks Lithuanian as well as any Lithuanian. His chances of surviving outside the ghetto are much greater than inside. How could I discourage him and why should I? There is no longer any doubt that the Germans with the help of the Lithuanians will liquidate us all." I never found out what happened to the young Remigalski. Many Jews decided to leave for Byelorussia, mostly to the district of Lida. There the situation was calmer and with the help of bribed Germans one could arrange to leave Vilna. Many Jews left the ghetto that way. Few survived.

One of the saddest experiences that we endured on a daily basis was the delivery of "living merchandise" sent by the large-ghetto Judenrat. They consisted of the old, the sick and the invalids and were almost a certain sign that the fate of our ghetto had been sealed. We knew full well that Hitler would not feed and maintain such "merchandise."

And yet, in those very days, a new rumor started circulating – the Germans were preparing new, yellow work permits. Among the working units the talk was that all work permits given out up until that point would be annulled. In their place new brown work documents would be distributed. Immediately the Jews took to calling the new document the "yellow *Schein* (document)." Once more all working units started chasing after the new documents. To obtain them, the Jewish brigadiers made lists of their workers and handed them to their German employers. Over the months we had become used to all sorts of work documents. We already had documents with photos; documents with the Lithuanian Horse; documents with the swastika; documents with the word *craftsman* and others. To this collection a new one was coming along – a colored document.

People knew from bitter experience that there was little safety from any of the documents. Thousands of Jews were taken out of the ghetto with the best documents in their hands! Nonetheless, everybody made an effort to obtain the new papers. There was a feeling that the new brown document was somehow different from all the previous ones. Up until now, every working unit had given out documents of their own. The German works department had not taken any interest in the matter. Now the German works department was well organized, with a special section for Jewish matters. The same works department on Vilna Street also had a special section to recruit Poles, Lithuanians and White Russians (Byelorussians).

As was the case regarding all other offices, Jews were forbidden to have direct contact with the works department. All matters regarding Jewish workers had to be taken care of by their German employers. Now the Germans received lists from the Jewish brigadiers to obtain the necessary yellow (brown) documents. The first information we received from our "good" Germans was that the number of workers was being curtailed in all units and the number of yellow documents would be severely limited.

We were informed that the works department alone would decide on the number of units and on the number of workers allowed in each unit. By this we understood that many units, considered unimportant, would not receive any yellow documents at all. In addition, we learned something more important: while all yellow documents given out until now had not been of uniform size, color or style, the new documents would all be of one format. They would be numbered and they would carry the seal of the works department. Thus far, nobody had seen a single new yellow document but there were already many legends revolving around it. We believed that whoever would receive the new document would receive a license for life for himself and his family.

In my unit, the work of fitting out the rooms in the large building for the German women who were telephone and telegraph operators had come to its end. We had outfitted the rooms with the highest-class Jewish furniture, carpets, bedding and linens. We had also finished the dining room and furnished it with elegant crockery and silver cutlery. We had prepared the reading room and the smoking room and a special office for the woman in charge. We had tried to work as slowly as we could but the work was done.

For days we wandered around the large courtyard, pretending to be busy but, in effect, doing very little.

When the matter of new work documents became serious, we asked our officer to obtain the new papers for us. At first, he accepted the list of all our workers saying he would do his best for all of us. A few days later he informed us that the German works department refused to accept the list our brigadier had given him. When we pressed our case he agreed to try again to obtain documents for a few workers. The real chase began. Everyone individually promised him a large reward. It became a competition; the price of the yellow document was quoted in gold, diamonds and jewelry. In the end the German officer himself made a list of eight people that included me. He explained the reason to his workers: "The pharmacist is my colleague. I am a pharmacist with a diploma." I was surprised and elated. I had never considered the possibility of such good luck. The others envied me.

Days passed but all the promises never materialized. Not a single new yellow document came our way.

I turned to the German woman who was in charge of the girls, promising her my wife's gold watch if she would obtain a works document for me. She promised very courteously to go to the works department and ask for the desired documents. A few days later she called me in to her newly arranged office and said: "Our department is not allowed to employ Jews."

*   *   *

As the days began to get colder we realized that we had not taken any warm underwear for our children. We had left stacks of underwear and dresses in the house when we were deported to the ghetto. As our Polish subtenant had remained in the apartment we knew that no outsiders would have come to take things away from the apartment. We sent a note to the subtenants, listing the things we would like them to deliver to us for our children.

Two days later, our young former neighbor, Zukowska came to us together with her husband, a simple house painter and a decent man. They brought us a large basket with things and at first sight I was happy. I took out half a loaf of bread, some potatoes, a piece of lamb meat that smelled bad and a few pieces of torn children's clothes – rags that were not ours and were totally useless. To my question about the whereabouts of all the food products, linen and clothes we left behind the young woman said: "The Lithuanians bandits took it all. The rooms are empty. What I have brought you is from our own things and our own bread." I was touched by her sudden generosity and thanked her. We took from her only the bread and the potatoes; all the other items we returned. I ascribed her generosity to the fact that a few days before she had come to me with the house caretaker and I sold her three tons of coal that we left behind in a cellar of our former house in Wielka Street in return for a few loaves of bread.

At home when I told the story of the basket my family laughed at my naiveté. "Have you already forgotten how she dragged everything out of our hands when we were still in the house?" my mother pointed out.

I realized the woman's trick and I resented her action. I decided to pay her back at the earliest opportunity. At that time the German officer in our work unit told me that he needed a nice office desk. We had brought to the building tens of beautiful desks but the officer wanted one additional one.

"I have a most beautiful writing desk," I told him.

"Bring it," the German said. I said that I could not go alone to where I had lived before. If he really wanted to see the desk he would have to take some workers and come with us.

He asked the foreman for six workers and we went. On the way I told the others what I wanted. I told them to fill their pockets with everything they could cram in. At what other time would I have such an opportunity?

When we entered the apartment and the woman saw me together with other Jews in the company of a German officer she turned white. She immediately turned to me to settle the matter between us. I pointed to the officer and said she should talk to him. The room was totally bare. The German officer asked her where the office desk was, as he couldn't see it in the cleared-out room. She did not reply. I opened the door and led the others into her two rooms. I stopped, flabbergasted; both rooms were full of our property. I pointed to the desk: "Here it is," I said. The officer liked what he saw: "Yes, truly nice."

He turned to the woman: "How did you get hold of the desk?" "The Jew gave it to me," she said. "To keep it for him," she added arrogantly.

I was filled with anger. If this is how you say you got it, I decided on the spot – I will teach you what "the Jew" can do.

"You see, sir," I turned to the German. "She is wearing my wife's dress and my wife's shoes. These are our linens and dresses," I went on as I tore open the wardrobe that was full of our things. "Take it all away!" the officer commanded.

It was all we needed. Within minutes we made packs of everything and we moved over to the writing desk. We opened the drawers one after the other; they revealed a veritable fortune: the most expensive new linen for men and women that my sister had bought in 1939 before the war, beautiful tablecloths, knitting wool. All the drawers were full of our possessions. In minutes, six pairs of hands took hold of everything and carried it all out of the house with a great sense of revenge.

We took what the officer saw and what we could put in our pockets. We left the apartment with more things than we had taken when we went into the ghetto.

When we reached our working place the German officer took all the valuable things for himself and left us the rest. It was a small part of what we had collected. But what he let me keep brought in a considerable amount of money. It was enough to sustain our family for some time. Most of the things I brought back remained in the ghetto during its liquidation; I did not get much out of the things. But we had our satisfaction. On top of our own satisfaction the case became known in the Gentile surroundings and was a valuable lesson for many other treacherous neighbors.

A few days later our caretaker came and told us that the neighbors kept gloating about the lesson I had managed to teach the Polish woman.

The Liquidation of the Small Ghetto

The situation of our ghetto was evidently terminal, with a considerable number of people leaving daily. On top of the ordinary people, the more educated who had been the backbone of our departments also began to leave. The first one was Dr. Poczter and his departure caused a serious problem. Once he departed we were left without even the minimum of medical help. The large ghetto came to our rescue. It sent doctors to us in the small ghetto every day. The doctors came in the morning and went back to their homes in the evening.

On Monday, October 20, 1941, at around eight in the evening, Buragas, the Lithuanian who was supposed to be the only man to attend to our needs, came to the ghetto for a conference about the number of yellow documents we were to receive for our inner administration. The Judenrat had made a list of two hundred employees, which had been handed to him earlier. Now, at the conference, Buragas said that the Judenrat would not be given anything close to that number. He told us the Judenrat in the large ghetto would receive 350 yellow documents (in the end they received 400) and we would be given 75 such documents.

He spent a long time with us during the conference. I discussed with him the way we were to pay rent for the dwellings in the ghetto. The city authorities had earlier sent us an official letter demanding full payment of rent for all dwellings in the ghetto. This was the text of the letter:

> To the chairman of the Jewish Committee
> in the Ghetto Number 1:
>
> For Jewish use of dwellings in the ghetto, occupied and nonoccupied ones, as well as other buildings, the Vilna city authorities, with the agreement of the mayor, will deliver to the Jewish Committee an invoice, the sum of which the Jewish Committee should collect from the residents of the ghetto. The full sum as stated on the invoice should be delivered to the cashier of the communal bank or to the cashier of the Fourth District of the city of Vilna, at 4 Sadova Street.

To this end the Jewish Committee should:

- Open an account to collect rent from ghetto residents and appoint a responsible cashier.
- Obtain books from the Fourth District of the city of Vilna to write out invoices for rent. The books given to the house administrators will be kept in accordance with a proper list and will be numbered.
- Keep an income book and a diary written up by the cashier. The cashier should accept money according to the amount on the invoice, confirm on the invoice that he has received the right amount and sign two copies. One should be given to the person making the payment and the second copy to be kept in the office. Having received the money, the cashier is to write up his income book and his diary. The daily income must be balanced and signed by the cashier and the chairman of the Jewish Committee, or by his appointee. The income book must be balanced once a month.
- The cashier is not allowed to write up any other payments in the income book, neither for the Jewish Committee nor for personal payment.
- The chairman of the Jewish Committee in the ghetto is responsible for the work of the cashier.

S. Narushish – District Administrator
Krushtshunas – Accountant
10.13.1941

Before leaving, Buragas handed Lejbowicz ten yellow documents, five of them already designated for five furriers. The furriers were to be immediately sent to live in the furriers' building at the Kailis factory. The other five were open to be filled in and sent to the recipients. At 10:30 p.m. the conference was over. We dispersed wishing each other a peaceful night.

Since our arrival in the ghetto we no longer said "good night"; we said "a peaceful night." Before Chairman Lejbowicz left, he filled in the names of the individuals entitled to yellow documents and sent them to their recipients by police messengers.

Arriving home I assured everyone that our ghetto still had some future, as Buragas promised seventy-five yellow work permits. This should be a sign that the ghetto would continue to exist. We went to bed only half-undressed, as had lately become our routine.

We were awakened by loud noises coming from the street. I went to the window to find out what was going on. At first I could not see anything as it was a dark autumn night. I looked down over the roof and noticed small lights coming from handheld torches. Lying stretched out on the roof I heard the wild shouts of the Lithuanians: "Quick, quick!" followed by desperate screams in Yiddish.

I realized that another "cleansing" was taking place. Within minutes all the family was awake, dressed and began making small bundles. We waited and talked among ourselves, trying to work out what it all meant. It was an hour after midnight. A few hours earlier Buragas left the ghetto assuring us that the ghetto would remain intact and he promised us the new yellow documents. True, he had not agreed to the number of documents that the Judenrat asked for but he had promised a certain number. What did the present situation mean? What did we have to do to save ourselves?

Without delay I helped my wife and the two children out through the window onto the roof. I found some warm covers and covered the children. My mother and I remained in the room.

Having attended to my wife and children, I covered the windows with heavy blankets to stop the light in the room showing outside and took a deep breath. It was dark outside so my wife and the children would not be noticed – we were, after all, on the fourth floor – and from the room they would also not be noticed; at least they would be secure.

We sat like this for an hour…and another hour, waiting impatiently for the moment when the raid would be over. We already knew that the Germans were working according to a prepared plan and timetable. But this time it seemed to take much longer. The "cleansing" had gone on for already three hours and it was still continuing. We noticed that the desperate screams kept coming closer and the torchlights were approaching closer with every minute.

Suddenly a frightful thought hit me. I was the last man to come home and I had locked the gate downstairs. When the killers would arrive and find the street-level door closed they would know that people were in the building; they would break down the door.

Leaving my mother alone, I crept down, unlocked the door and opened it. From the street level the wooden staircase led to the first floor where we had created a provisional old people's home and a few paralyzed elderly people brought to us from the large ghetto had been accommodated there.

We heard the Lithuanians breaking down doors with heavy iron bars, smashing windows and closed cellars and beating people mercilessly. It was nearly dawn and a new problem was arising. It would be impossible for my wife and children to remain on the roof much longer. They would be noticed in the daylight.

Distraught, I paced around the room trying to work out a way to save the family. Every few minutes I went to the window to exchange a few words with my wife and children, trying to comfort them, telling them that soon the raid would be over.

But there was no end this time; on the contrary, the raid was getting more intense and the noise and screams of the desperate women and children were coming nearer, nothing short of driving us mad. People driven like a herd of animals kept looking for hiding places to save themselves and the Lithuanian human beasts kept chasing them and beating them mercilessly.

Suddenly, out of despair came the solution. I turned to my mother: "There is nothing to be lost, the 'cleansing' is still going on and it will soon reach us. Make me a white armband. I'll put it on like a policeman and go down to the Lithuanians."

It was already cold outside. I put on my fur coat, pulled on the white armband, locked the door and went down to the first floor. There I stopped outside the door of the old people's home and waited.

After some time I heard the approaching steps of the Lithuanian murderers. I froze in my place. Two Lithuanian soldiers, more like young scoundrels, arrived. They went up the few steps and one of them asked what I was doing there. I told him: "I was put here by the Jewish police to guard the old people. Soon the cart will arrive and take them away." Without saying anything, he gave me a mighty push throwing me down the staircase. By some miracle I fell without breaking any bones.

Only half-alive, I lifted myself and began running as fast as I could. I stopped in a corner behind a building in the courtyard to catch my breath. When I felt a little revived I realized my situation; what was I doing here? The bandits would walk up to our room and God knows what they might do?

Collecting my energy and my wits I ran back to the house. On the first floor everything was open and the people had gone. I ran higher up – the same thing. At our room the lock had been forced and the door was half-open. I trembled at the sight that met my eyes. The younger of the two Lithuanians was standing at the bed where my mother was lying, her head was pushed toward the floor by the young murderer who was choking her: "Give us the gold! Money! Give us!"

Near the bed a few Soviet rubles were spread on the floor. The murderer was choking my mother and she was fighting for air.

I ran forward to the bed and pulled a bundle of notes out of my pocket: "Here. Take it! Here is the money; let her be. She has no money." The bandit took the money (three hundred rubles) and without saying anything they left.

I ran to the window, exchanged a few words with my wife and children; they sounded terribly shocked. They had heard what had gone on.

It was already broad daylight. My wife and the children could no longer remain on the roof. I helped them back into the room and I went back, like before, to my "police position."

It wasn't long before a Lithuanian dressed in a leather jacket with a brief-case in his right hand (he must have been in charge of the Lithuanian Gestapo), came along. In answer to his question about what I was doing there, I gave my previous answer: "I am a Jewish policeman. I have been put here on guard wait-ing for the cart to take away the old people." He asked: "Is anybody up there?"

"No. They've all been taken."

"Are you telling the truth?" he asked.

"Please, see for yourself," I half-encouraged him.

He went up to the second floor and found open doors and empty rooms. He ran from one room to the next and finding nobody he went down cursing in the most vile language. My heart was pounding so hard that I actually felt its beat in my chest… All right, I got rid of him but for how long? How many other demons would still come up? When would the tragedy come to an end?

From that moment on the "visits" continued. To every officer who showed up I gave the same answer. Some believed me and went on their way. Others went up to the first floor; a few went up to the second floor and seeing the de-struction they had already managed to bring about – they left. Some however decided to see for themselves, and went right up to the highest floor. I went up the staircase with these officers. When the ones who were the least trusting reached the fourth floor and saw the lock on the door they demanded to know why I had tried to cheat them. "I told the truth," I explained. "Nobody remains in the building except my family. The chief of the Jewish police ordered me to keep the door locked and if asked, to say that this was done on his order, with the understanding of the Lithuanian authorities."

While saying this, I also handed the murderers some money. In two cases I had to unlock the door and show them that my family were the only people in the room.

This too passed "only" with fear and money. I counted seventeen such parties. The money I had was going fast. After the first payments, I reduced the amount from three hundred to two hundred rubles; later to one hundred rubles and in the end to as little as fifty rubles.

Time was passing. It was 10 a.m., noon, 2 and then 3 p.m. and there was still no end to the raid. I couldn't work out what was going on. I could not ask the Lithuanians what was taking place and I failed to understand what exactly was happening around us.

I stood at my position until 4 p.m. I had so far managed to chase off all the enemy attacks. Ten hours had already passed since I came on duty. What now?

At that moment I noticed Pawirski, the chief of our police. I ran down and asked him what was happening. He replied, somewhat absentmindedly: "The ghetto is being liquidated. I am running to the other ghetto. Save yourself the best way you can." Saying this he ran off in the direction away from the gate, possibly to climb the fence or to pass through the gate that went out to Wielka Street to get himself out of the ghetto. Now I understood why the raid had been going on for so long. I was angry with myself for having waited until the last moment. I could have at least saved myself and the family the long torment. I was guilty for all their tragedy. But what was the good of being angry, of accusing myself? I had to find a way to save the family. But where was I to start? What was I to do? First of all I went back to my family.

It was around 5 p.m. Luckily the "visitors" had stopped coming during the past two hours. It had been quiet for some time and then I heard voices coming from the side of the courtyard. Carefully I peered out of the window. There were no Lithuanian guards and the people were not screaming. I noticed that the noisy group was surrounding a German. I ran down and asked what was going on. One of them informed me that the German is ready to lead the Jews out of this ghetto into the large one, but he was asking for a watch. "Good, I will give him a watch." The man was not a fool. "Then give it to me," he said. "Wait," I told the man. "I will have a talk with him first."

With this I went over to the German and told him: "I have my family here. We want to go over to the other ghetto and in exchange, I am willing to give you a beautiful watch." The German easily accepted: "Good, show me where your family is."

I felt my blood freezing. Had I trusted the German too much?

But there was no way to undo what was done. The German had already pulled out his revolver and said to me: "Come, show me your family." I had no choice and began leading the German. Behind me I heard someone saying: "Let's get lost – the German is from the G," meaning the Gestapo.

Everything is lost, I told myself, walking up the steps. For the second time I had brought it on myself and my family.

Walking up the old, twisting staircase I said to the German: "You don't need a gun, there is nothing to be afraid of." To which the man replied: "I am not afraid but it does no harm – just in case."

I unlocked the door and led the German into the room with his gun at the ready. Seeing the German with his gun pointing in their direction the children screamed. I calmed them immediately: "Don't be frightened, the man is a 'good' German. He came to take us to the large ghetto. Here everything has come to its end."

"Right, right," the German confirmed. "Don't be frightened," and he put the gun away on the table. "Take your bundles and let's go," I said, "and take as little as you need." At that moment I took the alarm clock off the table and handed it to him: "Here is your clock."

The German become angry: "Curse you! I don't need such a clock! I want a watch! A pocket watch or a wrist watch!"

I pulled out of my pocket two Soviet one-hundred-ruble notes and handed them to him: "I have no watch but here is the money to buy one. In the other ghetto I will buy you a watch, exactly as you want."

He took the money and put it in his pocket, asking: "Have you any gloves?"

"Yes," I replied. 'I have elegant leather gloves with fur lining."

"Let's see them…"

My wife began looking for the gloves but in her state of mind it took some minutes before she pulled out a pair of beautiful gloves, leather with fur lining, just as I had told him.

The German was delighted. "Very nice, yes, very nice!" he said, handing me his old gloves. There it was – the "good" German.

The gloves saved us. They had their own interesting story.

During the winter of 1940 Advocate Reichman arrived from Lodz. Winter that year was particularly cold. Reichman's feet became frostbitten, and he reached Vilna close to death. I took him to the Jewish Hospital. My daughter looked after him and provided whatever he needed. For a short time he lived with us. Not wanting to live on communal charity, Reichman, like many others, became a dealer in the town market to earn his living. One day he came and showed us some gloves that he had bought for his business. I liked his self-confidence. "You know what," I said to him, "I will give you a lucky start. Give me a pair of gloves." I paid him the equivalent of three dollars for the gloves and put them away. They lay untouched for two years; now they fulfilled their destiny. They saved us.

Wanting to have the German fully on our side I said to him that he would be the only one in the whole of Vilna with such elegant gloves.

We started to get ready. Already experienced from the first time we went to the ghetto, I told the family to take as little as was absolutely necessary – not more.

We took the bundles and the suitcases and had a last look at our latest home where we had spent tragic days. We locked the door and in the company of the German we went down into the courtyard and out into the lane, trembling and praying that it would all pass peacefully.

We went through the central streets of the ghetto, the family in front and the German at my side with the gun in his hand. The streets were empty. Passing Szklanna Street we saw masses of Jews surrounded by Lithuanian guards. Some Lithuanians tried to take us over from the German but he stopped them harshly: "Get away, get away! They are my people!" he warned them with his gun in his hand.

From Szklanna Street to the ghetto gate was no more than a minute but to us it was like eternity, walking in the valley of death and seeing masses of Jews being led to the slaughter... Did they envy us? Who knows? Probably yes, seeing how we were being led to the gate, to life.

Let us already be on the other side of the gate!

At last we reached the gate. Fate was playing its game of life and death, the outcome to be decided every second. At the gate the Lithuanian didn't want to let us pass. The German approached him with the gun in his hand: "Let it go, you cursed dog! *Scheisse*! Let my people through!" Our "good" German shouted at the Lithuanian and tore open the gate while pointing his gun at him.

We were now on the other side of the gate!

God…how are we to thank Thee. God?

Quickly we moved on away from the ghetto and turned into Szwarcowy Lane. Here we stopped for the first time to catch our breath. Now we noticed that though we had taken much smaller packs than the first time, we had still taken quite a lot. Our energy was giving out. Up to now we had been driven by superhuman energy, by total fear. Now that we were nearly saved we felt how exhausted we had become.

We didn't dare risk too much and were soon on our way once more. It was the same way we had been driven to the ghetto on Black Saturday, but in the opposite direction. We passed by our house in Wielka Street and looked at the windows of our apartment. But how different was the situation now! On September 6 we had a spark of hope that "there," in the ghetto, we would be left in peace. Now we were walking again into a ghetto with far fewer illusions. Now we knew that the ghetto meant concentrating Jews in one place to make it easier for the murderers to liquidate us. The ghetto meant a passing island of tears where we were forced to await our death at any hour or any minute. The ghetto meant final doom.

The ghetto also meant weakness, helplessness. The six short weeks that we had been in the small ghetto had shown us that in a ghetto one is not even allowed to die a hero's death. For each act of vengeance by a hero who might kill his deadly enemy – a German – hundreds or thousands of helpless Jews would have to pay with their lives. In the ghetto we asked ourselves if it was permitted to be a hero when others would have to pay for it.

Scared, unsure and frightened to the core, we walked through the wide street. At last we were in the small lane. When we reached our childhood landmark, the Zavalkin House, we stopped for a second time. A peasant on a horse cart passed. I stopped him and asked the German if he would allow us to put our things on the cart. "Yes," he said, "if the peasant will permit it and you'll pay him." What more was there to say – if one is a "good" German that's his way. The peasant agreed – and we walked behind the cart.

The entrance to the large ghetto was close to the Church of All Saints. We took our packs off the cart, I paid the driver and within a few paces we were at the gate of the large ghetto.

Neither the Lithuanian guard nor the Jewish police inside the gate stopped us. We lived through another miracle – our family had survived the liquidation of the small ghetto and we were inside the large ghetto! "Our" German kept leading us right to the building of the Judenrat of the ghetto. Outside the building, in the street, stood the chief of police of the large ghetto, Jacob Gens, with his assistant – Dessler. Seeing me and my family in the company of the German, Gens asked: "Balberyszski, where are you coming from?" I replied: "From the other ghetto."

"Quickly, go to the police station," he half-advised and half-ordered.

I knew Gens from two previous meetings regarding the evacuation of the elderly and the sick that he had been sending to the small ghetto. I didn't know his assistant at all. I didn't even know his name was Dessler. I knew old man Dessler, his father, very well. Between the years 1919–1925 he was the chairman of the medical society Mishmeret Hacholim, of which I was a committee member.

Hearing Gens order us to the police station, I thanked the German and immediately went with all the family to the station, which was located in a shop. An old friend, Haim Malczadski, now a policeman, took charge of us. Malczadski was a former pharmacist and we had worked together in the pharmacy of Mishmeret Hacholim. At one stage we had been on the committee of the Union of the Employees of Pharmacists. We were friends. Seeing me with my family in our condition, he embraced and kissed me like good friends do at such a moments. He comforted us, saying that if we got out of the hell of the small ghetto we would not get lost here.

Malczadski immediately introduced me to Flesher, the sergeant of the police. Malczadski and Flesher made a place for us in the back room of the station. We found a few iron beds there and we settled in temporarily.

It was the evening of October 21, 1941. This was our first home in the large ghetto of Vilna. After a short time, Flesher brought us tickets for the evening meal, to be eaten at the police kitchen. He came together with Malczadski and both of them assured us that Gens had told them we could spend the night in the police station. We were grateful for it.

Together with the children, I went to the police kitchen located in the same court. The kitchen was large but dark, lit by a few candles. The soup consisted of a few carrots with water. But at the time the hot water was much tastier than the best food at other times. When we finished eating we went back to our room at the police station. I found a mattress for my mother and the rest of us fell on the iron beds and slept like the dead.

*   *   *

Where did we get the energy, the courage to do what we did in order to survive that fateful day, how did we manage to escape the maze of death that surrounded us every minute – it all remained beyond our comprehension. In any case, the welcome we had received so far in our new "home" gave us new courage, hope and faith for the future. The tragic chapter in our lives known as the small ghetto of Vilna came to an end. We were now opening a new chapter – the large ghetto.

At a later stage we learned the blood-chilling details of the liquidation of the small ghetto. Throughout the night and during the whole day of October 22, 1941, the Lithuanian murderers kept breaking down doors and forcing closed entrances, attics and cellars. They worked enthusiastically, with sadistic glee on their faces. Often, one of them would murderously beat a victim while others would laugh and encourage the sadist. They had brought iron bars and axes to the ghetto to assist in their "holy work."

The fate of the Judenrat members was no better than that of the other ghetto inhabitants. A few days before the small ghetto was liquidated, Lewit, a member of the Judenrat received a yellow document as a worker at the Kailis furrier factory. Two other members of the Judenrat, Levin and Schneiderman managed to survive in a hideout and a few days after the liquidation of the small ghetto they reached the large ghetto. A few days later Schneiderman fell victim during a "cleansing" raid. Levin was about to leave for Byelorussia when he fell into the hands of the Gestapo. The German who was to help him escape changed his mind and denounced him.

Lejbowicz, the chairman of the small-ghetto Judenrat, managed to reach the large ghetto by the proverbial skin of his teeth. Fried, the chairman of the large ghetto, made Lejbowicz humble himself before he gave him a yellow document. In the end, Lejbowicz decided not to remain in the ghetto. He took his family to Byelorussia, where they all perished. A little later his brother-in-law, Pawirski, former chief of police in the small ghetto, also left the ghetto. Feldman, the fifth member of the Judenrat, arrived in the large ghetto financially well off. For a large sum of money he had obtained a yellow document and remained in the ghetto throughout its existence.

Of the five members of the Judenrat, two are alive at the time of writing – Feldman and Lewit. The other members who took part in setting up departments in the small ghetto shared to a great extent the fate of the general community. Remigalski and Smilag came to the large ghetto, remained there for a few days and perished through a provocation of the Jewish police. They trusted the police announcement that the small ghetto was being reestablished. They went back there and were taken to Ponary a few days later. Dr. Poczter died on September 19, 1943, in the Klooga (Estonia) Concentration Camp. It seems that Sackheim died during the liquidation of the large ghetto. Kaszuk, the accountant of the small ghetto, came to the large ghetto and worked there in the financial department.

At first the Jewish police of the small ghetto tried, as always, to help save as many people as possible. When they realized that the raid meant the liquidation of the ghetto they tried to save themselves and their families, but they didn't have much success. Many policeman of the small ghetto went together with the others to Ponary. Some managed to reach the large ghetto on the first day while others saved themselves in well-prepared hideouts. But there were few such places for the simple reason that there had not been sufficient time to build them.

One good hideout was in Yatkowa Street. It had a large apartment that had been left untouched after the owners were taken away. By making a secret opening in the wall it was possible to climb into another apartment, also untouched. The hole in the wall was made in a built-in cupboard and the opening was covered with a painted board to match the rest of the cupboard wall. Around thirty people successfully hid in the second apartment. They were betrayed by the senseless act of a young woman who had received a yellow document. She had registered her father on the document as part of the family, but the father was in the hideout with the others and she wanted to take him out. The young woman had found a "good" Lithuanian who had helped her obtain the document in the first place. She asked him to take her to the hideout and help bring her father back into the ghetto. The "good" Lithuanian did. The next day the Gestapo arrived and took the others away – to Ponary.

The Gestapo did not catch all of them. Some instinctively felt that helping the young woman did not mean the Lithuanian could be trusted by others. As soon as the Lithuanian left with the father and the daughter they left the hideout. Among them was Rosa Bunimowicz, who had worked as administrator of our building. All those that remained were lost. Among those who were betrayed was one of the Bender brothers, who had been my assistant in the housing department. It is worth noting that throughout the month that the people were in hiding, the Gentile caretaker of the building provided them with food and all other necessities.

My cousin Sonia Kulbis told me of another unusual case. Some thirty people were hiding in a primitive hideout at 10 Zydowska Street. When they felt that it was about to be given away, they saved themselves by running to another place equally primitive. There they found a cellar and all thirty people went down to hide in it. Among them was a young woman with a baby. The baby was crying and the mother could not silence it. The situation was tragic and dangerous. It was clear that were the bandits to hear the child cry, all would be lost. When nothing could be done to silence the child, the others called to the mother to choke the baby. The mother wouldn't do it. Others tried to take the baby away from her to choke it. The mother cried bitterly but would not let the baby out of her arms.

Seeing that she could not silence the baby the mother said: "I cannot kill my baby and I cannot let you kill it. I am leaving. Whatever has to happen – let it happen. This is my fate and I accept it. May God protect you all. I don't want to be the cause of death of so many Jews."

The woman with the child left the cellar and covered the opening from the outside. She remained with the boy in the room above. It didn't take long before the people in the cellar heard the screams of the Lithuanian bandits who had entered the room. Seeing the woman and the baby they beat her first, and took her and the baby away. They didn't search the place any further. All the Jews in the cellar survived the raid. A few survived the war. Among those who survived were my cousin and her husband; both of them were in the cellar.

The final liquidation of the small ghetto took nearly a full month. Both Germans and Lithuanians kept searching for whatever might have been left by their victims at the last moment. Unfortunately there were also Jewish traitors. They denounced hideouts to the Germans and Lithuanians and helped the bloodthirsty cannibals to drag the Jews from the hideout to Ponary.

The walls of the ghetto were not taken apart. They had still to play a sad part in our martyrology.

Ten days after its original liquidation, the small ghetto was filled once more with Jews. This time it was filled by Jews with yellow documents who were taken under guard to clean up the ghetto. When they went home after work, they allowed Jews from the hideouts to join them. The lucky ones that had not been found by the Lithuanians managed to arrive in small groups to the large ghetto where they remained.

We learned in time of many great deeds of heroism that remained unrecorded. We heard of cases where the Lithuanians were willing to help young, beautiful woman escape death, children to run away and parents to save themselves. But the beautiful young women did not leave their husbands; children didn't run away from their parents and parents did not leave their children. The strength of the bond uniting the Jewish family, the devotion of a husband, a wife and children to each other in those tragic times was a mass phenomenon. In some cases the Germans were astonished to the point of losing their calm. They could not understand Jewish devotion and love while they stood at the brink of death. Later when we were in the concentration camp we often debated the phenomenon, trying to decide if the action was right or wrong; we could never decide one way or the other. Soul-disturbing moral greatness at the brink of destruction.

Reliable Lithuanian sources told me about another case of true heroism at Ponary. A German Gestapo officer in his arrogant way ordered a young woman in an elegant fur coat to undress. Instead of undressing, the woman replied by spitting in the bandit's face. She did not reach the pit alive. A hail of bullets ended her life immediately. But the Jewish spittle on the German face must have remained in the psyche of the Gestapo officer for some time.

Great historical injustice is being done to tens of thousands of Holocaust heroes by interpreters of history who deliberately and consciously minimize Jewish heroism during the Holocaust. They reduce the word *resistance* to its lowest denominator of *armed resistance*. We didn't have the means to put up physical resistance. Individual resistance in the ghettos was an agonizing moral question. Did one have the right to carry out an act of physical resistance such as killing a German or even a Lithuanian knowing that the price would be the lives of hundreds or thousands of Jews, many of whom were still under the illusion that they may survive? It is only when hope for survival was totally shattered that armed resistance became possible. By then, however, it was too late.

There were thousands of passive heroes who showed great moral courage and strength. If we consider the acts of individuals when they knew that the Germans would have no way to punish others for their heroism, we discover a phenomenon that was unique: resistance that left the murderers astonished and with no means to punish anybody for it.

The story of the woman who spit in the face of her murderer was one of the highest acts of moral resistance; it must have haunted and enraged her killer for some time, without him being able to do anything about it. Killing additional Jews? He did that. The woman who resisted him was already dead. She committed a supreme heroic act which her tormentors had no way to avenge. Thousands of similar actions have been recorded.

The German people will never be able to wash off the Jewish spit in the face of the German at Ponary. We should erect a monument to the memory of Jewish heroes without a gun in their hands and we should make pilgrimages to such a monument. It should honor the men who did not want to save their lives by leaving their wives, mothers, sisters and brides; the Jewish women who were unwilling to stay alive for the price of leaving their husband, children, parents or siblings. They sanctified the human spirit at the edge of the death pit. The heroic actions of thousand upon thousands of Jews stand in testimony to the greatness of the human spirit. And this testimony will remain in the annals of history for centuries to come.

*   *   *

Thus the dramatic chapter of the small ghetto of Vilna came to its tragic end. It had lasted from September 6 to October 21, 1941 – a total of forty-six days that resulted in the murder of nine thousand Jews.

It defies imagination that all the events described so far took place within four months of the German occupation of Vilna on June 24, 1941. During that short period of time Germans and their Lithuanian helpers succeeded in destroying centuries of Jewish endeavors and murdering more than half of the Jewish population of "Jerusalem of Lithuania," the pride of the Jewish people.

◆

PART THREE
In the Large Ghetto

Prologue

The gates of the large ghetto opened wide on Saturday, September 6, 1941, just as they did in the small ghetto. At dawn, as soon as the first rays of an unusually beautiful early autumn day appeared, thirty thousand Jews, the remnant of the magnificent Jewish community of Vilna, were herded into the streets that were cordoned off by German and Lithuanian forces. They were quickly divided into three streams in accordance with a well-prepared German plan. Those destined for the large ghetto were driven in the direction of Rudnicka Street. On Sunday, September 7, 1941, the large ghetto became reality and the process of settling in began. It was a mirror image of what was happening several hundred yards away in the small ghetto. Same harrowing scenes of parents looking for their children, children looking for parents, husbands looking for wives only to realize that they were lost somewhere along the way and did not enter the ghetto. Hungry people who were driven out of their homes on Saturday morning and were not allowed to take any packages as well as people who had taken bundles and lost them during the march to the ghetto were looking for food. And everybody was looking for shelter. Over the next few days the ghetto was a macabre scene of disoriented, confused people in turmoil. Hundreds kept wandering around asking for lost members of their families and friends. During the months before the creation of the ghetto we were really not aware of the vast number of people that had already disappeared. Due to the dangerous situation that had prevailed in Vilna during the weeks preceding the establishment of the ghetto, we had not gone out, we did not meet. Now we began to learn the true magnitude of our tragedy.

The march into the large ghetto had taken the whole day and night of Saturday, September 6. By the time it was over approximately twenty thousand Jews were behind its walls. Nine thousand were in the small ghetto. Some six thousand Jews never lived to see either of the ghettos. They were herded into Lidski Lane and from there they were taken directly to Lukishki and Ponary.

CHAPTER 8
Surviving in the Large Ghetto

Surviving the First Cleansing

After spending the first night in the large ghetto at a police station, early in the morning I went to the courtyard of 6 Rudnicka where the police headquarters were located. This was also the address of the Judenrat and various other ghetto institutions. The hierarchy of the ghetto lived in this courtyard. The present courtyard had once been divided into three separate courts. Now they were joined together.

At this early hour the place was already full of people who had managed to escape the liquidation of the small ghetto the previous day without falling into the hands of the Lithuanian murderers. Most looked lost and helpless. Some of them had worked in the Judenrat of the small ghetto. They surrounded me and asked me to see that they get some bread, as they had not eaten for the last two days. I made a list of the people and went to Advocate Grigori Jaszunski, the director of the food department. He signed the list and I received a loaf of bread for each person. I immediately handed out the bread to the people in the courtyard according to the names I had on the list.

While I was distributing bread, the music conductor Jacob Gerstein, a former activist of the Vilna community, approached me and poured out his bitter heart: "You see, I am old, sick and hungry and have no document. I have no near ones with whom to find a little comfort. The young ones are quick and energetic, they are the leaders. For money one can buy a good document but I have no money and no one wants to know me." His words cut through me like a knife but what could I do? I was with four souls of my own, standing like a dog without an owner, temporarily homeless. I had just escaped from the inferno called "liquidation." I took my loaf of bread and handed him half of it; a few days later I did the same again. He thanked me, crying with gratitude and

I cried with him. I found a number of friends in a similar condition, including Haim Levin, the past editor of a Zionist paper; Haim Semiatycki, a well-known poet; Haim Remigalski; Kaszuk, the past director of the Bunimowicz Bank; Ms. Trokman, the teacher; and Israel Segal, the stage actor. All of us had managed to save ourselves when the small ghetto was liquidated, but we now remained without that life-protecting paper, the yellow document.

Together with my family I settled in an empty room in the building of the Judenrat. It was without furniture, so we spread out on the floor with the bundles we had brought from the small ghetto. We knew that we would not be allowed to remain in the place for long, but the short relief was better than nothing.

I went to see Burstein, the house administrator, who once had a bicycle shop. Hearing my name he became attentive: "Are you Balberyszski from *Der tog* (The day, a Yiddish newspaper to which I was a contributor)?" he asked. "Yes," I replied hopefully. "So, you are the man who organized the self-defense when Professor Chamiec tried to start a pogrom in Vilna?" "Yes," I said once more, surprised that he remembered an incident that took place back in 1922. "That is an old story. Today the situation is totally different." "I don't agree with you," Burstein replied. "You deserve to be helped," he added. He promised to do whatever possible. The happiness that my family experienced when I came back to our empty room and told them about it was indescribable. When I returned the next day he led me into an empty shop, dark and in need of a good cleaning; this was to be the promised dwelling. I looked at it and in a moment it became "the Palace of Graf (Duke) Potocki."

We moved into our new home. We opened the shutters and had a good look at it. It was a small shop that had not seen a broom for a long time and had no stove. The only furniture was a small table and a broken chair. After making our home livable we went out into the courtyard and were met by a new rumor that made our blood run cold – there would be a new "cleansing" operation the next day. We had not yet managed to catch our breath after the final "cleansing" of the small ghetto and another slaughter was already waiting for us at the gate.

We knew that we could not remain in our room for a second longer. It was an open store with entrances from the street and from the court. What kind of a hiding place would such a shop be? And we had no yellow work documents. The previous evening I had gone to see Chairman Fried, almost begging him to save us. He replied in Russian: "I don't have any yellow documents. You can do whatever you want."

Early the next morning, October 23, a few thousand people, all with old, white work permits, besieged the building of the Judenrat. None of them had any prospects of obtaining yellow permits and they were desperate. They shouted in anger that the Judenrat members had taken all the yellow permits for themselves and thought only of saving themselves and their relatives.

Seeing that yelling would not achieve anything, I climbed up to the highest step outside the building and addressed the people: "Brothers and sisters, Jews. Our shouts and accusations will not help us much. The situation is most dangerous. Our lives can be measured in hours. If we won't find a solution we will all be lost." The reaction was soul-searing. People started crying and I could hardly hold back from joining them. "Our only solution," I continued after a moment, "is to collect a large sum of money and hand it to the Judenrat. Let the Judenrat see if it can help. Do you agree?" The response was as I expected. We elected a delegation of five people and went in the name of the thousands to see Chairman Fried and the commandant of the police – Jacob Gens.

Gens was not in the office. We spoke to the chairman and asked that he call the police commandant and within minutes Gens arrived and confirmed there would be a "cleansing" raid the next day and all those who did not have a yellow document would be taken away. There was no way to save anybody. When we told him about the collection of money he said he didn't believe that we would be able to collect a sufficiently large sum to satisfy the Gestapo. We undertook to collect a large sum and asked him to check if this would help. "Good," he said, "I am going to town and will do whatever will be possible."

Fried admitted that the Germans had issued thirty-five hundred yellow documents that would cover families of up to four people. This meant that fourteen thousand people including wives and children could be saved. Any

Jews above that number would not be allowed to remain in the ghetto. Everyone else would be taken away.

The outcome of the intervention was that we left Fried's office with more despair in our hearts than when we entered. We let the large mass of people know that Gens had left for the Gestapo and the hopes were not very high. The people slowly dispersed.

I waited for Gens's return at the ghetto gate. When he returned he said straight out: "I couldn't achieve anything."

"What shall I do, Commandant, I have a family of five people."

"If you have a place to go outside the ghetto, go." He left me standing and walked away.

I came back resigned to my family. We were trapped in a net from which we could not escape. Was there anything we could do to survive the "cleansing"?

The whole afternoon we walked around in our overcoats, full of despair as we saw the clock measuring the hours left to our bitter end.

I found out where Maks Kantorowicz, the son-in-law of Pak the pharmacist, lived. I knew that he had a yellow document as a worker at a high-ranking German department. I went to him with my two children. To reach his address we had to cross through walls that had been knocked down to avoid walking through open streets. The apartment consisted of two rooms and a small kitchen. The Kantorowicz family lived in the first room and two other families in the next one. His family consisted of four people, the parents and two children. Together twelve people lived in the apartment. When we arrived,

helped, but please help me save the children. Take them in for tomorrow until the "cleansing" will pass and after that we will see what we can do." Kantorowicz immediately agreed. But the neighbors of the apartment who had listened to our conversation did not agree: "No, we cannot and we will not allow people without documents in our home. We would like to help you, to save you – but we cannot. You should not ask this of us. You have no right to demand of us that we all be taken because of your children." Kantorowicz did not say anything after that and we left without taking leave. I felt as if I were looking into the grave of the five members of our family.

On the way back I could not look into the faces of the children and they did not say anything. We entered our room without saying a single word and fell on the floor.

How well the German murderers understood human psychology! They knew how to turn closest friends into enemies. Of course there were many households and many people who had a different approach. They were willing to help as much as they could, often with a measure of risk to themselves.

We spent the night in despair and at dawn we were once more in the courtyard without having any idea what we might be doing next to save ourselves. We heard that Gens had ordered all employees of the Judenrat who had yellow documents to assemble in the building of the theater. I took my family and went there. But to no avail – police stood guard at the door and did not allow anybody without a yellow permit to enter.

I racked my head for a way to get into the building that appeared at that instant to be the inner sanctuary where death would not enter. I went around the building and found a door to the sanctuary – the stage door of the theater! Carefully, without letting others know of our move, we managed to enter through the rear door into the fortress of life. The theater auditorium was already full of people with yellow cards and so was the foyer. All were workers of the Judenrat and their families. Time was moving on and with it the suspense of the people. "Who knows," we heard whispers from one side or the other, "who can tell what satanic game the Germans have got for us this time?" It reminded us of the police raid at the end of Yom Kippur when the Judenrat and the police betrayed the community and handed over two thousand Jews possessing yellow documents to the Germans. The only comfort was that among the assembled in the hall were the leaders of the ghetto together with their families. We, the few people with white documents, were less agitated. We had nothing to lose. The time for the "cleansing" was approaching.

Suddenly there was a commotion. We could not hear clearly what was happening, but when we heard it we realized that it meant the end of everyone without the yellow document. On Gens's order, everyone inside the theater should move outside, where the control of the yellow documents would take place. What was I to do now? To go out meant going to our certain destruction. A single person or at most two might have a shred of a chance, one person might find a way to get around the control but we were five people! I was frantic for a solution. "No," I said to my wife, "we have no reason to go outside. We must stay here." But where could we hide inside without being eventually noticed?

We had been standing on the stage the whole time. Looking around for a nonexistent solution I noticed an opening in the floor at the end of the stage. I bent down and found myself looking into a pit leading under the floor of the stage. It was the place for the stage prompter. Without any further thought I pulled my family down into the pit. Half-sitting and half-stretching on the floor we were out of sight and when seeking a little more space we found others who had found the place before us. In total silence we heard the last people leaving the hall. The pit and its darkness now became our common grave in which we had buried ourselves in our lifetime – to escape death.

The total silence didn't last long. German and Lithuanian voices began reaching us from inside the hall. We understood that the "cleansing" had begun. We remained in our tomb for two or three hours without whispering and in the meantime we heard Lithuanians and Germans shouting, cursing and running in and out of the hall. Suddenly a voice was heard from the hall calling in Yiddish: "Mother, where are you?" Before we even realized the danger to which the caller was exposing us, a voice in our pit replied: "Chayele, I'm here." In that very moment we heard steps of the girl running toward the stage and right behind her the heavy boots of a Lithuanian. The Lithuanian, with a torch in his hand, looked into the pit, swung the torch up and down and said, "Oh, there are quite a few here." We remained frozen in our places. Our minds paralyzed, unable to utter a sound – not a word, not a cry, not a whisper. So this is how it ends – in a dirty prompter's pit under a theater stage? And all because of a girl's search for her mother! The Lithuanian kept looking at us.

His face expressionless, his eyes glistening in the light of his torch. Seconds went by, seconds that seemed like eternity. And then he turned off his torch, turned around and left. Paralyzed with fear we waited for him to return with his fellow murderers. A minute passed, and another minute and a third one – we were sure he was going to bring his helpers. Every second became an hour and every minute an endless agony. But nothing happened; nobody came for us… After a while we noticed that the outside had become very quiet. Probably the "cleansing" had been completed. Not being certain, we stayed in our pit.

We remained entombed until 5:00 p.m. when we heard single steps in the hall coming toward the stage. We recognized the voice of Burstein the house administrator calling to his mother-in-law: "You can come out now, the "cleansing" has ended, they have already left the ghetto." The old woman left first and a few others with her. We were nearly last. Only then did we notice that some thirty people had been hiding in the pit together with us. The prompter's pit under the stage had not been our living grave – it had become our life-saving sanctuary.

My family decided to remain in the pit overnight. After all what was the difference between this floor or that floor?

The "cleansing" that took place on October 24, 1941, claimed the lives of almost four thousand Jews – men, women and children.

It had been executed by a few hundred Lithuanians, who had fallen on the helpless Jews like a pack of excited dogs, ready to tear apart their prey. They had been assisted by the Jewish police. In many cases the Jewish police managed to save individuals – mostly family members, or those willing and able to buy their lives. On that day, half the residents of the ghetto were "illegal Jews" with no valid work documents. Those who had no money had only one way to try to save themselves – by hiding.

Many people with yellow documents had also gone into hiding. They remembered how valueless such documents had been during the Yom Kippur raid. During that cleansing many worthy communal activists were sent to Ponary.

One of them, details of whose death I know about, was Leib Shriftsetzer, a gifted and beloved stage actor, no longer a young man. When the cleansing began, his whole family left for the hideout. They pleaded with him to join them but he would not budge. "I won't go anywhere," he told them. "I have no more power and no will to keep living like this. Let happen what has to happen." He remained in the house and the murderers took him away. In a similar manner Haim Levin, the editor of *Di Tzait*, the Zionist paper in Vilna, was also lost. He was a house administrator in the ghetto but had no yellow document.

The cleansing went on throughout the day and took the lives of more victims than any previous raid. After it was over the ghetto had the appearance of a place that had gone through a pogrom. All the dwelling places stood open, the cupboards empty. Items of little value had been strewn about while everything of real value had ended up in the pockets of the Lithuanian bandits.

In the morning, after having spent the night in the pit we dared to leave and returned to our home. It was ruined, as were all the other homes in the ghetto. The doors had been forced, the few suitcases that we had saved from the small ghetto had disappeared. We were left with the clothes we wore on our backs. But at that moment who could think of clothing? "Oh, you are here, thank God that we meet again," was the way friends met after the "cleansing."

We had unexpected visitors – Ms. Trokman, the teacher, and Israel Segal, the actor and director of the Yiddish Theater, both originally from Lithuania. Segal was somehow related to the Police Commandant Gens. At first he had landed in the small ghetto and I found work for him as house administrator, and we became friends. At a later time, Ms. Trokman taught our children English. I was pleased but also surprised by their visit but they had come for a reason. During the "cleansing" ordeal they had been in a hideout that they had vacated after the Lithuanians left the ghetto. Passing our "home" they noticed the doors that had been forced open and a few suitcases standing on the floor. They took the suitcases and a few other things and put them in the next room. Now they had come to tell us about it. We found most of the things untouched. The consideration of these two people under the prevailing conditions in the ghetto, only hours after the great slaughter, touched us to tears and we thanked them warmly.

We moved back to our room and, thanks to Burstein, our electricity was repaired. We had a little food in our suitcases and after we made some order in the room we arranged our "beds" on the floor and considered ourselves as on top of the world. My mother cooked a warm meal in the electric kettle and we shared the food with Ms. Trokman and Segal.

We also found a small iron stove and used a ghetto weed as heating material. But nothing gave us the least feeling of security. The only security now would be the yellow work permit. While previously no document had ever been fully accepted during raids, we found that during the last raid the yellow document had been fully acknowledged. With that in mind the price of such a document rose sky high. Already before the last "cleansing" the yellow document sold by the highest echelons of the Judenrat was fifty gold rubles. Now it had become priceless – more than tenfold the original price.

The pursuit of yellow documents became an urgent and frantic activity. It replaced the pursuit of food and work.

The Germans had printed thirty-five hundred brown (we called them yellow) documents; they were numbered and the names of their owners had to be filled in. The first documents had been handed out to workers of German units, according to prepared lists. During that operation the Germans reduced the number of Jewish workers drastically. A number of Jewish brigadiers in the German units had their own business interests in the new documents, together with "their" Germans. They saw the new yellow documents as a golden opportunity to make small fortunes. But not all brigadiers were shameless traders. Many were honest men who tried to obtain as many yellow documents as they could and hand them out according to merits. The Jewish works department also had its hand in the trade in yellow documents and more than once people who were entitled to receive them went to their death because their documents went to a higher bidder.

The greatest number of yellow documents went to the furriers of the Kailis factory, probably because of the approaching winter. After all, the largest customers of fur coats and gloves were Germans.

The Judenrat received around four hundred yellow documents for its personnel and the orgy around them knew no limits and no shame. Most employees of the Judenrat did not receive the document they deserved. Their documents ended up in the hands of relatives of the ghetto privileged and their friends. Well-known prewar community activists employed by the Judenrat who did not belong to the "right" ideological group were totally ignored and remained without a document.

In the same way that the ghetto population had begun to hate the Jewish police after the first "cleansing" betrayal, they now hated the politicians from various parties who were at the helm of the ghetto. The yellow documents that had been given to those who had once pretended to work for the people revealed their true selfish natures; morally deficient and without shame, they were no better then underworld characters. There were few political activists and ghetto leaders who were ready to share the fate of the common people. At the very end, however, they were forced to do so, when there were no longer other lives to offer in their stead.

The yellow documents were valid for the owner "and the family" and had to be registered in the Jewish works department. The Germans probably laughed themselves silly seeing what their latest document had caused to the Jews in the ghetto.

A bachelor who received the coveted yellow document immediately registered his "wife" and "two children." Relatives were naturally the first ones to be chosen. When a single woman received a yellow permit, she had an instant "husband" and "two children." In many such cases a mother or a daughter became the "wife," and fathers became "husbands." Elderly women cut their hair short and put on short dresses, colored their lips in order to be a "wife" or a "daughter." There were cases that worked the other way around, when young girls became the "wives" of elderly men and young men became the "husbands" of women who could have been their mothers. Terrible as the tragedy of this was, it brought a smile to more than one pair of lips in the ghetto.

Relatives and friends helped each other by registering family members, but there were others who would demand payment for their service. There was a regular fee for becoming a "husband" or a "wife."

Our minds worked overtime devising all kinds of schemes to mislead the Germans. But with all our Jewish wisdom there were cases when the wisdom came too late. The Kantorowicz family was such a case.

The elder Kantorowicz received a yellow document and so did his fifteen-year-old son. To his own document, Kantorowicz senior appended his wife and his daughter. But the fifteen year-old son considered himself too young to have a wife and family. During the "cleansing" his grandmother, aunt and young cousin were all taken away. All three could have been saved. His grandmother could have become his mother, his aunt could have become his wife and the child – his child. During the "cleansings" the Lithuanians counted only the number of people registered in each document. But by the time the family realized that such a possibility had even existed it was too late.

On the basis of the thirty-five hundred new documents the Germans distributed, twelve thousand people became "legalized." This was later confirmed by the number of bread cards given out in the ghetto. During the month of October the ghetto administration had handed out over twenty-five thousand bread cards but in November the number had fallen to only twelve thousand "legal" Jews. The number rose a bit in December 1941 to thirteen thousand, thanks to "corrections" in the registration of families.

During those tragic days in the Vilna Ghetto, when each one of us was seeking a way to survive a little longer, the height of the human spirit reached right to the Heavens in expressions of love, friendship and readiness to endanger oneself to help another soul. On the other hand, there were acts that reached to the darkest depths of the abyss – where human demons made a business of buying and selling friends of a lifetime for the value of a gold ruble.

The most prominent dealers in this corrupt, morally degrading and soulless business were those who had access to the yellow documents. The Judenrat and the high-ranking police officers were at the forefront of the business. Next came the Jewish works department and the brigadiers. The ghetto higher-ups robbed many Jews of their legal right to remain alive, thus sending them to their deaths in Ponary. At the beginning of 1944 when I was in a concentration camp in Estonia, a Jewish worker told me the following heartbreaking story: "I was a worker in a small unit toiling for the Germans. The unit received a very limited number of yellow documents. My German employer considered me a good craftsman and when I begged the German officer for a yellow document he obtained it for me. But protocol dictated that he not hand the document to me directly. The officer sent the document to the Jewish works department of the ghetto. It was sent a few days before the "cleansing" was to take place. Day after day I ran from my work place to the Judenrat, to the works department and wherever there was an office to run to. Everywhere I received the same answer: "Your yellow document has not arrived." In the meantime the "cleansing" took place and my wife and two adult daughters were taken away. I somehow remained alive.

"After the 'cleansing' I turned once again to the works department and made a frightful scandal there, giving vent to all the bitterness in my heart. I had nothing to lose anymore. I told them I would go to the German officer and tell him that the Jewish works department in the ghetto had given my yellow document that he had received for me to their relatives. Within three days I received my document with a strange woman and two strange children already appended to it. My wife and my two children went to Ponary in order to save a strange woman and two strange children. The Judenrat had surely not done it out of pure charity."

The man who told me this story cried while telling it, and added: "Who can tell if my wife and the children would have survived, who can tell if we will survive. But to send my wife and my beautiful children to Ponary and register a strange woman and two strange children to my yellow document for money – such a person deserves a special place in hell."

How Do I Save Five Souls?

Day after day I kept knocking on the doors of the ghetto leaders, both those whom I knew personally and those I did not know. The answer was always the same: "We cannot help. Try another office." The only one who did something for me in the end was Dr. M. Brocki, the director of the Jewish Hospital. He didn't have a yellow document for me but his attitude was humane. He started by giving me a friendly hearing. He knew me from the time of the First World War when we worked together at the head office of the medical-sanitary department, assessing and providing restitution for war damages in Vilna and the surrounding area. He said with sincere regret: "You came to me too late. I distributed all the documents I had for hospital personnel as soon as I had them in my hands, I saw to it that every document should be fully used. I no longer even have a place to register you."

His declaration was absolutely true. The hospital personnel knew that he had made sure when handing out the yellow document that it carried four people. From the hospital workers I learned that individuals without the document were grouped to see that not a single place be wasted. In the first instance the doctors received documents for themselves and their families. Next it was the nurses and the administration. By the time the pharmacists' turn arrived only a single yellow document was left. The pharmacists and the sanitary workers remained helpless and illegal. At first I did not take Dr. Brocki's words literally but later when I was working at the hospital I found out that nobody, including the ones who had remained without any help, accused the doctor of any improprieties. Everyone admitted that Dr. Brocki distributed the documents with the greatest responsibility and total honesty. There were simply too few yellow documents and too many doctors. A great many hospital workers lost their lives during the "cleansing" operation, among them my close friend Adler, the former director of the Pharmacists Association in Vilna, and his family.

Once more my mind was consumed by despair as I struggled with the problem: How do I save my family – my mother, my wife and my two children?

I spent many days in the court of the Judenrat at Rudnicka 6. I met the same people, provided they had not been taken away by some minor "cleansing" and the answer was always the same: "No documents."

Vilna, my hometown Vilna! There was not a stone in all the footpaths of the town that hadn't felt my step. Now I was standing in the ghetto of Vilna, without a spark of a future, unable to save myself.

Over the next few days a rumor began circulating in the Judenrat court that a new "cleansing" was about to take place. On the day I first heard of the new "cleansing" I met Mrs. Niemencinski. I knew her husband Maks since my earliest heder years. Mrs. Niemencinski told me that her husband had left Vilna and was at the moment looking to find a quieter place in Byelorussia. She was waiting for a letter from him and as soon as she would hear from him she would join him there.

As the situation in the ghetto had once again become very insecure Mira Niemencinski proposed that I follow her to a possible hideout place. She led me to the third court of 6 Rudnicka to the building leading out to Konska Street. She took me up to a very long attic that was as dark as a dark labyrinth. She told me that at the last "cleansing" a few hundred people were hidden in the attic. From that day onward my family spent nights in the attic, just in case. One night the neighbors wouldn't give us the keys to the attic because "the ghetto was quiet." We spent the night on the steps leading to the attic.

Meanwhile, rumors about a new "cleansing" became more and more persistent. People started running from the ghetto to Byelorussia, particularly to the Lida area. There, people kept on saying, it was a real paradise. Quiet, peaceful and no "cleansings." Jews there were left alone. Leaving for Byelorussia took on the form of hysteria. Not only people who had no documents were running to Byelorussia but people with good yellow documents also became infected with the need to run. The Judenrat took back the yellow documents from those who were leaving and made good business out of them.

People traveled to Byelorussia in various ways. The most popular way was by a German car. A new kind of middleman cropped up from nowhere and began arranging passage to Lida, Voronovo, Bialystok and other places –

always for a fat fee. Jewish middlemen and "good" Germans never missed out on this kind of work.

Of course trusting Germans was a risky venture and treachery was a constant fear. One such disaster happened to a former member of the Judenrat of the small ghetto and his family. Levin, who had not received a yellow document in the large ghetto, decided to leave for Lida. He paid a very high price for the arrangement and the car carrying him left the ghetto – it was driven straight to the Gestapo.

Among those who left for greener pastures were Leib Mincberg, a former member of the Polish parliament; Jankiel Trokenheim, a former member of the Polish senate; and Lejbowicz ,the former chairman of the small ghetto and his family. All of them had yellow documents but decided to leave. Their end was tragic. They died in the "peaceful" places much more quickly than the people with yellow documents who remained in the Vilna Ghetto.

Seeing that everybody who had any chance was leaving, my family pressured me to follow suit. I was against it: "All right," I said, "we risk our lives. We smuggle ourselves across the border of Byelorussia. For this we will give away whatever we still have. Let us say we arrive in Byelorussia alive, what will we gain? We will still be in the hands of the same murderers. Do any of you really believe that the Germans have a different plan for Jews there than they have for Jews here? I believe that they have the same tactic everywhere. Isn't it therefore more reasonable to stay where we are? Here we at least know the people and we have a roof over our heads."

But my words didn't convince the family. And one nice evening we decided to leave the ghetto. The plan was that my wife and my mother would go back to our apartment while I would go with the children to my Gentile colleagues and we would see what would happen next. The plan was no plan; it was a decision made in a chaotic state of mind, decided and acted upon out of resignation and despair.

We went to the ghetto gate but the Jewish police drove us back in a brutal way. We waited a little while and tried again with the same result. While we stopped to decide what to do next, a man named Naftali Weinik, a journalist, came and told me that he had arranged with a Jewish policeman to let him out of the ghetto for one hundred rubles.

I immediately went to the policeman and handed him the one hundred rubles. Within a minute he nodded to Weinik and let him out. A few minutes later my wife and my daughter approached the gate. When he opened the gate a civilian Lithuanian Gestapo officer met them face to face. He took hold of my wife and daughter shouting: "So, you want to escape!" He took them to the Jewish gate police and ordered them to keep the two until he would return. The police immediately searched their small suitcases and found nothing but personal wear. When the Gestapo officer left, I ran to the two policemen on duty pleading with them to save the two poor souls. Again a matter of luck – I met with understanding. When the Lithuanian returned the policemen informed him they had searched the women's suitcases and there was only underwear. They had asked the women what they were doing at the gate and both had said that their men usually come back from their work much earlier. As they had not returned in time they became worried and came to the gate to wait for them. The Lithuanian let the two women go.

We were in total despair and it was an exercise that certainly didn't strengthen our nerves or our health. When my wife and daughter came out of the police room we embraced them as if they had returned from Ponary. In abundant joy we returned to our "home" and there we noticed another piece of luck. We had forgotten to hand in the key to our home! I said to the family: "We have tried three times to leave the ghetto and we did not succeed. Let this be a sign that we should stay here and we will survive."

My mother made us all a royal evening meal and we celebrated our luck.

The next morning once again I began to work the round of offices to obtain the yellow document, but the earthly gates of mercy, like the Heavenly ones, were hermetically closed. The mood of the people without the yellow document was becoming ever more despondent; despair filled the air. At dusk we feared the night – and at dawn we were afraid for the day. People avoided looking each other straight in the eye. Those who had the lucky document felt guilty greeting their unlucky friends, and anyone who did not have the yellow document felt embarrassed to face their friends, knowing that they could not hide the envy they felt.

And so we, the unlucky ones, stood together in the courtyard of life and death, with death looking out of their eyes. We were no more than homeless dogs. No, I am wrong. We were a thousandfold more unlucky than dogs. Dogs would only feel abandoned by an earthly owner. We felt that we had been abandoned by men and by God.

Several times a day I used to visit Mr. Burstein, the administrator of the Judenrat buildings on 6 Rudnicka. He was an honest man dedicated to saving as many Jews as he could, often at considerable risk to himself and his family. As administrator of the Judenrat buildings he was under a constant avalanche of work. He was the first to meet every German and Lithuanian who entered the ghetto. His uninvited "guests" were an endless bunch of criminals that had become rulers over Jewish lives. Burstein had to know how to deal with each of them; he had to know who was actually powerful and who was just acting important. He was well trained for his job and mentally agile. What he had already done for my family since we had arrived from the small ghetto was nothing less than save our lives – finding a roof over our heads, a small heater, electricity and above all – showing me his dedicated friendship.

But all his attempts to obtain a yellow document for me came to naught. As the rumor of a new "cleansing" became more persistent, I began asking him to find a hideout for my family.

Outwardly the rumors did not interrupt the "normal" life of the ghetto. Every morning thousands of workers left the ghetto and went to work in German and Lithuanian work places. The workshops in the ghetto were also busy. And every day people went out of the ghetto without documents, risking their lives in an attempt to obtain the life-saving yellow document from "good" Germans, their past employers. In all those cases in which people ventured outside the ghetto something was brought back. After all, life had to go on.

On Saturday, November 1, the news became official: the next "cleansing" would take place on Monday, November 3. The streets of the ghetto became full

and noisy like a beehive. There was no longer any doubt about it. The Germans
had decided to liquidate all "illegal Jews" who were still in the ghetto. Anyone
who was able to bought out the last few places left on existing documents. I
was helpless; I needed five places. Where was I to get them?

In the courtyard of the Judenrat I met Kantorowicz. I told him of my situation and he told me of his tragic loss due to the oversight on his son's document.
He told me that on his own document he had only three people registered: he,
his wife and his daughter. If I wanted, I could register my son as the fourth
person. The question "If you want" sounded unreal to me – of course I wanted!
We immediately went to the Jewish works department and made the necessary
registration. As soon as this was completed I ran "home" to tell the family the
good news, that one of us was already saved. Thank God for this. But the boy
would have to be at the Kantorowicz's home. We decided that he would leave
for his "home" on Sunday morning and he would remain there.

Now, what about the other four souls? As soon as the Sabbath was over I
was once more at Burstein's office pleading with him to find us a hideout. I was
moved by his answer, by his readiness to help: "You know, Mr. Balberyszski, I
can no longer see your pain and the ugly way you are being treated by people
who should remember you. I remember the way you were carried away from
Niemiecka Street bloody, beaten to a pulp after saving Vilna Jewry from the
pogrom that Chamiec was preparing. No! Come with me and I will give you
an apartment."

I was moved by his words. "I am grateful for your willingness to help, Mr.
Burstein. But right now I do not need an apartment! I need a hideout where I
can hide myself and my family from the hands of the murderers." "Come with
me and trust me," he said.

It was nighttime. I called my family together and we took the few things left
in our possession and went with the administrator. We entered the third court
of 6 Rudnicka. It was originally the courtyard of 6 Konska street, but openings
were made in house walls and the three courts had become one. The doors and
windows that faced the street outside the ghetto had all been boarded up. We
went along the court and entered a narrow passage leading to an apartment.

The door of the apartment was not locked and we entered. We found ourselves in a small kitchen which opened into a room full of old-fashioned furniture. In the center of the room stood a large wardrobe that divided the room in two. We entered behind the wardrobe and looked bewildered. We were facing a wall with a built-in cupboard and there was nowhere to go. Burstein noticed our confusion, went over to the wall, opened a door of the built-in cupboard and bent down: "Are you there, Mrs. Kremer?" he called. From the cupboard came back a voice: "Oh, it's you, Mr. Burstein, a good evening and a good new week to you." "And to you," Burstein replied. "I brought you new neighbors, take them in." "Of course, of course, welcome," the voice replied.

We remained perplexed, not understanding what was going on. Before we had time to say or ask anything an elderly man came forward: "Well, young man, don't just stand around. Make a move and get inside." I looked in all directions and didn't know what he meant. There was no door and no 'inside.' I turned around looking for Burstein but he had already left.

The elderly man came forward, opened up the cupboard doors wider and said: "well, bend down and go." I bent down as ordered. Only then did I understand what he meant. The opening was so low that I had to slide in on my belly.

The built-in cupboard had two shelves, the lower one about sixty centimeters above the floor. The depth of the cupboard was over forty-five centimeters. In the rear of the cupboard above the lower shelf a hole had been made in the wall, about sixty centimeters wide and forty-five centimeters high. You had to lie down on the shelf with your head forward, take hold of the inside with arms outstretched and slide in. Once halfway through, you had to take hold of the leg of a bed standing on the other side of the wall not far from the opening and move down to drop on the floor of another apartment. First I sent my son. The young boy made the slide quick and clean. After him we all went through the hole. I went in first. After me my wife entered and after my wife came my mother and my daughter. When we were all in, the man on the outside covered the opening with a board, threw some rags and papers on the shelf and closed the doors of the cupboard.

When we rose from the floor we were blinded by the bright light. We found ourselves in a large room full of furniture, mostly beds. Mrs. Kremer was already at our side: "Oh my dear Liba, how did you come to be here? You were in the other ghetto!" she said to my mother. It turned out that the two women had known each other for many years. Mrs. Kremer directed us to a free corner to arrange our things. The room had large windows, but the inner shutters had been closed and outside the windows had been boarded up. Heavy drapes had been placed on top of the inner shutters in order not to let a single ray of light stray outside. Any light in the room came from electric light bulbs.

Near the entrance hole stood a large brass bed and next to it a small table. On that bed Mrs. Kremer and her daughter Nadia with a small boy had their "home." Nadia's husband had fallen into the hands of the Lithuanian murderers. Old Mr. Kremer slept in another corner of the room on a sofa. Next to the brass bed on the other side stood another cupboard and next to it was a metal bed frame without a mattress. The bed became the "home" of my wife and daughter.

Close to Mrs. Kremer's little table, on the wall where the hole was made, stood a wardrobe and a little further away from it was a desk that reached right to the window. Between the two windows was another iron bed frame without a mattress. My son and I made our "home" on the iron bed. On the third wall there was a door to another room. Near the door on the other side stood a small table. This was where Tsalel Szkolnik and his old mother had their "home." A little further inside the room stood two brass beds with mattresses. One bed pushed up against the wall and the other opposite it. Between the two stood a tiny table. In that corner young Sasha Kremer and his wife Pola had their "home" together with their young daughter. Next to the desk stood a bed, the "home" of old Mr. Bakaturski and his wife. At night we put up two folding beds. My mother slept on one and Mr. Kagan and his wife on the other. The room was full of furniture. There were just three small floor spaces to get through. Next to my bed was the large oval table surrounded by a few chairs. This was the "living room," where we sat, ate, read and chatted together. We were a compatible group.

The Kremer family consisted of seven people. They had been an established family in Vilna dealing in paper and bookbinding. Old Kremer was an educated person and his son was an actor on the Yiddish stage. Kagan was a brother of Mrs. Kremer. He was a very intelligent man. For years he had run a pharmacy in Zarzecze. Haim Bakaturski was a talmudic scholar. During the Jewish High Holidays he led services at his prayer house. His wife was intelligent but mentally ill. Tsalel Szkolnik used to deal in down and feathers. His mother had been a very intelligent and religious woman with a good head for business. She had married off her daughter to a popular rabbi but unfortunately the daughter had died at a very young age.

We found five families there, altogether eleven people. With our arrival the group numbered sixteen people, including two small children and one mentally ill woman. We were overjoyed with the new place. For the last twelve days we had been roaming the streets of the ghetto like stray dogs, in attics, in dirt, we could not remove our overcoats and now – we were among people we knew who received us warmly. For the first time we had the opportunity to go into a separate room, remove our clothes and wash ourselves.

This second room of our hideout had once been a locksmith's workshop. It had two windows and a door leading out into a street outside the ghetto. It was boarded up outside and covered with heavy curtains inside. We found a small kitchen, a sink, a tap and a small toilet in the corner. Behind the little kitchen was a dark room that was once a smithy. The apartment had belonged to a Jewish master bed maker by the name of Frum. When Jews were driven into the ghetto he had been driven out of his apartment to another place and the home had been declared as outside the boundaries of the ghetto. The history of the apartment was very unusual.

The kitchen and the room through which we had entered the hideout belonged to Bakaturski. He was a producer of thin cardboard cigarette tubes which were later filled with tobacco. At his home, he kept a few hand-operated machines for producing the cigarette tubes. He had resided in the same apartment before the establishment of the ghetto and was among the few "lucky" ghetto dwellers who had remained in their own homes. It was to his home that the other eleven people had come in the first place. In addition to the people who had originally moved to the hideout, another few had come and remained in his home: Bakaturski with his sick wife and Kagan's son-in-law Kreimski with his wife and their small daughter. When the black Friday came on 24 October, only Kreimski had a yellow document. All the others had white papers and the older ones had none. They racked their brains to find a hideout.

Mrs. Kremer and Szkolnik knew that the Frum apartment had a common wall with the Bakaturski apartment but they did not know precisely where. On Friday morning when the butcher's knife was already at their throats Szkolnik tapped along the wall and found the place. Without a second's thought they broke open a sufficiently large hole in the cupboard to enable a person to crawl through. They all entered the apartment, thereby saving themselves. In order to cover the hole they made a board and covered the shelves with papers and rags, while Kreimski, who could remain on the outer side, closed the cupboard from his side. The Lithuanians entered Bakaturski's room during the raid, opened the cupboard but didn't notice anything suspicious. After checking out Kreimski's document that covered him and his family, the murderers left. After the raid was over those eleven people "settled" into the new-found rooms as "permanent" residents.

No matter how difficult the situation was, or how bitter our life became with the permanent fear of being discovered during the murderous "cleansings," we felt very relieved to have found that wondrous place.

* * *

Since the liquidation of the small ghetto on October 21 and the first "cleansing" raid in the large ghetto on October 24 the ghetto kept humming like a beehive. Those who had no good papers knew that only a miracle would save them. But even those who had good papers lived in constant fear. They too had seen how worthless the best documents were during the "cleansing" raid of Yom Kippur. And even those who trusted the new yellow document could not relax. They were also anxious about the ones without documents, the ones that Fried, the Jewish chairman of the large ghetto, had so flippantly named "illegal Jews."

After all, these people were their own friends, relatives, grandparents too old to receive yellow documents – their own flesh and blood.

Following the October 24 "cleansing" the Judenrat announced that the small ghetto would remain after all, and whoever wanted more comfortable accommodation with furniture and domestic amenities could move to the small ghetto. They also announced that people without documents who moved to the small ghetto would automatically become "legal." Many desperate people who had no documents left their hiding places and went to the small ghetto via a gate that the Jewish police opened for them. In addition to those who went voluntarily, the Judenrat and the Jewish police began to force people out of the large ghetto, particularly the old and the sick, the helpless, including our dear friend Paulina Prylucki. On October 29 the Gestapo carried out a "cleansing" raid in the small ghetto and took everyone to Lukishki prison and from there to Ponary. Among the people who might have stayed in the large ghetto but returned voluntarily to the small ghetto were Advocate Smilag, Haim Remigalski and his wife, and Sackheim from the Jewish People's Bank. They had all managed to get themselves out of the small ghetto during its liquidation and returned, only to fall into the flames waiting to consume them.

The small ghetto was again "cleansed" of "illegal" Jews but it remained as it was. The time for its total obliteration had not yet come. Its old, narrow streets and lanes had yet to witness the final cataclysm that lasted three days, from November 3 to November 5.

CHAPTER 9

The "Cleansings" Continue

Three Days of "Cleansings"

On our very first night in the new hideout we slept on the iron beds without mattresses and without bedding, but it was paradise. As the room had no open doors or windows, the light remained on day and night. On the rare occasion that meals were cooked, the food was cooked in electric pots and water was boiled in electric kettles.

Our neighbors advised us to go out as little us possible in order not to jeopardize the security of the hideout. We decided that only my mother would leave the place to buy food. All others were to remain inside. We already knew that on the next day, Monday, November 3, the Germans and the Lithuanians would start their work to liquidate all "illegal Jews." Somehow we could not make peace with the thought that this might be the last night that we would be together and among friends.

Early in the morning we were awakened by a very strong noise at our door – the hole in the wall. Haim Bakaturski opened the passage. He threw in a few parcels and with great difficulty pushed his sick wife through. Bakaturski, an invalid with a damaged leg, joined us with difficulty and a few new people followed him. It was now clear that the new "cleansing" had begun.

Beginning in the early morning of Monday, November 3, new people kept arriving at our hideout. Only God in Heaven knew how all those people knew about the place. A number of new arrivals had been brought by Mr. Burstein, the man who did everything possible to save Jews.

The first room became full to the brim and there was no longer any standing room. We switched off the light and no longer knew who was who. The only man around us who had a yellow document was Kreimski on the other side of

177

the wall. He let in anyone who came. We had agreed beforehand not to send anyone away, out of fear that we might be denounced in anger by the person who would not be let in. We had learned of such cases at a previous "cleansing." When the first room no longer had any place for newcomers we opened the second room where the workshop had been. We let people in without seeing anyone but we recognized some by their voices. I recognized the former pawn broker at the pawn shop, Abraham Kac. He had been the *gabai* of the Gemilut Hesed Study Hall in the courtyard of the synagogue where we used to pray for a number of years. All new arrivals found some "accommodation." One sat down on an iron bed and another remained standing and all in silence. We didn't let a breath escape out of our mouths. It was not long before we heard the arrogant steps of the murderers; the hunt had begun.

Once more the hole was opened and Burstein let in his mother-in-law. She had been with us in the dark pit under the stage in the theater when the previous consolidation of yellow card bearers took place. At that moment Burstein let us know that the Lithuanians were already in the ghetto. Everyone who had the yellow document would be sent over to the small ghetto and when this would be accomplished the ones left without documents would be taken away. How long this would take no one knew.

The present drive was to be thorough. The Jewish police went into all courtyards and announced that holders of yellow documents should leave their rooms unlocked and come to the courtyard together with their families. They would be escorted in groups to the gate where the consolidation of document bearers would take place.

As soon as this was announced, Kreimski covered the opening with the board from the outside and we tied the board from the inside. We heard him throw some things on the shelves and close the door of the cupboard. Now we were left all to ourselves, entombed away from the world. We listened for any noise and recognized Yiddish conversation coming from the outside. We understood it to be groups of yellow document holders going to the ghetto gate on their way to the small ghetto. For hours the march continued. We sat at our places in total silence, each one in his own corner. From time to time someone would whisper something. Once in a while voices broke out in the dark and then others would respond: "Quiet, quiet, don't talk!"

Throughout our vigil, the stream of people outside continued unabated. Toward evening it became quiet outside and we clearly heard the Lithuanians leaving. Through it all we sat in darkness, insensible to any difference between day and night. When we considered that it was dawn of the second day the young Mrs. Kremer lit the small electric light near her bed and put on the kettle. Immediately there were screams from all sides: "She is endangering us all!" The situation was getting out of control and we were in danger of the noise being heard outside. Mrs. Kremer had the last word: "What do you want? You want my child to die on the bed for a sip of warm water? If this is what you want it has to be the death of us all." I followed suit and put on our kettle next to our "home." I found some bread, spread a little butter and honey on it and forced my family to eat. This was our first meal in two days. The previous day we had all been so nervous and excited that we had completely forgotten about food.

Suddenly we heard the quiet voice of old Mrs. Kremer: "Quiet, they are in the other room!" We stopped wherever we were as if paralyzed.

Mrs. Bakaturski, as I have already mentioned, was mentally ill. The whole time she had been in the ghetto she had managed to control herself or her husband had managed to control her. Under the present conditions her mind became unhinged. She began to talk without a break. Not everybody knew about her illness and with our nerves already tense people on all sides began demanding that she stop. Her husband tried to make her stop but to no avail. As if to torture us, nothing we did helped. She acted deliberately against our pleas, becoming wilder and wilder. In the end she jumped on a bed, tore off her clothes and, completely naked, began singing Yiddish and Russian songs. The situation became unimaginably serious and people started demanding that she be strangled. The ones nearest her fell on her, kissing and hugging her until she fell exhausted on a corner of the bed and fainted... We all breathed a sigh of relief.

During the day the Lithuanians entered the room on the other side of the hole a few times in search of more victims. We couldn't hear it, but Mrs. Kremer who "lived" close to the opening heard them each time. In the end, most of us became resigned and apathetic and closed ourselves off in our individual corners. But there were others who reacted differently. Craving verbal contact, they tried to begin conversations and were aggravated when others failed to reply.

During the second half of the second day we survived another shock. Burstein's mother-in-law, an elderly lady who had been completely relaxed throughout the earlier commotion, suddenly began talking just like Mrs. Bakaturski had done before. She became wild and excited. Knowing her as a fragile person I was surprised by her sudden burst of energy. The previous story repeated itself once more. She tore off her clothes and began screaming and raging in a loud voice. People began screaming: "Choke her! Choke the old witch before she sends us all to Ponary!" By some miracle nobody outside heard the screams that took place. By the end of the day we were all exhausted and sweaty, without any fresh air. When at the end we felt that the murderers had gone we allowed ourselves to boil some water and wet our lips. The sick ones remained in their faint and the night passed somehow.

In this way we reached the third day of the endless "cleansing."

Although we thought that most of us had become apathetic the truth was somewhat different. The people in the other room who were near the boarded-up windows facing the outside of the ghetto were fully alerted to the sounds coming from the street outside. They would come in during quiet moments and inform us of everything they heard from the outside. The most disciplined were the children and the old people. They were alarmed by the least strange sound but they knew best how to keep quiet.

Sometime during the third day we heard voices in Yiddish approaching in our direction. Suddenly the noise was in the room on the other side of the cupboard! We were sure that we had been discovered. From the other side we heard the sound of the boards being torn away. We knew our torment, our suffering of the past three days was coming to its bitter end. Instinctively we drew closer to each other and I took my son's head and pressed it to my heart. He was not responding with any emotion. My heart went out to him. "*My dear child, why did you deserve such torment and such a young death. Why?!*"

Suddenly we felt a flow of fresh air coming from the hole and we heard the cry: "Get out, it is over and you are saved. The "cleansing" has come to an end. The people of the other ghetto are already coming back!" At that moment my son fainted in my arms.

Grisha Lewin, whose father joined us in the hideout with the latecomers had opened the hole.

We immediately switched on the light and saw a sea of faces, old and new. Some we knew and some were unfamiliar. One by one, people began to leave the hideout. At the opening we counted the number of people who had survived with us there and found we had close to sixty people besides the ones who had been there in the first place. It was incredible how so many people had saved themselves thanks to Mrs. Kremer and Tsalel Szkolnik, with the assistance of a thin board that divided us from death. This time it had been a very difficult "cleansing"; the murderers had to break open every door, basement and attic to find fifteen hundred Jews. It was to be the last "cleansing" for some time.

The November 3–5 "cleansing" had been organized very methodically. Early Monday morning the German Gestapo entered the ghetto accompanied by hundreds of Lithuanians. They ordered everyone who had a yellow document to leave their homes taking only small packets of food. They were told to take their family members registered on the documents and keep them close at hand for the control. From the courtyards they had to march to the gate of the ghetto in tight columns where the control took place. A strong force of Lithuanians and Jewish police worked together. The lucky owners of the documents went together with their families, who had been given numbered blue papers by the Jewish works department. If everything was in order the document owners were allowed to go on to the small ghetto. In cases where things were not as they should have been a rain of blows befell the unfortunate. Those who tried to smuggle through were pulled aside. The control took place accompanied by heartbreaking tragedies. Families were torn apart. Gens and his police cooperated with the murderers throughout but tried to save whomever they could.

The ghetto was emptied of people. Every house stood open and the Lithuanians spread out like released wild animals on the prowl to catch their victims.

This time ghetto inhabitants had hidden themselves much better than any time in the past. People buried themselves wherever there was the best chance of escaping the death verdict. The demons were forced to search courtyard after courtyard, house after house and room after room. They had to climb up and crawl in dark attics and drop down to murky cellars; they searched in every corner of the ghetto.

The workers of the Judenrat passed through a separate control. They were collected in the small garden in the courtyard of the Judenrat and afterwards were sent together with all the others to the small ghetto.

In the same complex of buildings where we had spent the raid three hideouts had existed and everyone hidden in them escaped the clutches of the Lithuanians. Throughout the three days the corner had been protected by the Jewish police. In the large building where our hideout was, a large number of Jewish police and ghetto dignitaries lived. But they were dignitaries only to the Jewish population of the ghetto. As far as the Germans were concerned they were no different than any other Jews. In spite of all the machinations of the Judenrat and the Jewish police, they too had old fathers and mothers without documents in their homes. The Jewish police guarded their own hideouts together with those of their neighbors. When they saw Lithuanians approaching they acted well to distract and divert them. Despite their efforts, the murderers came to our hideout a few times and opened the closet. To our great fortune they did not notice anything. Our friend Burstein told us about one such visit in his presence. It is hard to imagine how he felt seeing the murderers opening the closet and searching the place thoroughly.

But the most important thing was having luck at the right moment. That luck was unfortunately lacking in other places. One such case was in the hideout on Hekdesh Street. Some sixty people had managed to survive in a basement up to the third day. When they started to choke for lack of air they opened the cover of the basement for a moment right at the time when the Lithuanians passed. They noticed the movement and all the Jews were taken to Ponary.

The three days of slaughter that took place in the large ghetto left it in ruins. The Lithuanians took people away and robbed the houses of everything of value. To their everlasting shame, some members of the Jewish police joined them in both endeavors.

There was no longer any shortage of dwellings. After the three days, there was sufficient room for all, even for the destitute ones who had managed to remain alive. At the expense of those who did not survive, they were now able to have at least their basic needs met. And life went on…

The offices of the Judenrat presented the same picture of a pogrom as the rest of the ghetto. The offices had been vandalized, documents had been strewn on the floors; the system had to be started anew. The greatest damage was done to the great library.

On Thursday morning, the day after the slaughter, I went to see Burstein to thank him for having saved us. On the steps of the Judenrat building I met Chairman Fried. He was still in his elegant dressing gown, as if taking the day off work. I asked him (in Russian): "Well, will the beast now be satisfied?"

"How can they be satisfied when a few thousand illegal Jews still remain in the ghetto?" he replied, also in Russian. It took my breath away. The arrogance in his voice expressed what the words might not have made fully clear. It was the first time that I heard from his mouth the expression "illegal Jews." My family and I also belonged to the "illegal Jews" and he well knew it. The man with this ugly soul was the leader of the Jewish victims of the ghetto! As I passed I was mentally followed by the anger in his voice. If only he could get rid of the few thousand "illegal Jews" by sending them to Ponary he would be the rightful ruler over a quiet and peaceful ghetto.

A few days after the "cleansing" I met Haim Semiatycki. As we exchanged the details how each of us had survived the three days of "cleansing" he told me his story. It was more fantastic than the story of the Thousand and One Nights. Semiatycki recounted the following:

Not having any documents and unable to organize a place in a hideout for himself he saw that the only possibility of remaining alive was to leave the ghetto for the duration of the "cleansing." But where would he go? He had no Gentile friends or even acquaintances in Vilna. He met up with a few religious students in the ghetto and very early Monday morning, while it was still dark,

they climbed over the wooden fence at the point where it bordered with a
small street. Once over the fence they moved forward very carefully to the first
courtyard near the ghetto border. The place was empty and the dwellings had
already been cleaned out earlier, but not thoroughly. The Gentiles who showed
their "Christian compassion" to the thousands of houses whose owners had
been taken to Ponary or had gone to the ghetto had apparently been a little
afraid to come too close to the ghetto.

The religious students felt reasonably safe; they chose the most suitable
apartment and began leading very comfortable lives as befits any good household. They found large amounts of food prepared for the winter in the dwellings.
Pots with jam, oils, tea and white flour, sugar – everything that an organized
household normally has in store. They were afraid to do their cooking during
the daytime because the smoke would betray them but in the nighttime they
baked some bread for themselves. In addition to the good fortune as far as food
was concerned they had the good luck to have settled in the home of a Jewish
journalist. They found many books and journals and spent the day reading
and quietly talking. They slept like kings on soft bedding covered with the
highest quality down blankets and lived, as the Yiddish saying goes, "like God
in Odessa." "Such a wonderful three days," Semiatycki said, "we never had in
times of peace. We dined, as the saying goes, on nectar and ambrosia. When the
"cleansing" was over we didn't want to leave such luxury but we had to leave the
place. A few times we heard Gentile thieves robbing the neighboring homes. So
when the "cleansing" was over we collected as much of the better-quality food
as we could carry and returned to the ghetto in the middle of the night."

Haim Semiatycki had just become "married." The woman had registered
him as her "husband" for some enormous fee. But he never went to work
outside the ghetto. He started dealing in gold and diamonds and had many
clients among the wealthy elements in the ghetto – including the new ghetto
"aristocracy," some brigadiers and some high-ranking Judenrat and police officials. He could afford to buy a little butter and even meat. He no longer ate
in the communal kitchen.

The situation in the ghetto calmed down after the Grand Slaughter. Thousands of people went to work every day outside the ghetto and at evening time brought back various products. The yellow document had given their owners the possibility to exist. The ones who had no documents could not leave the ghetto at all, at least not legally. In addition they were afraid to spend too much time in the streets. The risk of being "accidentally" seen by Murer or any other German or Lithuanian officer was great.

My financial situation was becoming difficult. The price of food skyrocketed. A family of five people like ours needed large sums to be able to exist even on bread and soup. I needed to make contact with the city to see my friends. Here Semiatycki showed me limitless friendship. As soon as he received his yellow certificate he lent it to me for a few hours. It was nothing less than guaranteeing my return to the ghetto with his life. He gave away the security of his survival to help a friend!

I went to town and with the help of a Gentile woman in a small shop I let my friends know that I was alive and needed their help. On the way back to the ghetto I bought many loaves of bread and some vegetables. The foray into the city had been successful.

Alongside our food crisis, we also had to deal with increasingly crowded living conditions. When the "cleansing" had come to an end, we were asked by a family of five people to let them stay with us in the hideout for the night. The family, named Kac, had been in the large ghetto but missed out on getting hold of a regular place to live. They had reached our hideout through Burstein's generosity. Of course none of us who remained in the hideout were against helping them overnight. Kac himself was a very tall man, as were his wife and children. But after all we had survived together – what else are people for? We were now "free," though worn out from the last three days. We put together three chairs in one corner and the head of the family slept there. The wife and a daughter made their bed on the table and the boy lay down in another corner on the floor. The second daughter found a place somewhere and the night somehow passed.

The next morning the situation changed somewhat. Both husband and wife came to us saying they had nowhere to go and our place was very "strategic" and they intended to stay. We didn't have the heart to say no, and after all we had no moral right to do so. But a little later the Kac family noticed that we were choking for air. They moved into the other room and remained there for the rest of the day. In this way our two-room apartment became the living quarters of eight families consisting of twenty-three people. During the daytime the living conditions were already quite difficult for such a number of people but when nighttime came it was more "nightmare" than "nighttime." But one should never say "it could not get worse." A few days later we received an addition: the young Bakaturski couple.

The Situation in the Ghetto Stabilizes

Ghetto life began to "normalize" again. Only people with yellow documents went to work outside the ghetto. The same was true for the offices of the Judenrat, which had become a ghetto fortress of workers with yellow documents. Bread cards were only issued to holders of the yellow documents. The others, many thousands, had formally ceased to exist. Day after day I kept making the rounds from one office to the next, hoping against hope to somehow obtain the life-saving yellow document. I went to the director of the health department, Shabtai Milkonowicki, to Dr. Szadowski, the head doctor of the ghetto – with no result. Dr. Goldburs, a very decent and quiet man, worked in the health department. Seeing me coming so often he used the moment that we were together alone one day to say, "Why are you wasting your precious time and health here? What are you looking for? You can see that the people here look out only for themselves. The only way to save oneself is to run away." He spoke frankly and openly. He had the desired yellow document but in the end he left for Byelorussia where he perished.

I got together a few pharmacists and together we began visiting the offices of the "good" Jews. Among those who joined me were Klak, the prewar owner of the pharmaceutical factory ESKA; Gurewicz, a pharmacist who had worked for many years at Pak's pharmacy; and Masur, an owner of a pharmacy in a small town who had come to Vilna believing that he would be safer there. Together, we went to see Gens's deputy, Yosef Glazman, who received us very cordially. We told him straight out that the underworld characters had all been provided with yellow documents. We reviewed the corruption that was going on at the highest echelons. We pointed out that if, with God's help, a few Jews from the ghetto would eventually be saved there wouldn't be a single pharmacist among them, as 90 percent of pharmacists had already been sent to Ponary.

Glazman did not make any secret of his knowledge that the corruption and demoralization emanated from the highest ranks of the Judenrat but he was totally helpless to do anything about it. He told us that Gens was trying to obtain a few additional yellow documents for people who were useful to the functioning of the ghetto. If Gens should eventually succeed, pharmacists would certainly be added to the list.

Making our rounds from one office to another we reached the office of the director of the health department, Milkonowicki, where we once again presented our case asking him to let us have some of the yellow documents of the people who had left the ghetto. With a straight face Milkonowicki said that he had written to Hingst, the Gebietskommissar of Vilna, asking him to release a few additional yellow documents for Jewish pharmacists. We were at a loss for words. Not only was Milkonowicki obviously not going to help us, but he also intended to make fools of us. I was enraged and together with the others went straight to the office of the chairman of the Judenrat. Jakub Leib Mincberg, the former Aguda deputy in the Polish parliament (the *Sejm*), happened to be there. He was working at the hospital as a janitor and had a yellow document. Angrily, I told Fried what Milkonowicki had told us. Fried immediately sent his secretary to call Milkonowicki. As soon as Milkonowicki stepped over the doorstep Fried asked him what his words about Hingst were supposed to mean. Milkonowicki turned white and began to stutter some excuse. I did not wait for Fried's reaction. Before Milkonowicki finished, all my accumulated bitterness and anger burst forth and I interrupted him: "You have arranged positions in your health department for all your family and friends. But people like us, who have been associated with the medical industries and

who worked as Jewish pharmacists for nearly thirty years you treat like dirt!
I have spent a great part of my life in the service of the Jewish community, a
lot longer than you. Ask *Sejm* Deputy Mincberg about our work in the Jewish
community in Lodz for fifteen years. My family and I may end up in Ponary!
But don't delude yourselves – you will be there right behind us."

Nobody said anything after that and the delegation left the office, leaving
Milkonowicki alone with Fried. Mincberg left with us. When we were outside
Mincberg remarked, "I was astonished at your boldness – the way you dared
to speak to the second-highest-ranking member of the establishment."

A week later I was asked to come to Milkonowicki's office. He gave me
the good news: Gens had managed to obtain a few additional yellow documents and I was on the list. It was to remain a secret. But later that day it was
confirmed by Glazman. We were overjoyed. Perhaps, at long last, we would
stop being "illegals."

After a relatively quiet week, the situation in the ghetto stabilized. The
offices of the Judenrat began to function and the workshops in the ghetto
began to operate according to the "normal" routine. From somewhere came
the news that the Judenrat had decided to build a bathhouse, right across from
our rooms.

The ghetto needed a bathhouse like a blind person needs a seeing eye.
The whole ghetto was "impregnated" with lice. If anything in our life could be
considered "normal" it was the lice situation. We had been living in the most
squalid conditions for over three months without having a decent bath. Often
during that time we didn't remove our clothes for days on end while roaming
in attics, cellars and under the open sky. When we moved into our "new" home
we developed a routine for cleaning ourselves. Before we went to sleep we would
take off our shirts, men and women alike, and shake the lice down to the floor.
After the first night we gained wisdom and instituted a new rule: lice are not to
be shaken down on the floor; they must be destroyed. This became the daily task
in the hour before sleep. It was no real solution. It only alleviated the condition
for the next few hours. After "cleaning" ourselves we went back to our dirt and
squalor. We had no bedding and slept on iron beds, with our clothes as pillows.

While we were busy arranging our daily survival the Jewish police was busy with the final liquidation of the small ghetto. It was not a human liquidation any longer – there were no more Jews left in the small ghetto. When the workers with the yellow documents came over for thee days during the "cleansing" in the large ghetto the last people who had managed to survive the liquidation a few days earlier joined them on the way back and reached the large ghetto. Now the police of the large ghetto was making the "final liquidation" of whatever property had been left that could be of use to the large ghetto. I took advantage of their work. Getting hold of a small cart I went back to the small ghetto and went to our dwelling there. Everything had been vandalized. The furniture had been broken and the pillows had been cut to shreds, with the feathers and down shaken all over the place. I found a few pieces of bedding that had been left undamaged, a few pots and minor domestic things; I brought it all back "home" to the large ghetto. Nothing was left of all the expensive things that we had left behind when we left the small ghetto with the German. However, in our situation whatever I brought back was considered valuable.

After the "cleansing" at the beginning of November a whole month passed without further shocks. The holders of the yellow document had become an elite part of the ghetto. However even among them a "first among equals" system existed – that was the unit that worked for the Gestapo. They were a large group of people from various trades. They were known to be the "preferred" Jews of the Gestapo. For them the Germans had everything – security, bread, better dwellings. The Germans had ordered the Judenrat to assign to them two separate buildings where they lived with their families. Following their example, a new system of "blocks" developed in the ghetto. Every brigadier brought "his" German to the Judenrat. The German terrorized the council sufficiently to obtain a "block" for "his Jews." The brigadiers did not want their workers to become contaminated by "illegal" Jews who had only white papers, or no documents at all. This led to the development of a ghetto within the ghetto, which once more caused a transfer of people from one house to another, from one room to another. The Gestapo workers had their two buildings in one place, the workers of another German enterprise, the "Beute Lager," had another building, and the workers of the sanitary depot had yet another building. The rest of the ghetto were enraged at the brigadiers, who expelled the "illegal Jews" from their midst. The brigadiers tried to explain the "need" for such segregation with the excuse that they had to have their workers in one place. Considering the size of the ghetto the excuse was not convincing.

At the beginning of December the ghetto woke to news of another "cleansing." A number of people with criminal pasts – thieves, pimps and informers – known as *die Shtarke* (the Tough Ones) lived in the ghetto. They were recruited by Gens to provide assistance to the Jewish police as needed. On December 3, 1941, many of them were rounded up unexpectedly and taken away in a single night. According to witnesses, they were rounded up by the Germans and Lithuanians on the basis of a previously prepared list. Why? What was the reason? No one knew and no one understood. Later we found out that this had been done at the request of the Judenrat of the ghetto. They had become afraid to keep such a dangerous element in the ghetto. Although Gens had no moral compunction about making use of this element when it had suited him, he had delivered them to the Gestapo. Another 150 Jews were taken to their deaths.

Several days later, Jewish craftsmen working for the Gestapo started talking about an imminent "cleansing." Thus they were not surprised when the night of December 15 some Germans and Lithuanians came into their blocks on Straszuna Street and requested them to assemble in a column and leave the ghetto. They did so believing that the Gestapo would ensure their safety during the "cleansing" that was about to take place. Escorted by a small contingent of police the group of some five hundred people were quietly removed from the ghetto and taken directly to Lukishki prison. The next day their Gestapo employers arranged for the release of about two hundred "essential" workers who returned to the ghetto. The remaining three hundred, including some of the best craftsmen in the ghetto, were sent to their deaths in Ponary.

The shock waves in the ghetto that morning reached everyone, including Chairman Fried. These workers had not been what he termed "illegal Jews." They belonged to the highest elite! They had yellow documents and in addition, they served the Gestapo itself! If this could happen to them, was any Jew secure? "They probably got to know too many secrets," was one idea that circulated among the people, but few believed it. The ghetto leadership could not hide their fear. A few days earlier I had met my friend Moryc Grossman in the ghetto. I didn't recognize him as he had always had a large beard and now he was clean shaven. He recognized me, of course. He told me that he was appointed photographer to the Gestapo and his work had been well received. In recognition of the thousands of photos he had so far produced for them he was made administrator of the buildings of the Gestapo workers and leader of the group. Yet now Moryc Grossman was at Ponary.

We Live as "Illegal" Jews

My family and I were still living as "illegal" Jews since I had still not received the yellow document that Milkonowicki had said was on the way. I had no idea when I would receive it. We used to rise early but without the blessed document we avoided being in the street too much. We were afraid of the possibility of meeting up with Germans or Lithuanians, who had become constant visitors to the ghetto. To keep ourselves occupied we spent the first morning hours debating and discussing world politics, the situation at the fronts and similar "important" matters, as if our debates, opinions and conclusions were of any value. When we tired of this we read a little until we passed the first half of the day. Our day outside the closed room began in the afternoon when the workers started to return from outside the ghetto. They were the ones who brought the ghetto streets to life. They had news from the fronts and from the city and disregarding all danger we risked being in the streets when the workers returned.

In the late afternoon hours it seemed that all the twenty thousand-plus people of the ghetto were in the streets. During those late afternoon and early evening hours the commercial activity in the ghetto came to life. The streets hummed with people buying and selling all sorts of items, mostly food. Prices changed daily according to "the gate." If the search at the gate was strict, prices skyrocketed; if the police at the gate had been lenient the prices for the smuggled food were lower.

At that time, I received an invitation from Herman Kruk to come to the library where he worked. Kruk, a noted Warsaw journalist and librarian, arrived in Vilna after the outbreak of the war. In the ghetto he had been appointed to head the library and other cultural activities. He was not a member of the Judenrat and was a known critic of Fried. I arrived at the specified time to find several other individuals who had received the same invitation. Kruk made his point about the meeting in a few sentences. He declared that we should create a fund to help our comrades, particularly the intellectuals, who were in a very critical economic condition. After a lengthy discussion several people agreed to develop a concrete plan for the establishment of a fund and other operating details so that the practical work could begin. However, when everything was ready, the Judenrat informed Kruk that it would not permit us to go on with the work. The Judenrat itself would create a committee and no other body was allowed to do any social work.

Close to Christmas time there were some rumors about another "cleansing" and the Judenrat started to issue its own document, pink in color. The Jews in the ghetto named it the Pink Family-Protection Document and it was only valid for the ghetto. In conjunction with this "cleansing" the Judenrat released a circular that made it clear that the Judenrat was not keeping to its own rules and it employed "illegal" Jews. While no person without a yellow document was supposed to be employed at all and especially not in the offices of the Judenrat, the circular called on "those workers who still are without the pink document to present themselves the following day to receive the document."

There were two groups who were "illegal," yet employed by the Judenrat. In the first group were tradespeople who were needed in the workshops inside the ghetto. The second group was the protégés of the department directors, such as party members and relatives. I received my pink document on the night of December 21. On that night the office of the general department worked throughout the night. The next "cleansing" was supposed to take place the next morning.

My pink document was valid for myself, my wife and my two children. My mother was not included, since as far as the bureaucracy of the Judenrat was concerned she was too old. Overjoyed, I ran "home" in the middle of the night and caused quite a commotion – being the first one among the neighbors to receive such a document. After the initial euphoria I felt embarrassed and did not dare to look directly into peoples' faces; in particular, I could not face my mother. I comforted her with the idea that those who had received the pink document would soon be allowed to register additional persons.

On that night the offices of the Judenrat were besieged by masses of people who hoped to receive the pink document. After all it was not a small achievement to become a "legal" person in the ghetto. All in all, around three thousand individuals received such documents during the night and that was thanks to the efforts of Gens.

The next morning, December 22, 1941, Germans and Lithuanians appeared once again in the ghetto chasing after victims without documents. Those who had yellow documents had gone off to work, having left behind the blue documents that covered the family members appended to the yellow document. Those who worked in the ghetto were also covered by the pink ghetto document. Only those who had no document at all were taken away. At our hideout the rooms were full that day. Although I had a pink document I did not know how valid it would be in the eyes of the Germans and decided not to take the risk. On that first day I remained in the hideout together with the others. Sasha Kremer, a Vilna artist, was also in our hideout. He was employed as a laborer at the bathhouse construction project. Many of the workers at that project had not received any documents and did not turn up for work. This prompted Gens to appear at the bath and tell those who were there with documents to let the others know that they were "protected" and should come to work. A few days later the laborers received the pink documents.

The "cleansing" continued throughout the day. On the second day of the "cleansing" I left the hideout together with my family and we looked after those who were forced to remain inside. As it was close to Christmas we thought the raid would finish quickly. But for the holy work of murdering Jews there was no early holiday. The pursuit of the victims also went on during the third day until close to dusk of Christmas Eve. When the day was close to its end the killers left the ghetto, taking away the last victims.

The Christmas 1941 "cleansing" in the large ghetto took place exactly six months after the occupation of Vilna. Between the day the Germans invaded the Soviet Union and entered Vilna on June 24 and December 31, 1941, more than two-thirds of Vilna Jewry was slaughtered by the Germans and their Lithuanian helpers. During that period we did not have a single quiet day or night. We lived the entire time under a rein of terror and the outstretched hand of death. There is no doubt that Vilna was the first large city where the mass killing of Jews had taken place at such a frenzied pace.

Only at the beginning of 1942 did the Vilna Ghetto "relax" and the situation stabilized. Even then, however, it was a calm that could explode at any moment, erasing the city's last living Jewish souls.

The small circle of Vilna Ghetto dignitaries celebrated the arrival of the new year 1942 as Gens's guests. The celebration was lavish, with food, wine and entertainment until the wee hours of January 1, 1942.

CHAPTER 10

The Judenrat of the Large Ghetto

The Establishment of the Judenrat of the Large Ghetto

During our stay in the small ghetto, and after the joint meeting of the two Judenrate, I had become aware of the unlimited power of the large ghetto Judenrat and the ghetto police.

After the liquidation of the Vilna ghetto I found myself in the Klooga Concentration Camp in Estonia together with Fried. I asked him then just how the Judenrat of the large ghetto had come into existence. He provided me with a full account:

When the Germans liquidated the Vilna Jewish Committee a few days before driving us into the ghetto, they arrested most of its members. Two of them, Fried and Milkonowicki, escaped the Germans by hiding in the Jewish hospital as patients. There were many others who saved themselves in the same way. When the walls went up around the ghetto, the hospital was situated on territory that remained inside the large ghetto. On the Saturday morning, as Jews were driven into the large ghetto, Fried and Milkonowicki left the hospital. Murer, the German specialist on Jewish matters, was among the Gestapo officers who came that fatal day to make sure that everything was going according to plan. Walking in the ghetto, Murer came across Engineer Fried whom he had met before in the Jewish Committee. On the spot he nominated him as chairman of the Jewish Council. He ordered Fried to find another four people and create a Judenrat (Jewish Council). Fried appointed Advocate S. Milkonowicki (a Zionist and one of the leaders of the Vilna Jewish community) as his assistant and another member of the Vilna Jewish Committee, J. Fiszman (a shoemaker and a leading Bund activist) as a member. They were the first trio of the Judenrat. Under pressure Fried forced the fourth position on Engineer G. Guchman, who tried to get out of the offer. Unlike the others, Guchman was not an active party member. Fried assured him that the position was a purely technical one, as the ghetto had to have a technical specialist. The fifth spot that Murer had ordered was filled a few days later when a young lawyer, Grigori Jaszunski (a refugee from Warsaw and a leader of the Bund), joined the four.

Murer also gave Fried detailed instructions concerning the nature of the Judenrat. It was to be, he said, "a totally independent Jewish organization that had full authority to organize and manage all aspects of life in the ghetto. The ghetto is to be fully autonomous. Jews will go to work and be paid for their work. You will receive food to be distributed by you to the population. You must ensure that the ghetto is peaceful at all times. No one will cause you any harm. Whatever happened in the past is in the past. From now on you are safe."

While telling me all this in the concentration camp, Fried hastened to add that while he was hiding in the hospital he became acquainted with Jacob Gens, the temporary administrator of the hospital. A few days before the Germans attacked the Soviet Union Kagan, the permanent hospital administrator, had left for a rest cure and the city authorities had appointed Gens temporarily in charge.

Jacob Gens was not a native of the Vilna Jewish community. He was born in the Shavel area where he attended primary and secondary schools. After finishing school he joined the Lithuanian Army. He attended an officers course and graduated as a second lieutenant. Gens served in the army for several years, was promoted to first lieutenant and was demobilized with the rank of captain. He completed studies at the University of Kovno with degrees in law and economics. Gens first worked for the Shell Oil Company and later for the Lithuanian cooperative Lietukis. At the end of 1939, after the Soviets handed Vilna to the Lithuanians who made it their capital, Gens left Kovno and came to Vilna where he was appointed accountant of the municipal health department. He remained in that position until the Soviet Union took over the city in the summer of 1940. Gens was then appointed deputy administrator of the Jewish hospital and was there when the Germans entered Vilna. Fried found Gens to be the right man to be police commandant of the ghetto. He was reasonably young, intelligent, energetic and with past military experience. He offered Gens the position and Gens accepted.

Gens was married to a Lithuanian non-Jewish woman, the daughter of a Lithuanian officer, and the couple had a daughter. He was thought to have Revisionist-Zionist tendencies. The ghetto had a humorous ditty about Gens:

Gens wears an armband whitish and bluish

At home he has a wife who is – not Jewish.

When the ghetto was created, his wife and fifteen-year-old daughter remained outside its walls.

That is how six people became virtual rulers of the ghetto. They had received from the Germans the right to decide – as we say in our High Holiday prayers – "who shall live and who shall die." They were augmented by an additional twenty individuals who were recruited by Fried to provide administrative support in running the various functions of the Judenrat. Most of them were known activists in Jewish life and members of the three major Jewish ideological groups that were dominant among the Jews of Poland and Vilna: Zionists (secular, religious, socialist and nationalist), Bundists (noncommunist socialists and vehemently anti-Zionist, who emphasized Jewish cultural autonomy and Yiddish) and Communists. A fourth group, the Jewish Folkspartei (also known as the Jewish Democratic Party) was a non-socialist, liberal party which also advocated Jewish cultural autonomy based on Yiddish. The Folkspartei was much smaller than the major three groupings but was very active in prewar Poland and gained significant support among Jewish intelligentsia, small businessmen and artisans. In the ghetto, however, the ruling circles were essentially confined to the three major political groups. It is not surprising therefore that the strong ideological bond that existed between the members of the various groups in prewar Jewish life continued within the walls of the ghetto.

Members of the various organizations reorganized themselves within the confines of the ghetto into coherent and effective units with a hierarchy of leadership and party discipline. Tragically, the situation in which they found themselves in the ghetto did not lead them to eliminate the decades-long tradition of bitter animosities based on ideological differences. This, of course, led to many ugly instances of power struggles, favoritism and life and death decisions based on proximity to the circles of influence.

The Organization of the Judenrat

As soon as Fried was empowered by Murer to form the ghetto Judenrat he quickly started to organize its structure and activities. He established five departments and put himself in charge of the general department, which was responsible for the ghetto finances and for overseeing and coordinating the activities of all the remaining departments and functional units. The general secretary of the general department was A. Zajdsznur. Additional departments were food, headed by G. Jaszunski; health, headed by S. Milkonowicki; and housing, headed by G. Guchman. The fifth member of the Judenrat, J. Fiszman, was appointed as the liaison between the two ghettos. Contrary to the Judenrat of the small ghetto, Fried did not see the need to establish an education department. Some of the departments had a well-established base from which they could start their operations. For example, the health department had at its disposal the Jewish Hospital, which had become part of the ghetto and was very well equipped despite the Lithuanians having stolen much of its sophisticated instrumentation and other equipment. The director of the hospital was Dr. M. Brocki who held that position even before the establishment of the ghetto. The hospital also had a well-established pharmacy.

The wealthiest department was the housing department, which became the landlord of all the property in the ghetto and was responsible for the most desperate problem of providing accommodation to the ghetto population. A labor department headed by Aharon Braude – not a member of the Judenrat – was established to organize and manage the orderly supply of labor to German and Lithuanian work places. Several cultural institutions, including a major Jewish library, became active with H. Kruk as the head. As time went by, additional functional units were established to provide solutions for specific needs.

As soon as they started functioning as department heads, these administrators appointed their relatives, friends and fellow party members to various positions so that in no time the departments became centers of party activists.

During the many "cleansings," while the Lithuanians were looking for Jews who may have been hiding in the Judenrat buildings, most of the offices were vandalized, with the furniture broken and the files destroyed. In such tragic moments the preoccupation of the office employees was not to safeguard the offices but to save themselves and their families. But it is to their credit that as soon as the "cleansings" were over, the employees, at least those that survived, returned to their departments and resumed normal activity with energy and dedication.

As I mentioned above, as soon as Fried formed the Judenrat he invited the administrator of the Jewish Hospital in Vilna, Jacob Gens, to become police commandant and to organize a Jewish police force. Much later, at the end of 1943, when we were already in the concentration camp in Estonia Kruk told me that before the police force was formed there was an argument between Gens, Fried and himself as to the nature of that force. Kruk, who was appointed by the Judenrat to be deputy chief of police, was in favor of forming a militia, a people's security force, but neither Fried nor Gens accepted this.

Both were of the opinion that under prevailing conditions one could not wait a single minute or start with endless discussions. The police force had to be formed immediately and would have to rule with iron discipline. Thus Gens became the chief police commandant. Kruk asked to be relieved from the deputy commandant position.

Gens chose as his closest associates people who had either military experience or military training. Yosef Muszkat from Warsaw; Yosef Glazman from Kovno and Salek Dessler from Vilna were among them. Among the highest-ranking police officers was also a young German Jew named Oberhart. At first Gens appointed Muszkat and Dessler as his deputies and Major I. Frucht as a high-ranking officer. During the months of November–December 1941 when I ran around the offices of the Judenrat seeking a yellow document I already found a change in the positions of the police force. By that time Glazman had been appointed Gens's deputy and Salek Dessler was the contact man with the Gestapo. Dessler, a tall, overweight man with a facial expression that suggested retardation, was the son of the city *gabai* Felix Dessler, a rich businessman who for many years served as chairman of the well-known Vilna medical institution Mishmeret Hacholim.

During the early 1920s I was a member of the Mishmeret Hacholim board and would take part in board meetings held at Dessler's home. I never dreamt at that time that the young high-school boy would one day play such an evil and dramatic role in the life of the Jewish community of Vilna.

In the ghetto, old Dessler gave the impression of a man who did not know what was going on around him, even though he was very active in philanthropic work. Salek Dessler's wife was from Lodz and rumors had it that she was the cause of his slide down the dark path in his ghetto career.

Yosef Glazman, Gens's second deputy, was a completely different person. He was an intelligent, educated man, tall and handsome, with a warm personality and a Jewish heart. From the few conversations I had with Glazman when I was seeking a yellow document, I found him to be a good man with a sensitive soul. He understood the situation in the ghetto and judged it correctly. He wanted to help but by that time Gens and Dessler had already been hooked on the fishing rod of the Gestapo. They tried to drag him in as well but he managed not to get sucked in.

People in the ghetto felt Glazman to be a true friend and he gained the sympathy of the average person. Of course Gens and Dessler were jealous of his popularity. Gens did not relieve Glazman of his position but he and Dessler made Glazman's life sufficiently miserable as to make it impossible for him to remain in the police. He resigned from the police and took over the management of the housing department. There too he could not remain very long for the simple reason that he was honest and dedicated.

In time, the police force grew bigger. It established additional branches – a criminal branch and the gate police at the entrance to the ghetto – as well as a police command office, a cooperative, a public kitchen and a court.

The gate police were under the command of a young captain named Meir Levas from Kovno. He was a pathological sadist who trained his unit in his own sadistic spirit and the ghetto often suffered as a result.

The expansion of the police force reached its highest point during the summer of 1942, when the Judenrat was dissolved and the authority of the ghetto fell into the hands of Gens, who became the chief of police and the sole ghetto representative. At that time the police department employed more than two hundred people. Some had joined the force because they felt more secure there than anywhere else. The police also offered food and accommodation privileges. This influenced individuals to join the force as a way to survive the dark period. It should be said that many of the police did not cause any harm to the ghetto community on their own initiative. They "only fulfilled" their duty as police officers and one of their duties was to send other Jews to their death. According to their own moral understanding they were not guilty at all. They fulfilled their duties not by cooperating with the Gestapo but by order of the Jewish authorities. According to the police logic if there was any guilt in their work, the guilt was first of all that of the Judenrat and at a later stage that of Gens. I heard this often in conversations with many policemen whom I had known earlier to be decent and morally honest men.

Haim Malczadski was one such policeman. For many years he was the pharmacist of the Mishmeret Hacholim pharmacy; at the same time he was also known as an actor on the Yiddish stage under the name of *Malski*. He told me: "Yes, Mendel, what could I do? I could not go to work for the Germans. I have never been able to work physically hard. [He was already over sixty.] I had no capital to live on and I had to eat and provide for my family. I did the only thing I could do – I joined the police. I do not take bribes, I do not speculate like others in the ranks. I have not denounced anybody. I stand with the rod in my hand and regulate the street traffic or keep order in the lines at food distribution."

There were a number of people like Malczadski in the force. Decent ones who tried to remain decent. All they wanted was to survive.

But a tragic incident proved that Haim Malczadski could not always dictate his own actions. The case was both tragic and brutal. In the summer of 1942, the Jewish court sentenced to death five Jewish bandits and one informer. They were to be hanged in the ghetto. Gens did not want to appoint a Jew to the role of executioner so he ordered a large number of police to pull the execution rope together. Among the police that pulled the rope was Haim Malczadski. "Yes, Mendel," Malczadski confessed, "it is not easy bread that one eats as a policeman. That I had to live long enough to reach this point…"

"So why didn't you leave?" I asked him.

"Leave? And go where. What would my family and I live on?"

Haim Malczadski had a conscience that worried him a little. But there were many policemen who had no conscience at all. They were the ones whose power went to their heads as soon as they put on their police uniform. They used their position to live it up as much as they could, often holding drinking parties where food was served in overabundance. They used their position to become rich because they were sure that in the Jewish police uniform they would survive.

Other Jews became business people who dealt in the life and death market; still othere acted as agents of the Judenrat, informers. It was known in the ghetto that Dessler had his informers while he was the contact man with the Gestapo. At a later stage these police became open traitors to the Jews of the ghetto. They used to go around and seek out the hideouts and hand the people hidden there over to the Gestapo. They were nothing less than helpers of the Gestapo and the Lithuanians in destroying Jews.

Much Jewish blood lies on the conscience of many of the Jews who wore the police uniform in the large ghetto.

In the first weeks of the existence of the two ghettos people accepted as necessary the Jewish police in both ghettos. It was clearly understood that there was a need for a body to keep tens of thousand of people in an orderly manner, particularly under the extreme conditions imposed by the Germans.

In the small ghetto, the reasonably good relations between the police and the rest of the population lasted until the ghetto was liquidated. The same was also true at first for the large ghetto. The work of the police was to keep order in the bread lines and other food shops. They were often called to make peace between neighbors and to a degree were considered the leading elite of the ghetto population.

The break in the relationship between the police and the population in the large ghetto came suddenly, at the close of Yom Kippur, 1941. As I related above, on that day the police issued an order that the craftsmen of the ghetto come to the ghetto gate to register their yellow documents. The people came – only to be surrounded by Germans and Lithuanians and taken directly to Lukishki. It was the first act of betrayal. They deceived the Jewish population and handed over the assembled craftsmen to the Lithuanian murderers. At that "cleansing" it became clear that the Jewish police was established to help the Germans in their satanic plan to destroy the Jewish people.

The workers surrounded by the police saw the policemen as their angels of death. They sent their last death curses in the direction of the police, curses that were later repeated by the surviving members of the victims' families. A little later the police used another act of deception against the people of the ghetto. Together with the Judenrat they encouraged people to return to the liquidated small ghetto. Hundreds of innocent people, especially the elderly, sick and people without families, fell victim to police propaganda that stated that in the small ghetto accommodation and household goods would be freely available to all. So they went and fell directly into the hands of the waiting Germans and Lithuanians who took them to their death.

From that day on, the ghetto police was regarded as an instrument in the hands of Gestapo and the hatred of the police became universal.

The Judenrat and the police cooperated with each other during the early unstable period. However, after the first bloodletting came to an end and the situation "stabilized" Gens and Dessler began their work of undermining the position of the Judenrat in order to take over the ghetto. Fried, the chairman nominated by the Gestapo, quickly realized what they were up to and took umbrage at Gens's and Dessler's plans. In a letter in German dated April 6, 1942, Fried hinted about it:

Vilna Judenrat
Vilna, April 6, 1942

To the chief of the police, Mr. Gens:

In reply to your letter of the fourth of this month no.
2/667, a copy of which I enclose, I find it necessary to
draw your attention to the following:

Without entering into the principal aspect of the
problem, I must express my astonishment at a directive that is liable to destroy the stability that has been
established in the ghetto through much hard work,
especially since it affects the heating problem. This
directive has the potential to destroy the established
discipline.

In order to avoid repetition of such matters in the
future, I ask you to give the necessary instructions to
the police organs that are under your command that, in
all matters that have to do with the ghetto administration and economy, they turn to the Judenrat alone. At
this opportunity, I am informing you that on Saturday,
April 4, a police officer permitted the closing of all
offices of the Judenrat on the second floor, including
the cashiers, at 6:00 p.m., a full hour before ordinary
closing time. This was done without first confirming
the matter with me.

There can be no doubt that such an action by
police functionaries cannot be tolerated....
     (signed) The chairman of the Judenrat – Fried

A little later in the summer of 1942 this kind of friction led to the abolition of
the Judenrat. The German district commandant appointed Gens as the sole
ghetto representative and chief of police and Dessler as police commandant.

The winners in that struggle were Gens and Dessler because they kept permanent contact with the German authorities. The Judenrat with its Chairman Fried lost its high standing. But Gens did not remove Fried or any other members of the Judenrat. They remained in their positions and Fried became the director of the ghetto administration.

One has to admit that without the iron fist of police discipline there would have been chaos in the ghetto. To a large extent the order they established calmed people's nerves, and the fear of being arrested by the police deterred those wishing to act against the common good. The police carried out its basic functions under the most trying conditions. They kept order, they resolved disputes and they maintained ghetto discipline. And when some of them carried out unwarranted acts of brutality or were caught taking bribes, they were tried in the ghetto court and punished. Their names were also published in the ghetto newspaper *Geto Yedies* (Ghetto news). Had the police limited itself to "law and order," as did the police in the small ghetto, they would have received the full cooperation of the population and gained its respect. The tragedy of the ghetto police was that they went far beyond those tasks and many (but not all) became willing accomplices of the Germans in the implementation of their plans. Many of them also used their positions to enrich themselves by trading jobs and lives. For this they earned the people's contempt and their names were besmirched with everlasting shame.

A separate branch within the police force was the gate police, who were responsible for keeping guard at the entrance to the ghetto. The gate was always guarded by a Lithuanian guard outside and by the Jewish gate police inside. Next to the entrance was a small hut where the gate police had its office. The already mentioned sadist, Captain Meir Levas, officiated at the hut. In time, he became known for his brutality and sadism and was a hated symbol for the thousands who passed the gate every day to work in the city.

The work of the police at the gate was not easy. Their responsibility began as soon as the ghetto was created, with the German order that nothing was to be brought into the ghetto or taken out of it without their permission. Officially only the food rations that had been allocated for the ghetto were allowed in. The allocated rations were accepted at the gate by a representative of the Judenrat and delivered to the food storage center. The food department of the ghetto then distributed the food to soup kitchens, the hospital and the general population.

But even the little that the Germans allocated to the ghetto never fully reached the people. The Judenrat deducted large amounts from the general food rations for themselves. In addition, German allowances were only for the working "legal Jews" and their dependants according to their working cards. The "illegal" Jews in the ghetto had to rely on food smuggled in by the workers who went to the city everyday. Smuggling of food was not without danger, but it helped the smugglers earn a living and the "illegal Jews" to survive.

Everyday many thousands of Jews, both male and female, left the ghetto to work in the city. Each of them brought back a small amount of food, such as bread, potatoes, flour, vegetables, meat and eggs. Many of the products were immediately bartered or sold for cash. This kept the commercial side of the ghetto alive. Primary control over all this was in the hands of the gate police. When the German "expert" on Jewish matters SS Officer Murer visited the gate to meet the returning workers, the Jewish police were completely helpless. They had to be very strict and confiscate everything. More than one worker paid for this smuggling with his or her life. Even when there was no German control visible at the gate, the Jewish police still had to be on guard, because more than once Germans or Lithuanians appeared out of nowhere.

But on occasion the gate police confiscated food from workers when no Germans were around. The victims were usually poor Jews, individuals who relied on the little they smuggled to earn a living. The professional smugglers, working hand in hand with the gate police, brought in sack loads of food. Their smuggling was well organized. They used the carts that brought in the official rations to smuggle in double and triple the allocated amounts. They also used carts that were brought in for garbage removal, and even the black cart that carried the Jewish dead to the cemetery outside the ghetto was used for food smuggling. The gate police and the Judenrat made a handsome profit from it. Robbing the poor when there were no Germans around was an act of sadism and brutality. For not only did the gate police steal the bread out of the mouths of the smugglers, they also often beat the unfortunate ones. The workers used to say that the Jewish sadist Captain Levas was not better than the Germans, except that he did not sent workers directly to Ponary.

The brutality of the gate police at certain stages reached proportions that became unacceptable even to the Judenrat. Correspondence on the matter between Fried and Gens illustrates the matter:

> Vilna Jewish Council
> April 21, 1942
>
> To the chief of police in the ghetto,
>
> At the entrance gate to the ghetto many incidents take place between gate guards and the people who enter. Often the incidents are due not to reasonable action of the guards but to careless actions and unnecessary provocation of the gate guards. We are bringing this to your attention and request you to take the proper action to remedy the situation.
> > *(signed) The chairman of the Judenrat – Fried*

Like their captain, the gate police developed a criminal taste for brutality and lawlessness. They used to mercilessly beat anyone who fell into their hands. They divided the confiscated products among themselves or sent them to the kitchens of the police cooperative. On occasion the gate police decided to be charitable and sent the food to the children's home.

The Jewish ghetto police was generally disliked, but the gate police was hated by everybody – that is, by everybody except one man. That man was the German expert on Jewish matters: Murer.

Ghetto Finances

The Judenrat had very large financial expenditures. It had to cover the cost of its employees, the budget of the police, hospital, children's institutions, workshops and all other institutions of a general communal character.

In addition to this, the Judenrat needed large sums for social help, sanitary work and housing. All this was part of the internal budget. On top of the internal budget the Judenrat had to find large sums of money to pacify the ever-present greed of the Germans and the Lithuanians and to satisfy the occasional demands for "payments" and "contributions" to the outside authorities.

The ghetto administration had to find ways to get the vast sums needed. Considering that the Jewish community had already been pauperized by the time it got to the ghetto the budgetary work of the Judenrat was not easy. True, the ghetto had a number of people who had managed to bring significant amounts of money into the ghetto, but that wealth remained private. The ghetto administration had no way of knowing about it nor of confiscating it even when it became known. In addition, individual families had to live off their savings and valuables because the normal sources of income had totally disappeared. The ghetto administration had to start collecting its income from the new earners that ghetto conditions created.

In the beginning, money was obtained from the workers, both those who worked for the Germans outside the ghetto and the storekeepers and tradesmen inside the ghetto. The new "wealthy" group also included the "middlemen," who had their "good" Germans and became rich through them. Money also came from taxing those bright individuals who earned easy money dealing in gold and currencies.

The finance office was established after the first great "cleansing" in September 1941. Its director was a man named Kaszuk, a past director of the Bunimowicz Bank. At first Kaszuk was in the small ghetto, where he worked with the administration. During the first liquidation of the small ghetto he managed to save himself at the very last hour. When he reached the large ghetto, Fried invited him to become manager of the finance office.

The finance office based its income on three sources: 1) Income tax; 2) commercial, industrial and license tax including workshop earnings; and 3) a head tax.

The income tax was derived from the workers who went to work outside the ghetto for the Germans or Lithuanians. They received payment for their work, but they saw very little of their earnings. The brigadiers, who were in charge of tax collection, had to deduct a set percentage into the treasury of the Judenrat. On top of the income tax there were additional unforeseen deductions that left the workers without sufficient funds to feed their families. They had to live from the little they stole at work and smuggled in daily to the ghetto.

The overseer of the tax collection was Avraham Zajdsznur. He kept the workers' income accounts and reconciled the amounts with the brigadiers when they came to pay the collected tax. The income tax was the first tax to be implemented by the Judenrat.

When conditions in the ghetto had stabilized many people started entrepreneurial work. They began to build small industries and open restaurants, establish small stands where they bought and sold ghetto items and took in goods on sales commission. All these self-employed people had to buy a license from the Judenrat. At first, the license fee was relatively small, around ten to twenty mark. As the ghetto economy developed, the license went up to three hundred mark.

The self-employed and small industrialists were also obliged to pay income tax, though they were legal only in the eyes of the Judenrat. The Germans considered them illegal and criminal. When a German or Lithuanian came for a visit to the ghetto, the illegal shops closed and locked their businesses.

The third tax was the head tax. This had to be paid by everyone, "legal" and "illegal" Jews. It was the most controlled tax in the ghetto and its collection was a top priority for the Judenrat. The head tax made up a significant part of the Judenrat budget.

On top of all this, the ghetto administration had additional sources of income. They collected money from rent, electricity, and taxed income from the communal kitchens and restaurants . All these taxes were official and legal

income sources. Yet at best they covered only the official expenditures of the
ghetto administration.

The ghetto administration also had large expenditures that never appeared in the pages of the budget. These were illegal demands of Germans,
Lithuanians and other blackmailers. For such expenditures the Judenrat had
to have a secret treasury of gold, jewelry and foreign currency. The Judenrat
obtained this treasure by confiscation and forced secret "contributions" that
they extracted from large earners, such as the wholesale smugglers and middlemen who earned fantastic sums.

The financial documents of that period that were not destroyed indicate
that the bookkeeping of income and expenditure was kept in Russian rubles
and German marks. The exchange rate was ten rubles to a single mark.

The tax office was well organized and it included a complaints department.
One of the standard replies found in the archives states:

> Vilna Ghetto Finance Department
> October 1942
>
> To the Tax payer no..........
> We inform you that the ghetto administration
> has taken notice of your case of.........and decided
> that your tax for the month of September 1943 for the
> sum of.........should remain in force/should be reduced
> to.........
> We recommend that the final sum be paid. Oth-
> erwise we will collect the sum by force, adding to it
> the cost of collection.

The brigadiers were not always in a hurry to pay their collected taxes to the
finance department. But as they belonged to the ghetto elite, the language used
on them was somewhat more elegant;

"We request that you contact the tax section regarding this matter and
inform us within three days of receipt of this letter how the matter was resolved."

For head-tax collection the tax office used straightforward, even brutal language, as failure to pay this tax mostly affected the poorest section of the population. In one case, the demand for payment of this tax was issued on June 20 and on July 18 the Judenrat ordered the administrators of the buildings not to hand over the food cards for August to those who had not paid the head tax Overall, the taxation department was well organized and efficient.

CHAPTER 11

Under Gens's Rule

The First Half of 1942: Avoiding Starvation

Since the "cleansing" that had finished at dusk on December 24, 1941, the ghetto had been relatively calm. Thousands of Jews went out like slaves every morning to work for Germans, Lithuanians and various institutions. Others found employment in the ghetto, in the administration or, under various pretexts, became traders and self-employed. Many ghetto institutions were developed and anyone seeking work had no difficulty in finding it. The ghetto derived its spiritual energy from its desire to live and its unshakable will to survive its enemy. One of the great moral supports for this was the daily news brought back by the workers in the city. There was also a kiosk in the ghetto where the daily papers in Lithuanian, German and Polish languages were available. Of course, all three papers were full of anti-Semitic accusations. There was no good news in them but we learned to read the news between the lines.

The problem of surviving German "cleansings" now gave way to the problem of surviving hunger and starvation. Food distribution in the ghetto was in the hands of the food department of the Judenrat. The food department was allocated a certain quantity of products determined by the German authorities and supplied by a Lithuanian agency. The quantity of products was based on the number of individuals registered on the official work permits. It consisted of a daily ration of 120 grams of bread and some 30 grams of other products, and it meant starvation. But the ghetto also had thousands of "illegal" residents who, as far as the Germans were concerned, were nonexistent, yet they too had to be provided with food. Smuggling of provisions into the ghetto became a major undertaking and trading in food products became a flourishing business. Those who had money could buy anything their hearts desired. Jews who had left their property with Gentile friends outside the ghetto risked contact with them to obtain some of their belongings in order to sell them and buy food. For those who had nothing to sell the situation was desperate. They had to find some source of income in order to live, and for many that meant stealing. Whenever there was an opportunity workers outside the ghetto stole German goods at their working places. This was of course a very dangerous undertaking but life had to be risked in order to be sustained, and the Germans could not prevent it.

Bringing the stolen goods into the ghetto was another life-endangering process, but at least everything that was brought in from outside could be sold. A major purchaser was the Judenrat, which had the financial resources to pay market prices for the goods. The Judenrat was also able to bribe the official Lithuanian suppliers of food to double or triple the allotted food rations which they regularly delivered to the ghetto.

The Jews who worked in the ghetto and had no contact with the outside world were in a more difficult situation. In the ghetto there was no easy way to steal. The ghetto elite abused their power and took for themselves provisions that were earmarked for others – but the ghetto workers could hardly avail themselves of this method. To ameliorate the difficult condition of the workers in the ghetto administration, Gens introduced the distribution of *paiki*, a kind of additional food parcels. Gens' intention was good but the practical handling of the *paiki* was once more in the hands of the hierarchy and they knew how to use it for their own profits. In the end the *paiki* reached only the top echelon of the administration and their friends, with others deriving little benefit out of it. The workers who were in a better position in the ghetto were the self-employed tailors, shoemakers and other tradesmen. No matter how difficult the situation was one could not totally avoid using their services.

Organized smuggling was another means of getting food into the ghetto. Groups of smugglers in cooperation with the Jewish police brought in cartloads of food using all sort of tricks already mentioned.

A special case was the group of chimneysweeps. They went out of the ghetto and returned a few times daily. Their buckets went out empty but returned loaded with products from outside. When the control at the gate was strict they smuggled their goods across the roofs and through the attics. There is no record of a single case in which the chimneysweeps were ever caught with their contraband.

Women used to bring in food products in specially made corsets. These were specially useful for items such as flour, sugar and similar foods that were hard to distinguish during physical searches. A tragicomic case happened when luckily there was no German around. A woman's corset burst during the personal inspection and she began losing quite considerable amounts of flour that kept running down from under her skirt. It must have amused even the sadist Levas. As people recounted it afterwards, he dipped his hand in the flour on the ground and smeared it on the face of the poor woman, but did nothing more.

But the greatest smuggler of all was the Judenrat. When bringing in the official allocated rations it used to smuggle in considerable amounts of products bought from the Lithuanians.

During the winter months of 1942–43, when the situation in the ghetto was relatively calm, Fried and Gens wished to improve relations with the ghetto intelligentsia. At that time they brought in large quantities of food over and above the German allocation. They enlarged the number of midday kitchen meals provided free of charge in the communal kitchens, as the poverty was considerable. They also allocated additional *paiki* and bonuses for artists, intellectuals and employees of the Judenrat. It was a maneuver calculated to draw the people away from their sympathy to Glazman and other groups whose dissatisfaction with the Judenrat had started to become too obvious.

Over time conditions stabilized and the atmosphere became quieter. People who in the beginning had difficulty living with one another became friendly neighbors and sometime friends. Many homes became evening social clubs where neighbors came together and debated politics, discussed the latest orders of the Judenrat or exchanged the latest gossip brought in from the outside.

This kind of peace slowly penetrated into the life of the ordinary people of the ghetto. In the high society of the ghetto leadership, however, the bitter struggle for hegemony continued.

The Dismissal of the Judenrat

In the summer of 1942 the news that the German District Kommissar and the Gestapo had dismissed the Judenrat erupted like a volcano. In place of the Judenrat they nominated Jacob Gens as the sole ghetto representative and chief of police. Fried was named head of administration, reporting to Gens, and Dessler was made police Kommissar. The news was widely discussed and commented upon among ordinary people. In reality it made very little difference to most people whether Fried or Gens was head of the ghetto. The average person feared them both. As for their style of leadership there was also very little difference – both fulfilled the orders of the Germans. To the people of the ghetto the change brought only a single fear: will the change be good for the ghetto or will it bring more trouble?

The answer that the ghetto received was immediate and tragic. On the night of July 27 the ghetto police handed over to the Gestapo close to one hundred elderly Jews. The hundred Jews were relocated to a very elegant summer country house, the TOZ building in Pospieszki. Before the war, TOZ was a Jewish welfare institution for school children whose families could not afford to send their children on a summer holiday in the country. The building where the elderly people were brought to was named after a well-known Vilna personality, Dr. Tsemach Szabad. For a few days the Jewish police delivered bread and other products daily to the people. One day when they came with their delivery they found the house empty. The Lithuanians had found another "vacation spot" for the old people. A place called Ponary.

Once more a cloud of fear descended on the summer sunshine of the ghetto. For half a year it had been relatively quiet, half a year without "cleansing" raids and suddenly it had all started again. What did it mean? How did the "cleansing" relate to the change that has just taken place? Was Gens paying the Gestapo for his nomination, or did the "cleansing" happen to be "accidental," unconnected to the change in the ghetto administration?

A short time after the old people had been sent to Ponary, I met Gens at a circumcision ceremony. Gens arrived after the religious ritual had been performed, but a few people were still sitting at the table. The lucky father handed Gens the customary drink and a piece of cake. I decided to make use of the unusual opportunity to learn some news. I realized that an opportunity like this, to sit with the head of the ghetto at one table in an unofficial gathering, would not quickly repeat itself. Carefully I directed the general talk at the table to the subject of the old people. Immediately, Gens reacted: "The 'cleansing' of the old people has nothing to do with me. The Germans 'collected' an old account they had with the old Judenrat… They wanted a few hundred people and I bargained it down to the hundred old ones. It was not easy. I had to drink enormous amounts with them. All this drinking will be the death of me in the end," he said and after a moment of silence he repeated: "The 'cleansing' that came at the beginning of my new position was only accidental, it should all be noted down to the account of the Judenrat. My aim is to save the ghetto." Before I had time to think I said: "You might save the ghetto but without the Jews…"

I had said the words and could not take them back. I bit my lip in fear; *God knows what I'll get for my comment.* But Gens said nothing and after a short while he left.

I have no doubt that Gens meant to save the ghetto. I am convinced that at the start of his career he had the best intentions to help save whatever was possible to save. I believe that even when he handed Jews over to the German murderers he believed that in this way he saved the remainder of the population of the ghetto. It is my opinion that Gens believed that in the end he would be the new Moses who would one day lead the Jews out of the ghetto. If there had to be sacrifices – that could not be helped. But the ghetto had to be saved. And to save the ghetto, according to his thinking, Jews had to work for the Germans, to drag out the process and win time. I say that this was his thinking, because Gens was not the only one who thought this way. Many people in the ghetto, driven by the inner wish to survive, clung to the illusion that survival was possible and if in the process some Jews had to be sacrificed by meeting German demands, than that was what needed to be done. The Germans, of course, through their diabolical planning, did all they could to nurture and perpetuate such illusions.

This also explains the effective cooperation between the Judenrat and the Gestapo during the first months of the ghetto. After the "cleansing" on Christmas Eve of 1941, Gens believed that the dirty work had come to an end. He was not alone in such thoughts. Fried also spoke of "illegal Jews" who caused the ghetto such great difficulties. Now that the dirty work had been done and the Jews who survived had a future, Gens wanted to be remembered by history as their savior. He managed to convince the Gestapo officers with whom he drank and partied to make him the ruler over the ghetto and they did him the favor; after all why not? It was not going to change anything in the end and Gens was already much deeper in their net than the Judenrat.

After the "cleansing" of the old people, life in the ghetto settled down again and the daily routine returned. The cultural side of the ghetto came to life, with all kind of concerts, theaters, schools for children and general entertainment evenings. These activities were coordinated by the Department of Culture that was established by the Judenrat and headed initially by Guchman. At a later stage, the Department of Culture and the Department of Education were consolidated into one Department of Education and Culture and Judenrat member Jaszunski was appointed as its head. In April 1943 Gens replaced Jaszunski with Dr. Bernstein. One of the key cultural activities of the ghetto was the library and reading room established soon after the formation of the ghetto and managed from its very beginning by Herman Kruk, a well-known Warsaw journalist and librarian. Under Kruk's leadership, the library succeeded in attracting thousands of registered readers and visitors to the reading room. On December 13, 1942, a festive evening was held to celebrate the one hundred thousand books that the ghetto population had borrowed from the library during the period September 1941–December 13, 1942. In addition to the central library, several smaller libraries were established in various ghetto institutions. My wife, my son and I all had subscriptions to the library so our family always had sufficient reading material.

The "Work Means Survival" Philosophy

The Gens obsession with "work means survival" led to the transformation of the labor department of the Judenrat into the most critical activity of the administration. The department was headed by Aharon Braude, a young man from a wealthy Kovno family, who was also the contact man with the labor department of the Gebietskommissariat. Braude was not a member of the Judenrat and over time, with the support of Gens, the labor department evolved into a semiautonomous authority. We may assume the reason for Gens's support was his desire to minimize the influence of the Bund activists on matters pertaining to employment, work allocation and brigadier appointments.

Over time, Gens used many occasions to articulate his "philosophy." One of the occasions was a public meeting held in the ghetto theater at which Gens declared:

> Let us state clearly, without fooling ourselves, that from the political point of view we Jews mean nothing to the Germans. We do not exist and should not exist. That is the Nazi law concerning us Jews. If some of us still survive, that is only because certain economic factors are in our favor. We provide a most valuable commodity – labor. The more workers we provide, the more products we produce – the more important becomes the existence of the ghetto. That is the foundation for our existence. Should our economic usefulness disappear – we become useless. Therefore, if we want to live, if we want to survive – we have to work. We have to be economically useful to the Germans....

And on May 16, 1943, *Geto Yedies* published an article under the heading "*Zum Moment*" (Right now) which stated:

We are obliged to increase the percentage of productive workers among the ghetto population, which has
grown. We must become a true working society, cre-
ative, productive, and earning, through its economic
viability, the right to exist.... Consequently we have
lowered the finishing age in the schools to thirteen
years. We cut them off from their teachers, their lessons and their childhood, and throw them into a hard
life, so as to swell the ranks of the workers. We shall
see to it that young girls also learn a trade. Our workshops are expanding. We already have industries in
the ghetto, both light and heavy: furniture workshops.
tin smithies, forges, a turnery, a locks smithy, fine me-
chanics, a syrup-producing plant, a pottery workshop,
a sewing workshop which receives large military and
private orders, and the Technical School. And above
all, the work being done outside the ghetto in numerous Wermacht units....

It has to be said that the above argument fell on fertile ground within the
ghetto population. People believed it because they desperately wanted to hope
that survival was possible and Gens showed them the way. In more somber
moments some tried to reconcile the "importance of work" with the fact that
many strong, young Jews, many craftsmen, were sent to their death in the
various ghetto "cleansings." But there was no question that for those who were
still alive work and a work permit were key to survival. The labor department
worked day and night trying to identify skilled labor, craftsmen and others who
would meet the German and Lithuanian demand for labor. The department
was also in charge of issuing the all-important work permits. Overall it did
this very well, although not without some ugly cases of issuing work permits
for bribes and payments.

By the end of 1942 some ten thousand Jews were employed, eight thousand outside the ghetto and two thousand within the ghetto walls.

It was the ambition of Gens, as published in *Geto Yedies*, to increase the number of workers to sixteen thousand – 80 percent of the ghetto population – by mid-1943.

The daily supply of thousands of workers to German and Lithuanian enterprises was the responsibility of the labor department. In order to ensure an orderly process, one brigadier acted as foreman of each group of workers in a given enterprise.

In most cases the foreman was the most outspoken member of the group, who managed to place himself in a leadership position and was accepted by the German employer as such. Within a short period of time the foreman established a close relationship with the Germans and became quite influential. When the need arose, he could influence the distribution of work permits, he could intervene in cases when a worker from his group would be sent to Lukishki prison during a "cleansing" and for an appropriate payment have him released. In many cases, the foremen were most active in trading with their German or Lithuanian employers. Many enriched themselves in the process. Two of them were Foreman Weisskopf who became known as "king" in the ghetto, and Foreman Woron who was able to resolve any problem – for a price. But there were many foremen who carried out their responsibilities honestly and did their utmost to help their workers both outside and inside the ghetto.

The ghetto administration, and particularly Gens, became quite concerned with the growing power of the foremen and the contacts they were developing with German authorities. In November 1942 Gens appointed a foremen's council with David Kaplan-Kaplanski as chairman and N. Kammermacher, Lidovsky, Pinsker, Steinhauer and Golomb as members. In time, the council became a de facto arm of Gens and Braude in dealing with labor problems.

The interaction between the foremen and their workers, and even between the workers themselves, led to many disputes and conflicts. In order to ensure that such problems would be resolved without the intervention of the ghetto police, on February 11, 1942, Yosef Glazman, at the time the deputy commandant of the police, suggested to the Judenrat the formation of a labor arbitration committee that would be empowered to deal with all labor disputes. Fried did not respond but after Glazman's second request the Judenrat dealt with the matter and on March 18, 1942, decided to form an arbitration committee that would deal with problems involving foremen and workers working outside the ghetto.

At about the same time as the formation of the arbitration committee, a Judenrat employees committee was formed. It included representatives of all employment units of the Judenrat elected by the employees. I was elected as one of two representatives of the hospital employees. Most of the other representatives on the committee were either Bundists or Communists. The first meeting of the committee dealt with the Public Committee for Social Welfare. This committee was established by Herman Kruk and other public activists but by order of the Judenrat was converted into a Judenrat institution. Bund members on the committee resigned in protest.

The second meeting of the Judenrat employees committee was held in June 1942 and dealt with the Judenrat decision to distribute *paiki* to selected Judenrat functionaries. Committee members were outraged at this decision and after a lengthy discussion it was decided to send a memorandum to the Judenrat requesting that the additional food parcels should be distributed to all employees and not just to a selected small group. On June 27, a few days after the committee's memorandum was delivered, all members of the Judenrat employees committee were summoned to Gens's office. They were informed that the decision about the restricted food distribution was his; that he made the decision in order to ensure that the key employees could carry out their duties and that no one had a right to question the decision. When Herman Kruk tried to say something, Gens cut him off saying that there would be no discussion. "No one has the right to interfere with me," he added, "and whoever does will find himself working in the forests outside Vilna." We left Gens, stunned by this outburst, and the activity of the Judenrat employees committee came to an end. But there was one positive outcome of our intervention – in time, the number of people receiving extra rations slowly increased.

The Health Department

The Department of Health and Sanitation was under the control of Judenrat member S. Milkonowicki. At first, the head doctor was Dr. Szadowski, who created a medical management group of five doctors. Four of the five came not from Vilna but rather from Kovno. I cannot say if this was accidental but the fact remains that Vilna doctors did not attain positions in the highest medical ranks.

It was relatively easy to organize the medical work and its departments. The old Jewish hospital remained inside the ghetto and nearly all the Jewish doctors of Vilna had come into the ghetto, as they had all been previously protected by yellow documents issued by the German military physician.

The health department organized its work in three departments: 1) hospital; 2) infirmaries and 3) epidemiology. The largest of the sections was the hospital under the direction of Dr. Michael Brocki. He held the same position at the hospital already before the war. The infirmary was established by Dr. Kalman Szapiro and he guided it from its inception to the very end. The epidemiology section was headed by Dr. L. Epsztajn.

As soon as I received the pink document (during the night of December 22, 1941) I reported to the head physician of the ghetto hospital, Dr. Brocki. I was informed that as the head physician of the hospital he had kept patients hidden there before the ghetto was established and in that way had saved many people from the hands of the "human-catchers." Among the people he had secretly kept as patients were two personalities who later became the leaders of the Judenrat: Engineer Anatol Fried and Advocate Milkonowicki.

After the ghetto was established Dr. Brocki once more turned the place into a hideout to protect a considerable number of "illegal" Jews. However this was no longer acceptable to the Judenrat leaders, the very same ones that he had earlier saved. Fried, the chairman of the Judenrat, and Milkonowicki, the head of the health department, now considered Dr. Brocki to be "too independent." They removed their one-time savior from his position as head physician. and gave the post to Dr. E. Sadlis, the head doctor of the women's hospital in Zwierzyniec. They also nominated Dr. Wajnryb as his deputy.

If his attempt to keep the hospital as a hiding place was Dr. Brocki's "sin," as far as the two highest rulers of the ghetto were concerned it was not the only one. As it transpired, he committed another unforgivable sin. As I recounted above, as head doctor of the hospital Dr. Brocki was in charge of handing out yellow documents. He insisted that every document should have as many people registered to it as was allowed, thereby preventing the Judenrat from using some of the documents for their own purposes. Dr. Brocki handed out the yellow documents to the medical staff according to their position in the hospital. He did not recognize party membership or personal friendship and he did not accept bribes. The leaders of the ghetto could not hold him in their grip and as a result, they removed him from his high position and handed it to someone more to their liking.

Dr. Brocki sent me to the hospital, where on December 27 I was made night watchman at the hospital gate. It was a bitter cold night. I dressed myself as well as I could and took over the keys to the gate. Next to the gate was a small guardhouse outfitted with a metal stove. There was enough wood to keep the stove going throughout the night. When one dozed off the cold woke one up.

Next to the hut was the mortuary, but I was satisfied. Let it be as a night watchman, let it be next to the mortuary, anything but not to work for the Germans. But there was the irony of fate. My first customer at the gate was none other than Fried. He was surprised: "Oh, it's you, well, good evening," and this was the end of our conversation.

I did not remain at the gate for long. Unbeknownst to me, some older Vilna doctors who knew me told Dr. Sadlis of my situation. He changed my position from night watchman and made me the person responsible for accepting the food parcels that people brought for their friends and relatives in the hospital. The handling of these parcels was also the duty of young doctors and students who worked at the hospital.

I did not last long there either. I was relieved of my position and sent to the "observation section" of the hospital. The observation section was only partially legal and as a result it was placed in separate wards throughout the hospital. The wards had patients suffering from scarlet fever, diphtheria, suspected typhoid and typhus. All these diseases were "legal." The Germans were prepared to tolerate them and the hospital was permitted to treat patients who were afflicted by them. What the Germans would not tolerate was spotted typhoid, of which they were more afraid then death. But among the hospital patients there were several who suffered from spotted typhoid. They were not from the ghetto but from the working camps outside Vilna. Their sickness was not surprising. Hygienic conditions in the camps were atrocious; dirt and lice rapidly spread the disease. Residents were brought to the ghetto hospital and they were taken to the observation wards, where they were registered as "status febrilis." When the crisis passed, their status was changed to abdominal typhus. Keeping the patients with spotted typhoid at the hospital was playing with fire. We knew that when the Germans had found out that the Jewish Hospital in Kovno kept patients suffering from spotted typhoid, they burned down the hospital together with the patients, doctors and staff. To the honor and praise of the hospital in the Vilna Ghetto it must be said that there was not a single moment of hesitation.

It is self-evident that all institutions in the ghetto had the same purpose, to save as many Jews as possible or at least to ease their tragic fate. Every department was a fighting post. But the hospital was more than that; it was a resistance post. A true military resistance movement that fought not with guns but with knowledge and dedication to save more and more Jewish lives from falling into the hands of the Germans. The Germans wanted to cause epidemics in the ghetto as an excuse for their beastly plans. They sought any sign of spotted typhoid as an excuse to burn down the hospital together with its dedicated workers as they had done in Kovno. But the 180 hospital workers accepted the danger of their positions and their work and maintained wards of spotted typhoid patients as well as prenatal wards for women, where abortions were also performed.

After Dr. Brocki was demoted and his place taken by Dr. Sadlis, the Gestapo said that they knew about typhoid patients being treated at the ghetto hospital. They threatened to shoot Dr. Sadlis and a few others if the physicians would not inform them within twenty-four hours of the real state of the hospital and assure them that the place was safe from spotted fever. Dr. Wajnryb, a young and intelligent physician, took over responsibility for the daily report. He began to fill out two reports every day: one true one and one that was falsified. The true report went daily to Gens and the false one to Dessler, who was at that time the contact man with the Gestapo. Gens read the true report and handed it back to the hospital.

This went on for a considerable time. The dedication of the hospital workers was highly recognized by the ghetto population. Nearly everybody knew that people with spotted typhoid were being treated at the hospital. It is well recorded that there were denouncers in the ghetto who worked not only with the Judenrat but also with the Gestapo, but not one of them ever betrayed or denounced the hospital. It is no exaggeration to say that the entire staff of the hospital, as a team, were a resistance movement against the German plan without ever firing a deadly shot against their enemy.

When I joined the observation wards, Dr. Szumeliszki was in charge. At intervals Dr. Emily Szalit used to visit the ward as a consultant when patients were discharged. The person in charge of the practical running of the wards was Ber Lewinson, an elderly, experienced medic. He was dedicated to the patients with body and soul. One could find him in the wards at any time of the day or night. He worked together with a team of nurses that was on duty at nighttime. Some of the nurses fell victim to the infection and became patients of the wards but the dedication of those around them helped pass the crisis; not one of the nurses died of spotted typhoid.

When I joined the section, Dr. Szalit handed me a list of my duties: I had to provide enough wood daily to keep six to eight ovens going full time. It was also my duty to collect the patient's soiled clothes, record the collected items, bundle the clothes in linen sacks and deliver them to the storage place for the duration of the patient's stay in the hospital. At discharge time, it was my duty to hand the bundle back to the patient.

My most difficult task was providing wood every day. Often there was no readily available cut or chopped wood. I had to saw the timber and chop it. It was hard work but I got used to it. After I became friendly with my coworkers, the doctors used to ask me to allow them to saw and chop wood as physical exercise. Here I found my place and I remained at it until the ghetto was liquidated.

There was no great diversity of entertainment to be had in the ghetto. Due to my hard work I did not participate much in the various events that did take place. I spent most of my free time talking with Ber Lewinson. He was much older than I and a walking medical encyclopedia of the last fifty years of the Jewish medical world in Vilna. Among the stories he told was how old medics used to "iron" the stomach of sick people with a warm iron. This was before there were any electric heaters or hot-water bottles. Another time he told me a story that I could not quite believe but he assured me was true: The ward of the mentally ill was once located on the second floor of the hospital. One day one of the patients wrapped himself in a white sheet, opened the window and decided to fly out. At the very moment he was throwing himself out of the window a peasant with a horse-drawn cart happened to drive by. Seeing that something white in the form of a human being or an angel was descending on him from above, the driver dropped dead on the spot. However it was never established if his death was due to fear or to the white body that fell on him. The mad patient was taken back to the hospital without any injury.

Lewinson also knew the details of the last days of Dr. Grigori Gierszuni, one of the most prominent and active Jewish doctors in Vilna. He was older than Lewinson, but for years they worked at the same hospital. Dr. Gierszuni was chairman of the doctors' union, chairman of the Zionist Organization, councilor of the Jewish Council in Vilna and the most important activist in the Moshav Zekeinim (old peoples' home) that had been built by the Jewish banker Israel Bunimowicz. After World War I, Dr. Gierszuni was chairman of the central office of sanitary works of the Jewish community. Together with the honorary secretary, Dr. Brocki, he helped restore the Medical Center of Jewish Communities around Vilna where I was the administrator. Dr. Gierszuni was a guest at my wedding.

He was over eighty years old when he entered the ghetto. A few days later his wife committed suicide. In the ghetto Gierszuni worked with the gifted surgeon, Dr. Solowejczyk. One night when they went to bed in their hospital room, some young Jewish scoundrels who were near the end of their medical studies broke in to their room. The scoundrels pulled the two doctors out of their beds, complaining: "You old ones can sleep throughout the day, we have to rise early in the morning to go to work. You can sleep on the floor." The two old physicians had to do as they were told. They never entered their room again. Several days later, Dr. Solowejczyk left the ghetto and Dr. Gierszuni committed suicide. His suicide reverberated in the ghetto. It was a shock to the community. Suicide! Dr. Gierszuni committed suicide!

Very few suicides happened in the ghetto. It was one of the things the Germans could not understand. They made no secret of their difficulty to understand this phenomenon: "You live in such extreme conditions," they used to say, "and you are not even able to commit suicide. Why?" But the fact was that no matter how much our situation worsened from day to day, our will to survive grew stronger and stronger. Under our living conditions, suicide was probably the easiest way out, but we did not seek death as the easy way out. We wanted to survive! Our heroism was to stay alive, to fight for it! We knew that the greatest defeat of the Germans lay in staying alive despite their terrible plots to destroy us.

We found out about the suicide of Dr. Gierszuni when we were still in the small ghetto. At the first meeting of the Judenrat and the advisory board in the small ghetto we paid tribute to that very dedicated man.

There was never an epidemic in the ghetto. It was a divine miracle on one hand and a result of the well-organized work of the epidemiology experts on the other. The two baths built in the ghetto functioned well and the constant series of lectures about hygiene and inspections produced good results.

However, the situation of Jewish workers in the working camps around Vilna was very bad indeed. Workers there succumbed to lice and dirt. I remember one particular case: A Jewish worker from the Rzesza Labor Camp was brought to the hospital with a high fever. The worker was literally as dark as rich soil. He reminded me of the cholera patients I saw during World War I. We put the patient in a bath to wash him and it took five baths of water to bring the patient back to the color of a normal human being. His clothes were overloaded with lice to the point that it was impossible to disinfect them and they had to be burned. We could not understand how the man could have walked around with his body infested with lice.

Naturally there were cases of death among the typhoid patients. One of them was a young artist named Simcha Lipowski. I received him when he arrived and carried him out of the ward after he died. The greatest number of patients passed through our wards during the winter months of 1941–42. By springtime, nearly all the patients had left the section. The last two patients of the observation wards were my own two children. When they left, the last ward of that section was closed.

Spending the whole day among the infectious patients I took particular care to avoid becoming infected. I was not afraid for myself, as I had caught spotted typhoid in 1918. I was especially careful for the sake of the family – but no one is stronger than fate and obviously I had to go through the test. At the very last moment, when the bout of typhoid was at its end it touched my family. Truth be told, it was no surprise – the opposite would have been surprising. Living so close to each other, it would have taken a miracle for my family to have not become infected.

Soon after Passover, my daughter broke down. She had a very high temperature and my friend, Dr. Kolodny ordered us to take her to the hospital immediately. It took a considerable effort to get her out through the hole of the hideout room where we were living. Not wanting to draw too much attention to her case, I took her under my arm and walked her to the hospital. Three days later she was diagnosed as suffering from three kinds of typhoid: para-, spotted- and abdominal typhoid. It was a very unusual case. A few days later my son became ill with high fever. He too was taken to the hospital and diagnosed with "only" two kinds of typhoid: para- and abdominal typhoid.

It was early springtime April 1942. The number of patients was diminishing daily and most were already after their crisis. Now, with my own worries about both children I was at the hospital day and night. My daughter's sickness took a very difficult turn. She kept talking deliriously in her state of high fever, running out of bed and behaving very strangely. She had to be constantly watched. We lived our own hell in hell until the crisis passed and we nursed the children back to reasonable health.

There are no sufficient words of gratitude to my colleagues for the help I received over this difficult time. They displayed more than help. They demonstrated their love, their loyalty and their empathy in my suffering.

The sanitary police drove everybody out of our dwelling and took us all to the baths. They thoroughly disinfected the whole dwelling. All soft material was taken for disinfecting. The people in the dwelling were not happy with all the bother that the sickness caused them but nothing stopped us from doing what had to be done. All necessary protective steps were taken. This was the way we kept the ghetto guarded from an epidemic and our case was no exception.

While my children were at the hospital, unconscious and with high fever, an incident took place that made me and the whole hospital staff feel that we were but a single step away from Ponary, or worse. A German medical commission arrived to inspect the hospital. Inwardly, we all became paralyzed with fear. The fear that the Germans might discover that patients with spotted fever were being secretly kept was beyond words. It might have been the end not only of the hospital but also of the ghetto. But outwardly we had to present a picture of hospital efficiency – and we managed it.

The whole hospital, and our section in particular, was extremely stressed, seeking ways to protect the hospital from disaster. Medical cards were prepared as best we could without disclosing the true state of things. On all beds the signs read *abdominalis* or *status febrilis*. The German commission spent a long time at the hospital and it was unending torture for us. Besides our own section there was another "illegal" ward – the women's natal ward. According to the German order, giving birth in the ghetto was strictly forbidden.

We received constant communication about where the commission was visiting, where they had left and where they were going. While they were in the main hospital we cleared out nearly all the patients that could be moved from our section. I helped and by the end I was left with only my own children – and the the German commission was approaching! Even now I cannot describe my feelings As for myself, I was resigned to whatever would happen but what would happen to the children, to the patients, to the hospital if the German medical officers should come? We thought of hiding the sick patients but it was too risky and too late. While the inspection went on, I was out of my mind with fear.

I was not alone in that feeling. The other workers were in a similar state – the case of the Kovno ghetto was at our doorstep. The only clear thought that I can recall was thinking of the irony that we managed to survive all the "cleansings" only to die in the hospital, the place dedicated to keeping people alive and to healing them.

But people can be stronger than iron. We braced ourselves and at last we received the information that the commission had left the hospital. The director and the head doctors had shown the commission all the other wards and sections and succeeded in avoiding our section.

How the news lifted our spirits! We cried with relief and embraced each other. I fell on the beds of my children and kissed them. They lay there unconscious, without realizing that they had just received the gift of life and the chance to recover.

During this disastrous war I survived many terrible and tragic moments. But the day of the hospital inspection remains engraved in my mind as my most difficult moment.

A few weeks after the German inspection we finally closed the observation wards. It was an occasion for a special celebration. We organized a "grand banquet" to which we invited the leaders of the ghetto Judenrat.

Political Tension in the Ghetto

During the winter months of 1942–43 the ghetto was living under great political tension. We followed the fierce battles around Stalingrad, going from total hope to total despair and back. We debated the daily news as if our deliverance would be right outside the ghetto gate and could reach us any day if we made the right decision. As time went on and the news about Stalingrad became clearer we felt as if a new spirit had been given to our tormented souls – this even before the final outcome of the German defeat became official.

We received general daily news from the workers returning from the city. But there were a few individuals who made politics their daily task and specialized in interpreting the rumors. These experts gathered every evening at the "News Exchange" located at a popular corner in the ghetto. The chief expert for news was Dr. Yaszpan. As the police physician Yaszpan knew a few things that others did not know. He used to leave the ghetto frequently and return with radio news. Dr. Yaszpan was a tall, slim man who stood out from the circle of listeners around him. His listeners drank in his words the way Hasidic followers hang on the words of their rebbe. He loved to repeat every bit of news a few times and when the news was encouraging he would repeat it even more than a few times. From the News Exchange his commentaries spread to ghetto homes where they turned to discussions and political arguments. Will Stalingrad survive the German onslaught – or will it not? Will Leningrad fall – or will it not? Will Moscow be taken – or will it not ? These were the discussions that continued into the night.

In our apartment behind the hole-in-the-wall we had our own expert, Abraham Kac, who worked at the railway. Every day he came back with a few frozen apples. He reported to us the number of trains and carriages that had passed through Vilna transporting frozen and badly wounded German soldiers back from the Russian front. He said that the stink in the carriages was so great that it could not have been wounded soldiers inside, but rotting bodies. His words, "rotting bodies," smelled in our nostrils like expensive French perfume. "The nurses," he told us, "would not let us come close to have a look at the German cadavers. They did not realize that we did not need to see them, the stink was quite satisfying…"

When the news arrived that the German army at Stalingrad had surrendered to the Red Army our joy was boundless. The three days of mourning that the Germans declared were for us a declaration of three days of joy and happiness. We greeted each other with "Mazel Tov" and wished ourselves to hear such news more often. The optimists interpreted the news as a sign of good luck. When asked what kind of luck this was they smiled: "When they will be busy in their own misery they will forget us." Others were superoptimists:

"Now the Germans will see the great mistake they made killing thousands of capable young Jews who would have been useful for their needs."

We began to live in hope of having already survived the worst. This lasted until the beginning of March, when disturbing signs began arriving from surrounding places of the total liquidation of the last Jewish communities around Vilna.

During the month of March, at the first signs of spring, Jews from the surrounding areas began arriving in Vilna. They were from the ghettos near the Byelorussian border: Swienciany, Oszmiany, Michaliszki and Sol. Soon after, the Judenrat informed the ghetto population that Jews from Kovno and those who had relatives in Kovno would be given an opportunity to return to Kovno. If they wished to do so they should register at the Judenrat. Some 340 people decided to take advantage of that opportunity and registered. Rumors of an imminent liquidation of the small ghettos spread like wildfire and the ghetto was again gripped in the clutches of uncertainty.

To stem the panic and quell the rumors, Gens clarified the situation toward the end of March. In the *Geto Yedies* of March 21 he informed the ghetto population that the District Kommissar for the Vilna area had ordered that the area outside Vilna be made "Judenrein" (cleansed of Jews). He wrote that this was the reason why Jews from the surrounding towns and villages had begun arriving in the Vilna Ghetto. The population of the four small ghettos near the Byelorussian border would eventually be settled partly in the Vilna Ghetto and partly in the Kovno Ghetto. Gens announced that the Judenrat of the Kovno ghetto was already preparing homes for the arriving Jews. In order that the transfer should take place "normally" and peacefully, the District Kommissar had authorized Gens to be in charge of it with the help of the Jewish police, but without any involvement of Lithuanian or even German forces. To do this, Gens and a group of Jewish police would travel to one destination and Dessler with another police group to a second destination. They would assemble all Jews with their belongings on two trains, one headed to Vilna and the other to Kovno. The Kovno train would stop in Vilna to receive the Jews who had registered to move back to Kovno. The train was scheduled to pass through Vilna on April 5, 1943.

To any questions or expressions of doubt came Gens's categorical answer: "I, Dessler and our own Jewish police will be in full charge of the whole operation." We preregistered the people who were to travel to Kovno in the quarantine office in order to care for them during the few days they were to stay with us.

Gens and Dessler left with two police units on April 3, 1943, and collected the small Jewish communities left in Swienciany, Sol, Michaliszki and Oszmiany. They brought together four thousand Jews, put them on two freight trains as arranged, locked the wagons from the outside as ordered, and brought the two trains to Vilna as Gens had promised.

Gens's train, carrying the Jews from Oszmiany, Michaliszki and Sol, arrived first and on time on the night of April 4. After attaching the cars with the Kovno passengers, the train left for Kovno with Gens and the Jewish police traveling in the first car. As soon as the train left the station Gens realized that their direction was not Kovno but – Ponary! And, indeed, the train stopped at Ponary. At the Ponary station Gestapo Officer Weiss met the train and took it over. He took Gens and his policemen to the offices of the Vilna Gestapo, where a very fine table full of the best food and drinks was already prepared for them. When Gens asked why he and the police had been taken away from the train, Weiss told Gens in a short sentence that the role of his police and his own role had come to an end and the Gestapo had taken over the train to lead it to Ponary. Gens and his police spent the night at the Gestapo. Early at dawn he was brought back to the Vilna station to await the arrival of the second train under the leadership of Dessler that carried the Jews from Swienciany.

As soon as the train arrived, Gens pulled Dessler, his police and members of the Swienciany Judenrat with their families from the train. When they started to ask questions he drove them away. At the last moment Gens unlocked the last two wagons of the train and chased the people out of the station. Germans and Lithuanians immediately surrounded the train. Several hours later it started on its way to "Kovno" and arrived at Ponary. After the arrival of the Swienciany train Gens and his police were taken back once more to the Gestapo. They were kept there until daylight and only then were they allowed to return to the ghetto. As soon as they entered the ghetto it became obvious from their faces that something terrible has happened. Within minutes, a new calamity overtook the hopes of the ghetto. Over four thousand young men, healthy, strong and full of life had been taken to the slaughter! Once more the Gestapo had managed to trick Gens and his police to help them bring the Jews to the slaughterhouse of Ponary.

The next day Weiss and his Gestapo officers came to the ghetto with a truck and collected twenty policemen. The ghetto trembled in fearful expectation, not knowing what the new disaster meant. The distraught residents had to wait until the police returned to learn the frightful news. Neither of the trains had arrived in Kovno. They were stopped at Ponary, the locked cars were opened in sequence and the groups of people from the opened cars were brought to the prepared pits, shot and thrown into the mass grave. The execution went on throughout the day.

Seeing what was going on and realizing that they were not in Kovno, the Jews in the locked cars began breaking the small barred windows, floors and ceilings of the cars. A few people managed to get out of their death trap and run. They did not get very far. Lithuanians and Germans who surrounded the place finished them off with their machine guns. Nonetheless, the resistance must have been quite intense, particularly when the cars were opened, as was evident by the bodies that were strewn over half a mile away.

The Gestapo had taken the Jewish police to collect the bodies and to throw them into the prepared pit. The Jewish police did their work. They collected the bodies, threw them into the pit, covered them with shovelfuls of lime and recited Kaddish (the prayer for the dead). Coming back to the ghetto they told their families the horrible secret. The secret didn't last very long and the worst terror ever befell the ghetto. Nothing that had befallen us before was comparable to the latest slaughter. For the first time the Germans showed their murderous intentions quite openly, as if to say, "look, this is what has been happening in Ponary where we have already slaughtered fifty thousand Jews and you know what this means to you."

Until the latest slaughter, the Gestapo and the "good" Germans did their best to assure us that those taken away were taken "to work." Now they had taken off their masks. It could only mean that those still alive would not be around as witnesses to the German's inhuman crimes.

The German part in the slaughter was now beyond any doubt – their intentions had become clear by their own admission. But a very dark and painful question remained as to the Jewish part in the killings. Did Gens know that the transports would end up at Ponary, or did the Germans manage to trick him? The ghetto did not know the true answer.

A few days later, on April 10, 1943, a meeting was called at the theater building. Gens was the only speaker. He said:

"I was told that in order to make the surrounding areas of Vilna Judenrein I was to collect the Jews remaining in the smaller towns and villages and concentrate them in the two ghettos of Vilna and Kovno. In our ghetto Hingst would not allow me to take in more than two thousand Jews from the province. The other five thousand Jews were to be absorbed by the Kovno ghetto. The Judenrat in Kovno knew about it and prepared dwellings for the Jews who were to arrive. I was also told to make a "small selection" of the old and the sick. Dessler and I were of the opinion that as the Germans had given us a choice, it would be better, in spite of all the difficulties, to carry out the operation by ourselves rather than let the Germans do it. We would bring two thousand Jews to our ghetto and the five thousand to Kovno. But then the tragedy happened. At the last moment the Gestapo told us that the District Kommissar of Kovno decided not to accept that many Jews. The Kommissar for the Vilna area would also not let any additional Jews enter our ghetto. The two trains with people remained with nowhere to go. Not to Vilna and not to Kovno and the Gestapo found a way out – to Ponary."

Was Gens's story true? Who can tell? Was it all just a tragic incident due to the change in Kovno, or had it all been planned in detail beforehand and staged? Whatever the case may be, this was Gens's version of the slaughter. The people left the hall in despair, hopeless, rejected and resigned. Under the evening sky we returned to our homes with thoughts much darker than the night above our heads.

A few days later, horse-drawn peasant carts drove in to the ghetto bringing food and many bloodied items that the Lithuanians had collected from the people they had murdered. They brought only rags and items they would not use themselves. Better items had been distributed to the Lithuanians and the peasants. The Gestapo sent the clothes as a "gift" for the needy Jews of the ghetto. The "gift" caused a very sharp conflict among the ghetto people. Some spoke up loud and clear that the ghetto was not allowed to accept the clothes under any circumstances. Others were of the opinion that we had to accept the clothes to show the Germans how great was the tragedy of the Jews in the ghetto. Gens said afterwards that we were forced by circumstances to accept the items in order not to show the Germans that we lived comfortably to the degree that we could forgo their "gift" of clothes and food.

As the carts drove along Rudnicka Street, Jews stood on the sidewalks and cried bitterly. At the same time, other Jews ran to the carts and grabbed loaves of bread and pots of butter. Some of the people who snatched the pots did it not for the butter or fat that was in them but to look inside to see if the pots contained gold coins or jewelry.

We had believed that we were immunized against any shock the Germans could perpetrate against us, but the slaughter of five thousand Jews haunted us for days. Rumor had it that some of the Jewish policemen who participated in the "cleansing" had profited by accepting payments from the Jews they herded into the trains.

The Wittenberg Tragedy

On Friday, July 16, 1943, the people in our apartment, numbering about forty souls, were awakened earlier than usual. From the legal part of our apartment, that is, from the other side of the hole in the cupboard, we heard that the ghetto, was "not quiet." Within minutes we were all dressed. All tables, chairs and passages that we normally used for the night were immediately cleared away. The bedding was packed up and one by one we slid through the hole into the front room. Under the circumstances it was not quite the right thing to do but we did it. Passing through the cupboard into the front room I asked Haim Bakaturski, the owner of the place, "What is going on?" His reply was louder than usual: "How would I know? The police are running around like poisoned rats, they are searching and seeking…"

"Seeking what, or whom?" I asked.

This time the answer came from Mrs. Kac: "They are searching for a Communist."

Her husband, the tall Abraham who came to live with us after the "cleansing" in December 1941 helped out: "Yes, that's it, a Communist. As if we don't have enough trouble from the Germans, we need additional trouble from Communists to speed up our end…"

I could see that I would not learn much from the conversation. As this was not a Gestapo or Lithuanian raid I decided to go out and find out for myself what was going on. I went through our courtyard to what used to be the second courtyard of the building. The highest echelon of the ghetto, people like Fried, Milkonowicki, Braude and Dessler, had their apartments at that address. At the second courtyard everything was normal. Nobody was around and the place was as quiet as a cemetery. Moving further in the courtyard I came across a few people and police running to the police command.

The first part of the courtyard was always full of noise. Here were many of the workshops and the sawmill. Many policemen lived here. It was still very early and everything was closed. I went out from the courtyard into the street and came face to face with a ghetto that was wide awake. The noisy morning was nothing unusual. People were hurrying to their columns on the way to work outside the ghetto. But something was different from the usual early morning movement. Police kept running in all directions but nobody seemed to know what the disturbance was.

Suddenly I noticed a sight that was most unusual in the ghetto. A young man, short but well built was running. He was wearing elegant high boots like those of an officer, the short coat he was wearing was clean, well fitting and – he had a revolver in his hand. I was confused. In the streets of the ghetto with a revolver?! Who is he? And what is it all about?

I asked the group of people watching, like me, full of curiosity. Somebody knew the answer: "It's Henekhke Szapiro. Before the war he was an agent for the Polish political secret police. Later he became an agent for the Soviet NKVD. Now he cooperates with the police and works for the Gestapo…"

But none of us knew what it was all about. Based on past experience we felt that whatever was going on was not to our benefit. We intuitively sensed that something dangerous was going on, but we had no idea of its nature.

Seeing that the ghetto had not become filled with Gestapo or Lithuanians I remained calm. Obviously it was something of an internal character. And if it was an internal matter, I was willing to let Gens and his police handle it. They knew what they had to do.

From short pieces of gossip I caught as I moved around, I learned that it had something to do with a Communist. The police were looking for a Communist whose surrender the Gestapo had demanded. The Communist had been arrested late the previous evening but his comrades had managed to rescue him from the hands of the police. Now the police were trying to find him.

With that knowledge I went back to the apartment to calm the people who were waiting anxiously for some clear information. I calmed them by telling them that the ghetto was not surrounded. I told them it was some internal ghetto matter and said: "I can assure you that Gens and his police will know how to deal with it."

The people in the apartment became calmer but remained ready for any eventuality. I left them and went out once more to satisfy my curiosity and settle my nerves. Before long the story was circulating in the streets that the Gestapo demanded that the Judenrat hand over a Jewish Communist who was denounced to the Gestapo by a Lithuanian member of his own party outside the ghetto. The name of the Lithuanian was Kozlowski and he told the Gestapo that he was in contact with a Jewish Communist from the ghetto, by the name of Wittenberg. Now the Gestapo was demanding that Wittenberg be delivered into their hands alive.

There was not the least insinuation in the German demand that Wittenberg might be a leader of a Communist cell in the ghetto or part of a Jewish underground organization in the ghetto. As far as the Gestapo was concerned Wittenberg was a Communist in contact with the Communist organization in Vilna and they wanted him alive in order to learn more about Communist activity in Vilna.

Did the Germans know, or did they even suspect that an underground might exist in the ghetto? I am sure that they had no such idea!

Had they known or suspected such a possibility, they would have surely demanded that Gens also surrender the other leaders of the organization. We could be sure that Gens and his police would have fulfilled the demand in the name of "saving the ghetto." Especially as Gens had his own informers and knew the leaders of the various organizations that were active inside the ghetto walls. I am convinced that the Germans knew nothing about a secret Jewish organized underground; they only knew about a Jewish Communist who had contact with Communists outside the ghetto. When in the end they got the man they wanted they considered the matter closed.

Did the Jews in the ghetto know about the existence of an underground? The general population of the ghetto had no knowledge of it. An underground organization does not advertise itself to the public until, in the eyes of the underground, the time is ripe to take action. The existence of the United Partisan Organization became known in the ghetto only later as a result of what happened with Wittenberg. Gens and Dessler had been aware of the existence of the UPO since its founding in early 1942. It included members of all the youth organizations active in the Vilna Ghetto. Throughout the first year of its existence, the UPO was no threat to Gens and the ghetto administration did not interfere with its activities. By mid-1943, however, when the UPO intensified its activities and groups of UPO members left the ghetto to join with the partisan groups in the Vilna forests, Gens felt that the organization was endangering the stability of his "work to live" philosophy. He was particularly incensed when he realized that a number of ghetto police members, supporters of Yosef Glazman, the highly respected deputy commander of the UPO were involved. On June 25, 1943, he ordered the arrest of Yosef Glazman and his deportation to the Rzesza Labor Camp. This was the price Glazman paid for his integrity and courage in opposing Gens and his policies.

And, as if to continue the purge, on June 27, 1943, Dessler, the chief of police issued an order dismissing eleven members of the police force and reassigned a number of others to lower level positions. All of them were members of the UPO. After the Rzesza camp was liquidated, Glazman returned to the ghetto. He was a truly heroic figure and the voice of conscience in the Vilna Ghetto.

But for the moment the UPO was not under investigation. The Germans were not aware of its existence and were only demanding that Gens hand over a Jewish Communist to them. The pervading attitude in the ghetto was: "It's a pity to have to deliver a Jew into the hands of the Gestapo. It was obvious that if they asked to hand him over alive, they were not going to immediately put him up against the wall and shoot him. They would surely torture him first. But didn't he bring it all on himself? Why should the ghetto hold back and bring about its own end? If the man wanted to do Communist work, that was his business but he should have left the ghetto . Do what you want – but on the other side of the ghetto gate."

Gens made good use of the psychological state of the people in the ghetto. After all, he and his people were doing the "good work" to save the ghetto from the current danger by searching for Wittenberg. Gens was still under the illusion that the ghetto might survive and refused to see the signs of the approaching end. And so did the ghetto population, which was clinging to every German defeat on the eastern front and in Italy and ignored the fact that all of the Vilna district had been made Judenrein and that the noose around the ghetto was tightening.

The chase after Wittenberg went on for hours. The whole ghetto felt involved in the chase but the only ones who felt harnessed to the cause were Gens's people: the police, provocateurs, underworld characters and chimneysweeps. They were the privileged.

Perhaps if the ghetto population had been aware that the chase was not after a "Communist" as the Gestapo maintained, but after the leader of the United Partisan Organization which existed in the ghetto, the ghetto population would have been less indifferent. But the population was not aware and quickly made peace with the thought of handing over a Jew to the Gestapo.

However, this was only one side of the tragedy. There was another side to it. When Wittenberg, commander of the UPO, was denounced by the Lithuanian and the Gestapo demanded his surrender alive, the United Partisan Organization had several options.

First of all, after freeing Wittenberg from the hands of the Jewish police, he could have been spirited out of the ghetto and sent to the forests to join the partisans. Secondly, Wittenberg could have committed suicide. Thirdly, as commander of the United Partisan Organization, Wittenberg could have proclaimed an immediate uprising in the Vilna Ghetto. All three options were considered and rejected. Escaping from the ghetto would have left the ghetto open to the Gestapo's demand and retaliation. A similar consequence would have resulted from his committing suicide when the Gestapo demanded Wittenberg alive. The third option of proclaiming an immediate uprising in the ghetto was thoroughly discussed. In fact, immediately after Wittenberg's release from the Jewish police he did proclaim a mobilization of all UPO forces but after long and painful discussions the organization decided against it. A revolt at this juncture would mean armed struggle against Jews: Gens and his people. In addition, it was doubtful whether the general ghetto population would give its total support. By deciding against an uprising the United Partisan Organization forgot that it was formed for the purpose of proclaiming a general revolt when the ghetto was on the brink of liquidation – for unlike Gens, the UPO had no illusion that the ghetto was close to its end.

On July 16, 1943, the committee of the Communist Party in the Vilna Ghetto decided that Wittenberg should give himself up. The leadership of the United Partisan Organization reached a similar decision independently. Both decisions were communicated to Wittenberg and the final decision was left to him. Hearing the decision of the combined fighting leadership Wittenberg asked: " Is it really possible? Is it true?" and added, " There has never been a case when a movement gave up its leader to the enemy, unless the movement was morally bankrupt…" Wittenberg's objection was not out of fear of death. Rather, Wittenberg feared the demoralizing effect of the decision on the fighting organization and on the ghetto population. As a disciplined member of the organization Wittenberg decided to give himself up. He had a choice. The decision was his and he could have decided otherwise. But he did not. In that decision lay his greatness and his tragedy.

On that fateful day, June 16, 1943, I was at my work in the infirmary (my new position). My co-worker Chyena Borowska, a well-known Communist activist, did not come to work that day. I knew Chyena from earlier days as a leader of the Union of Workers of the Medical Profession in Vilna to which I belonged as a pharmacist. We used to meet at sessions of the committee where she was considered to be a very prominent member of the administrative hierarchy. Working together in the ghetto we were on friendly terms. She was a quiet and tactful person.

On the day of the Wittenberg tragedy she did not come to work. She was deeply engaged in the deliberations of the ghetto Communists regarding the Wittenberg affair. The happenings in the ghetto reverberated in many ghetto institutions. Attendance at the infirmary was very low, so I went home earlier than usual to meet my children who came from their workshops. We walked into the front part of our apartment and were just ready to slide through the hole in the cupboard when something in the front window attracted my attention.

The window of the front apartment faced the courtyard and the gate of the building led to a street outside the ghetto. The gate was always locked and we assumed that only Gens had the keys to the lock. Standing by the window, hidden from sight, we noticed two policemen running through the large courtyard. At the same time we saw the agent provocateur Henekhke Szapiro and Dreizin the policeman. They were walking not more than three feet apart. Behind them walked a man of middle height in a dark suit with a small parcel under his arm. I recognized the man to be Wittenberg. Behind him walked Gens with a revolver in his hand. Behind him walked Salek Dessler and Oberhart. They were placed like the number five on playing cards. We watched in shock and fascination as they passed in front of us and went toward the building gate. We heard the unlocking of the gate and after a short while we saw them walking back, all but Wittenberg. From the third room in our hideout, the one that faced the outside of the ghetto, they informed us that a Gestapo car that stood outside the gate had driven away. By sheer coincidence we were the only people who saw the last steps of Wittenberg and the final moments of the tragedy. The following morning Itzhak Wittenberg was found dead in his Gestapo cell. He committed suicide by taking a cyanide pill that was, in all probability, given to him by Gens.

CHAPTER 12

The Liquidation of the Large Ghetto

The Beginning of the End

On Friday, August 6, 1943, at about ten in the morning, the ghetto exploded with the news that the Porobanek Airfield close to Vilna had been surrounded and all Jewish workers, numbering about one thousand people, had been taken away. In the more than one and a half years since the last large "cleansing" of December 1941, we had become used to minor tremors such as the taking of the one hundred elderly people to Ponary, or the night raid that had been assumed to have been organized by the Judenrat. We had learned to live with the "incidents" as part of our "normal" life. Even the latest cataclysm that had taken the lives of five thousand people had been accepted, as Gens had explained, as a disaster that happened at the last moment and nobody could have foreseen it. But a raid on one thousand workers with yellow documents after one and a half years of "normal" existence shook the ghetto like the "cleansing" raids of the ghetto's early days. It did not take more than an hour before we learned that the same thing had taken place at another large German working place, Beute-Sammelstele, where a few hundred young and healthy Jews had been working for the last twenty-two months. Within another two to three hours we learned that Jewish workers everywhere had been "taken" from their working places.

The narrow, dark streets of the ghetto became overrun with people. Workers from the workshops inside the ghetto left their work places. Women whose husbands had left in the morning to work in the city ran into the streets believing they could learn something. The men whose wives had gone out in the morning to work in the city did the same. The ghetto population congregated in the courtyard of the Judenrat to find out what was going on.

The shock of the sudden "taking" of people with yellow documents was particularly frightening as it came after a rumor had been going around for

some days that the German government had ordered the Gestapo to stop killing Jews. We had believed that rumor (because we wanted to believe it) and
then this new disaster exploded before our eyes.

"Our time has come," was heard repeatedly. "Now they are taking the last
drops of blood still left in us." It was the voice of the last twenty thousand Jews
crying in the wilderness of the ghetto streets. Panic-stricken people crowded
about, their faces filled with questions but without hope of any answers. The
largest group gathered outside the office of the ghetto representative, in the
hope that he might know something. But he too did not know much.

The workers "snatched" from their working places were assembled at the
railway-yard awaiting the train that was to take then to their new "working
place." Many did not believe that and tried to run away. They were shot on
the spot. The Germans had difficulty understanding why the workers did not
believe them. But the past perfidies of the Germans had been endless. When
for once they told the truth – they could no longer be believed.

Hours passed in turmoil before we heard the first calming rumor that the
people had been taken to Estonia and not to Ponary. Who started the rumor or
how it came into the ghetto no one knew. It was a rumor like many hundreds
of others had been before. Nobody knew at the time that this one was not just
a rumor – but true.

The people snatched from their working places were taken to the train just
as they were. They were loaded into cattle cars and transported to Estonia. They
were sure they were being taken to Ponary. A little later when the rumor about
work was confirmed to be true the ghetto had its own difficulty to work it all
out. If the Germans really needed people to work, why did they do it in such
a brutal way? They could have ordered the ghetto representative to organize
whatever number of people they needed. Gens had always given the Gestapo
the number of people it wanted for Ponary, surely he would have carried out
their order for people this time when they were needed for work in Estonia.
We could not understand.

At last, after many hours, Gens returned from town and confirmed that
the people were sent to Estonia and not Ponary. He appealed to the people

to calm down since Jews had been sent to work camps – to life, not to death. Some Jewish foremen had been sent with them and the Germans had given Gens their assurance that in a few days those foremen would return with handwritten letters from those who had been sent to Estonia. Though the word of Gens was not fully believed the situation calmed down a little. The ghetto still buzzed like a beehive but the total despair had given way to "let's wait and see…"

At Gens's request a few Germans entered the ghetto at evening time to a special meeting of the brigadiers. The Germans asked that people be patient and calm as the workers had been sent to Estonia to work. "Nothing bad will happen to them," the German speaker calmly assured the listeners. "In a few days the foremen will return and bring letters. After their return it will be possible to send parcels of clothing, underwear and food to the workers. The main thing is not to be nervous and have patience," the "good" Germans calmed the ghetto, giving their word of honor.

Believing or not believing, it didn't make any difference. There was nothing we could do but wait. And we waited for the return of the foremen.

But the inner voice of experience could not be silenced. Would they really return? And would they really bring letters from the deported? People walked around like shadows for the next day. Hardly did we speak our doubts in words but our eyes spoke more than the words we held back. Men, women, children and old people whose near ones had suddenly been torn away streamed in the ghetto streets. One had to be harder than iron or completely without conscience to be calm during those days of waiting. But once again, the ghetto Jews showed their strength and waited.

On Wednesday, August 11, the ghetto was awakened to life once more. The news spread like wildfire throughout the ghetto that the foremen had returned and had been led to the office of the ghetto representative. The courtyard of the Judenrat overflowed with people. Everybody talked at once, impatiently waiting to see the foremen with their own eyes. At last they appeared and managed to say only: "All are alive! The workers were taken to Vaivara in Estonia! They are staying there and working."

When they lifted the parcels of letters they had brought back pandemonium erupted. People pushed, screamed and fought each other to be first to reach the foremen and see the letters written by their near and dear ones with their own eyes. The police had a hard time holding back the great mass of people.

The general wording of the letters was very similar: 'We are alive and we hope to stay alive…. Please send clothes and warm underwear as the area has a sea climate and the winds are cold. Food is scarce.' The wording of one letter went from mouth to mouth: "We are alive!" People calmed down a little. "Let it be Vaivara but let it be life. We Jews are used to 'oy vei' – it is the right name as long as it is not Ponary."

People started to prepare large packs of bedding, clothes, underwear and food – all that they could afford.

Gens announced that whoever wanted to could travel to join the people already there and take with them all their belongings. A number of people signed up as volunteers. At the end of the month Gens announced that the Germans were demanding a new transport of a few thousand workers for Estonia. He proposed that people should sign up voluntarily. However in spite of his assurances, there were not too many volunteers. Since the first euphoria when the foremen returned, people had learned a few things about Vaivara that were not very encouraging. The news was that the work was very hard and food scarce, the climate was difficult for the people of Vilna, so the result was that not many volunteered to leave the ghetto. Gens sent out letters demanding that the families who already had members in Estonia should leave the ghetto and travel to join their relatives in Vaivara. The letter caused a storm in the ghetto. A few young people volunteered to go, because someone had written in his letter that "Uncle Josef" (meaning Stalin) lived not far away and it would be possible to meet him. The interpretation was that the front there was nearer than to Vilna.

However, the few volunteers did not make up the thousands that the Germans demanded. People began to worry what the end result would be, how the Gestapo would react.

They did not have to wait very long. On Wednesday, September 1, 1943, the ghetto awakened to the news that the new Gestapo officer in charge of ghetto matters, Bruno Kittel, had entered the ghetto with a group of Germans and Estonians and was taking people to send to Estonia. During the few hours Kittel and his soldiers worked in Rudnicka Street they had managed to get hold of one hundred people, without regard to the position the individuals had in the ghetto hierarchy. So far none of the people sent to Estonia were from the establishment or the skilled working class. Seeing what was happening, and wanting to prevent the loss of the privileged labor class, Gens suggested to Kittel that he should give him a few days and he and the Jewish police would deliver the required number of people. Kittel agreed and left the ghetto together with his soldiers.

Gens immediately began to carry out his task. This time the ordinary police was not enough. He quickly organized an auxiliary police command comprised of members of the "*die shtarke*" (the "Tough Ones") who still remained in the ghetto. They undertook to find the hideouts on condition that they would not be sent to Estonia.

The entire Jewish population knew about the defeats that the Germans had suffered one after another on all eastern fronts. They knew that the end of the Germans was very near and it was only a matter of enduring for a short time. Some time earlier, people had begun to prepare better hiding places for the duration. They were built for longer-term survival. They were underground apartments that the Germans would never have found. Some were constructed in basements with an exit outside the ghetto. Electricity was taken directly from underground cables. Water installations and sanitary piping were connected to the city grid. Food, light and radios were stored. The hideouts were constructed to allow people to stay in comfort for months if need be. The entrances to such placed were most ingenious – through false toilets, under mobile stoves, even under a floorboard held in place by nails that could be removed in seconds.

But all these clever hideouts had been built against the Germans. For the Jewish "*shtarke*" that ran around like poisoned rats, the hideout might as well not have existed. They knew every trick and every place and they were giving it all away to the ghetto representative for the price of saving themselves and their families.

Our hideout was good because we had an exit to the outside. We had also added a new part by lifting the floor and reaching a cellar underneath. In the cellar we had provided only a large barrel of water. It was primitive when compared to other hiding places but it was sufficiently secure.

Gens called a large open meeting in the courtyard of the Judenrat. Together with his adjutants, he spoke to the people from the balcony of the building telling them that they would all have to travel to Estonia to work. He stated that there would not be any exceptions and that no one would be protected. Several times he stressed that this time hiding would be totally futile because his police force would find all hideouts and the people in them would be punished; they would have to leave as they would be found. On the other hand, volunteers would be able to take their clothes, linen, food and underwear.

The people listened to Gens, knowing that they had to make a decision. The only thing that was clear to the listeners was that the speaker, the police and their near ones would not be going voluntarily to Estonia. At the end of the nice speech of the ghetto representative the people decided that it would be healthier to hide. I did the same.

We went down to our underground cellar together with a considerable number of other people, leaving the apartment and all its contents ownerless, free for the taking. After a few hours in the living grave we learned that the police were dragging men out of their hideouts but women were left in peace. Hearing this, our women left the cellar-grave and moved back to protect the apartment. While in our hideout we heard reports about the Germans blowing up houses in Straszuna Street and about shots that were fired at the Germans. Many people died in the explosions and under the ruins.

This went on Wednesday, Thursday and Friday, September 1–3, 1943. By Friday it was observed that there were still too few people for Kittel's satisfaction. Gens found a way. He went to the Jewish hospital and drove out the sick, the doctors, nurses and pharmacists, leaving just a few in the wards. With a revolver in his hand he chased the hospital staff to the gate of the ghetto without letting them collect anything. Seeing what went on, many people started moving to the gate without being forced. My son and I, and the others in the cellar, remained in hiding. But soon after our hideout was denounced by a woman who had been with us. After she left her male friend was taken away, and she denounced us in the hope that her friend would be released. Police arrived with a detailed plan of our hideout and told us to come out as they intended to throw in grenades. Listening to the frightful screams of our women, we went out. The police took us to a collecting point. At the last moment my daughter convinced the police to release my son and me, promising that we would go voluntarily the next day. The artist Sasha Kremer was also released with us. The police were less generous to the others. They took away Haim Bakaturski, Abraham Kac, Szkolnik and several other of our hideout residents.

The next day, Saturday, the hunting game changed. Men were left in peace and women were driven to the gate. We hid my wife and daughter together with other women while we remained in the apartment to guard them. This was the fourth day of the frantic joint police-auxiliary police activity. Just before the raid was terminated, Gens called the auxiliary-police together, thanked them for their "faithful" work and sent them away to Estonia as a reward.

On Saturday night it was announced that the raid had come to an end.

People left their hideouts and filled the streets for a breath of air. The appearance of the ghetto was dreadful. The place looked like it had been through a pogrom. Furniture had been broken and thrown into the middle of the streets; everything was upside-down. The people looked white as ghosts, pale from lack of food and sleep.

As soon as the raid was over many people ran to the empty houses and cleaned out whatever they found. Many policemen joined in the robbery. Some of them had also made considerable fortunes during the four days, releasing people from deportation for payments in the form of currency, gold and jewelry. They became rich with goods soaked in Jewish blood and tears. During the days of the police raid Kittel spent a considerable time in the ghetto. He walked around its lanes and courtyards, watching how the Jewish police raid was progressing.

After the raid, we learned about the events at Straszuna Street. An armed group of the United Partisan Organization had holed up with its arms cache at 6 Straszuna Street. Gens and his police, who were aware of the group and maintained contact with them, were afraid to go there and left the group in peace. They even provided them with food for a considerable time. During the first day of the "cleansing," a group of Germans passed the building of 15 Straszuna, called for the people in the building to come out and when they didn't, they blew it up. They then passed 12 Straszuna, where a smaller UPO group was located, and the Germans fired at it. When the UPO returned fire the Germans blew up the building. Yehiel Szeinbaum, the commander of the Jewish forces at 12 Straszuna, was killed instantly. Others managed to disperse. Another version circulating in the ghetto, which may or may not have been true, was that after the shooting at 12 Straszuna it was Gens who gave the order to destroy the building in order to prevent any future clashes between the UPO and the Germans.

During the four days of the raid, five thousand Jews were sent to Estonia. On Sunday, September 5, the ghetto was free once more. The streets were full of people again but there was now much more space. Thousands of ghetto dwellers had left their rooms and their dwellings stood empty. Very few workers still went out to work, the price of food became astronomical and bread was difficult to obtain. During all the time that the ghetto had existed the price of a loaf of bread had been around forty to fifty rubles; now the same loaf went up to one hundred rubles and more. The many thousands who had been working for the Germans and Lithuanians in the city were now walking around unemployed. Only the workshops inside the ghetto were still working and their income was a drop in the ocean compared to the needs of the ghetto. People kept asking: "How long can such a situation continue? The Germans are certainly not going to keep feeding us at their own expense." We were expecting something to happen, but what that something was, no one knew.

The Germans did not keep us in suspense long. On Monday evening, September 13, the ghetto was rocked to its foundations: Gens had been taken to the Gestapo!

Although Gens used to visit the Gestapo from time to time, whenever there was official business he usually sent his deputy, Dessler. This time, however, he was asked to report to the Gestapo headquarters together with Dessler. In addition to the tremor of his arrest came the information that before he left his home he said to his mother: "If I don't return home for the night, don't wait for me any longer."

It is hard to describe what this single act meant to the ghetto. Gens has been taken to the Gestapo? Gens?! The only conclusion in the ghetto was that this was either the end of the ghetto, or there was something brewing in which he was to play some special role that the ghetto should not know about before the Gestapo initiated it. That evening, the shocked ghetto population forgot about the front, about politics or about food. The only subject of the evening was Gens.

The next morning Dessler, who returned the previous evening from the Gestapo, informed people waiting outside the offices of the Judenrat that he knew nothing about Gens. By that time there were people who already knew that a day or two earlier Gestapo officer Weiss had warned Gens that he would be arrested and had advised Gens to disappear. Gens had rejected the advice.

On Tuesday, September 14, the day after Gens's arrest, Kittel appeared at the offices of the Judenrat in the company of another officer. He ordered an immediate assembly of the Jewish police at the coffeehouse where they used to meet. There, Kittel told them that Gens had been shot because he had not fulfilled the demand of the higher German authorities. Kittel also announced that until another ghetto representative would be appointed, Dessler would act in the capacity of the ghetto representative. (Two weeks later when we were already in the sealed train on our way to Estonia, we got more of the story from a man named Woron who was in the wagon with us. In the ghetto he was one of the successful businessmen who dealt with their "good" Germans. Woron ended up in the Gestapo jail. He told the people in the sealed wagon that one evening he together with other prisoners had been ordered to bury some important ghetto personality. He believed that the body they had buried was that of Gens.)

The Jewish police left the assembly bewildered, frightened and lost. How could Gens have been shot?! Gens – their god, their bread giver – shot?! Kittel's announcement became known in the ghetto within minutes and people were at a loss to understand it. Was this the death knell of the ghetto, or was this a shot at the man who had dealings with the Gestapo and knew too much?

The police, of course, were the most affected by Kittel's announcement. Had the Jewish ghetto police been told that the whole of the ghetto was to be liquidated and only Gens and they would be left, they would have followed their master's order to the end. Had they not followed Gens's orders obediently and sent thousands and thousands of people to Ponary? Had they not just finished four days of slavery on Gens's orders and sent five thousand Jews to Estonia? They had done it all to save their master and themselves and what was the result? If this was the end of Gens, what could they expect?

In the afternoon the police organized a memorial service at the *Katzevisher* ("butchers") prayer house. The rabbi began his sad oration with the words: "We have no father." After the rabbi's speech, Solomon Gens, Jacob's brother, led the congregation in the evening prayer and recited Kaddish. Muszkat the police inspector gave the closing speech. Throughout the whole time of the memorial service Salek Dessler stood at the foot of the center podium with his bent head leaning on the brass walls surrounding it. Not once did he lift his eyes. He gave the impression that either his conscience was not clear – or he was trembling for his own fate, knowing that he was now next in line.

The mood of the ghetto was more depressed than at any other time. It was as if a dark cloud hovered over us, covering all, obstructing even the tiniest ray of light. Very little was debated. One silent question gnawed at us: "What will the next day bring?"

The fear that death was only one step away was reflected in the eyes of the people roaming the now half-desolate streets of the ghetto. It was more than a feeling – we knew that we were condemned, but how could we get out of the situation? Where was I to go now with an old mother, a wife and two young children? The worst of it was that with all our senses we saw death approaching and we had no escape. Together with my wife, my daughter and I racked our brains asking ourselves and each other what could be done…

Our only comfort during these agonizing days was the news from the eastern front. The German reports did not tell the full story of how badly they were being mauled and decimated on all fronts. But from slips or hints we learned that the beginning of their end had already begun. There was no longer talk about taking Moscow, or about reaching Leningrad. They had lost Stalingrad many months earlier and that had become a reason why the front at Smolensk, six hundred miles to the west, had to be shortened.

News did not reach us as it used to when thousands of workers were in the city every day but we knew enough to realize that we must play for time as much as possible. Taking one day at a time was our only hope. Maybe a miracle would occur and the Germans would suddenly collapse! This was our only hope.

Tense days followed. When we were already fully resigned and almost ready to give up, a new turmoil awakened the few thousand people who remained in the ghetto: "They are taking people to HKP."

HKP was a large German company that used to repair cars, machines and armaments. The workshops of HKP were spread all over Vilna, and Jews used to work there. But since the new law forbade Jews to work in the city, hundreds of workers who had been employed at HKP remained in the ghetto without work. Now we were told that HKP was opening a large shop in Subocz Street, in a housing project built in 1904 by a Franco-Jewish philanthropist to provide accommodation for Jewish workers. A few hundred workers and their families would be leaving the ghetto to live in the apartments of HKP in the same way that Kailis workers lived. The ghetto offices of the works department began to register workers and everybody was ready to move over. But, as usual, those who went were those who could buy their transfer.

This went on for a few days. On Saturday, September 18, Gestapo Officer Kittel appeared in the ghetto with a few trucks and declared that he immediately needed a few hundred workers for the workshop. At first a few hundred registered individuals came forward. But when Kittel showed no desire to take those who had registered, something made the people suspicious about Kittel and his needs. Later, when the police called on those registered (who had paid the police for the favor) to come forward, no one responded. Now Kittel ordered the new ghetto representative, B. Biniakonski, to collect the registered workers by force.

Once more the police began their mad rush to collect people. A new panic broke out but it didn't last very long. Kittel let the people who had been collected by force return to their homes. Nobody understood what it all meant. The only conclusion that we may now make (many years after the event) is that Kittel read the confusion that the death of Gens had caused to the ghetto. Having already planned its total liquidation, his intention was to leave us in a state of uncertainty in order to prevent any cohesive resistance. There is no other explanation.

Kittel walked around the ghetto, most of the time by himself, He walked around and talked to the women, who asked him: "Sir Kittel, please take me to HKP." As if talking to children he would reply: "Not today. Today it is only men but your time will come as well." Yes, their time would come too… "Sir Kittel" was in a light mood and spoke with anybody who approached him. After several hours he left the ghetto. The representatives of the Judenrat had disappeared like rats leaving a sinking ship. For two years these "representatives" lived at the ghetto's expense and now when the ghetto came to its final moments and needed coherent leadership, the leadership was absent.

The Liquidation of the Ghetto

At 2:00 p.m., September 18, the ghetto had a new sensation: Salek Dessler, the man who acted as the supreme contact between the ghetto and the Gestapo, had run away together with his wife and family. Detailed information reached us that Dessler's wife had left the ghetto with a small suitcase in her hand and her husband followed soon after. Sources at the office of the Judenrat informed us that before fleeing Dessler removed from the Judenrat safe many thousands of rubles in gold and diamonds. It was also confirmed that a few hours earlier Salek Dessler's wife and father had left the ghetto. Obviously the end of the ghetto was very close.

Bit by bit there were more revelations. The Desslers had not been the only ones to abandon the ghetto during the last hours. A number of people who had ruled the ghetto with their iron fists for two years also ran away.

The commandant of the gate police, the infamous Meir Levas, with his wife and father-in-law, also ran. So did Chief Prosecutor Czeslaw Nusbaum-Altaszewski (a former editor of the major newspaper *Republika* in Lodz, Poland). The ghetto was leaderless and in the grip of despair.

During the last few nights, groups of young people also left the ghetto to join the partisans in the forests. Many people who had friends among the Gentile population went to hide with them. Others managed to be received at Kailis or the HKP but for the rest of us, numbering about twelve thousand people, there was no escape. Nowhere to hide and nowhere to run. We had to drink the poisoned chalice to the end.

In the leaderless ghetto everything became surreal. A loaf of bread reached the astronomical sum of 250 rubles, or 25 marks. Butter and meat were still available – at exorbitant prices. The Lithuanian *Rute* shops responsible for delivering the official rations of 120 grams of bread per head smuggled in large amounts of bread illegally for very high profits.

Except for the Jews who were living in Kailis buildings and those who had managed to secure a place at HKP, no one was allowed to work in the city any longer. The days dragged on like endless eternities as we waited for the final explosion that had to come. The Germans knew how to destroy our will to resist by letting us wait; they knew we could not escape.

In the workshops things still appeared normal. The workers went on with their work. All other ghetto institutions were like ships without rudders. The hospital and the infirmary presented the picture of starving skeletons in their last hours. The doctors, nurses and pharmacists had been sent by Gens to Estonia in his last attempt to "save the ghetto." Nothing was operating any longer.

But who needed institutions now, what for? We were all waiting for the last fall of the axe. After three days we heard that on Tuesday night, September 21, there was to be a meeting of the ghetto council. The new ghetto representative Biniakonski together with, Milkonowicki, Fried, Guchman, Solomon Gens and

Fiszman were to meet to review the situation. The meeting took place. The decision of the meeting was that the leaders of the council should each take a new pair of high boots, warm underwear and appropriate clothing from the workshops.

On Thursday, September 23, we were awakened at 5:00 a.m. by screams coming from outside our apartment: "The ghetto is surrounded!" We jumped out of our sleeping places and within minutes we were running to the courtyard at 6 Rudnicka. The ghetto was already wide awake. The Jewish police were running around as if they had lost their heads, totally confused. Through a slit in the boarded-up windows that looked out beyond the ghetto we saw a military patrol walking up and down along the street speaking in Ukrainian.

People started gathering voluntarily at the courtyard of the Judenrat. Police went from house to house asking people to gather at the courtyard where an important announcement would be made very soon. This time it was clear that there was nothing more to be lost. There was no need to convince people that this was the end. Without putting it to a vote, the population accepted that what had to be might as well be now. There was no more energy, no more nerves or patience to keep on fighting. Half-resigned and half-dead, we assembled in the courtyard across from the balcony of Dessler's residence. Kittel appeared on the balcony together with Biniakonski, the new ghetto representative and Lakner, Murer's replacement as well as a representative of the District Kommissar. The representative of the District Kommissar began reading from a prepared paper:

> In the name of the Reichskommissar for the Eastern District, I decree that the Vilna Ghetto which existed for over two years shall forthwith be liquidated. All its inhabitants shall be deported throughout the day; some to Lithuania and some to Estonia. It is in the interest of the population to remain calm and follow orders. All residents have until midday to pack their things and then leave via the gates of the ghetto.

Biniakonski twice repeated the words in Yiddish through a large horn and Kittel added: "According to the order everyone must leave the ghetto. If anybody will remain here, the houses will be blown up with dynamite."

After that speech the officials left the balcony.

People remained glued to the spot. After days of preparing for the final axe, when the axe fell, the expected verdict was hard to absorb. What was going on? Leave the ghetto? Where to? To Estonia, to Lithuania? And could it not be a walk to Ponary? Dear God, why are You driving us out of our tormented minds? Why is there no end to our pain and torment! Leave the ghetto!. Did it mean that everyone would leave the ghetto or would the privileged remain? We had to know in order to decide how to handle the situation.

Without waiting for an answer to my unasked thoughts I pushed my way through to Kittel and Lakner and asked: "Is everyone leaving the ghetto without exception or would you leave some privileged group as has happened up until now?" They stopped for a moment and Lakner replied: "There are no privileged ones this time. The ghetto is being totally liquidated. Everyone has to leave, but it should be done in a quiet fashion, yes, quiet." The main interest of the murderers was that it all should pass "quietly."

After a few minutes of talking with my wife and daughter we made our decision. They would go start packing and I would try to find a way for us to remain in Vilna. Instead of starting to pack, a number of people ran out of the courtyard and began looting the ghetto warehouses. The people had been starving for the last few days and the warehouses were full. Without any logic people began carrying away full sacks of flour, bread and other products. Only when the looting came to an end did people go home to prepare their bags. I gave some thought to tryng to find a hiding place.

In the meantime, I was told that some of the privileged ones had received permission to enter the HKP block. If that was so, I thought, it meant that not all of us would be going to Estonia or Lithuania. Again it was the privileged ones. If they could remain in Vilna it meant there were ways to remain. My thoughts kept going in circles: Where would we travel to? Would we succeed in getting anywhere? How long could my family last in a concentration camp with an elderly mother and two children? Maybe there was a way to remain in Vilna after all. No matter how dark and bitter this would be, at least we would be among people we knew.

While I was contemplating all this, I saw an officer who had come from the HKP to the ghetto. After a short conversation, he gave me a note that allowed me to move myself and the family to the HKP as a disinfector. Overjoyed, I took my wife, mother and children, threw the few bundles we had and entered a waiting truck ready to travel. At that moment the workers from the nearby mechanical workshop came out under the leadership of their foreman and started to interfere, screaming that we had taken their places. They threw themselves on us, beating us and throwing our bundles off the truck. The end of it was that the German driver went over to the truck, chased everyone away and left with an empty truck. It is impossible to describe our despair.

While we stood lost and seemingly without any hope, my friend, the poet Haim Semiatycki, approached me: "Mendel, what are you going to do?" I answered: "I have no idea. What are you going to do?" His reply was: "I am going to stay in a hideout." I never saw him again. I know that he managed to get a place at the HKP. Some months later in Vilna the Gestapo arrested a Jewish family living on false papers. As a punishment for the "crime" the Gestapo shot fifty Jews from the HKP. Haim Semiatycki was victim number 48.

A little while later I met Avraham Zajdsznur from the Judenrat: "What is your decision?" I asked. "I am staying in a hideout," was his reply. Zajdsznur spent two months in a dark hiding place. He was eventually given away by a Jewish provocateur.

We were standing hopeless in the courtyard with the bundles and parcels next to us and suddenly we realized that my mother was gone! When? How did she disappear? "Mother, Mother!" My wife and the children burst into tears. Mother, grandmother, mother-in-law – gone. Disappeared like a ghost into the unreal world in which we stood.

The tragedy that held us in its grip did not allow us to even contemplate for a few minutes what had just taken place. Now we were forced back to the four living souls that were still together. We had to save ourselves; we had to save the two children who could not remember a single happy day.

People began walking out of the ghetto. The columns began to thin out and slowly the night took over. We decided to hide somewhere overnight. Observing who was walking out, I noticed that among the many thousands who had already left there had not been a single one of the privileged. They were obviously waiting for something. We decided to do the same, to see what was really going on. Could there be a new arrangement between the last Judenrat members and the Gestapo?

We managed to get into the headquarters of the police command and found a large number of people there. All the family members of the police were there. An interesting hideout, the police command. If it suited them it might as well suit us to stay there overnight. We remained inside in spite of the effort that was made to send us away. The place was full of people and luggage. Every few minutes the police commissioner kept taking bottles of drinks, expensive wines and candied fruit to the cabinet at the other side of the passage. There, Kittel and his German friends were holding an all-night party.

As usual, a deal had been struck even at this last moment between the ghetto hierarchy and the Gestapo. For a very considerable amount of gold and other payments a large truck would take some scores of people to the HKP. Once I knew that there was to be another truck I took my wife and children and a few things (leaving the rest behind) and went to the ghetto gate. Outside the police command the night was quiet and the streets were empty in God's cursed ghetto. It was four in the morning.

At the gate it was not quite the same. Here a few "strong ones" ruled together with the police. They kept pushing us from one place to another, preventing us from waiting for the truck that was to come.for them. Seeing that we would not achieve anything at the gate we decided to return to the police command and wait there until daylight. At that moment Solomon Gens, the brother of the murdered ghetto representative, arrived and threw himself on us like an injured animal: "Are you going back from the gate? Do you want to bring a disaster on the whole ghetto?! Stay here, Balberyszski, with your people. Don't move!" I didn't give in. "What are you talking about, Gens. I'm bringing a disaster on the ghetto? You are still unable to forget your old tricks." He boiled in anger: "Keep quiet or I'll make you mincemeat!" he screamed and began beating me with his rubber truncheon. The children began screaming and he left, first giving his order to the police to guard me.

But after a few minutes, while the police were busy trying to save their own hides we managed to escape and went back to the police command.

Here we met with a new disaster. A policeman stood at the entrance and wouldn't let us in. We cried and pleaded that we had left our luggage inside – all to no avail. Kommissar Aster came out and began pushing us toward the theater building in the same court where they collected people who had not left the ghetto the day before. They had kept them overnight under guard. We were afraid to enter that building. As we were later told, the police played their last criminal card there. They made different lists: who shall go to Estonia, who to Lithuania and who to HKP. At this very last moment they were still interested in only one thing – collecting money.

Seeing that we would not get into the command building and not wanting to finish up at the theater building, I took my wife and children and went around and managed to enter the command building through a window in the next courtyard. We felt we had found a way out of the danger that had been haunting us for the past twenty-four hours. We were now close to the privileged ones. I was convinced that they had made some arrangements with Kittel and his murderous horde. We sat down and waited until dawn.

With the first daylight we heard the steps of heavy boots and German voices calling on people to get out. Through the window we saw large groups of people leaving the theater, but for the moment we remained untouched. And then came an unbelievable sight: from the other side of the theater building a group of police walked out with their families and large packs of luggage. We had not had time to absorb this amazing sight before we became even more surprised. Another group of people under German guard came out – but could it be? Fried, Milkonowicki, Guchman and the other high officials were being taken out of the ghetto. If this was the case, Lakner, the German slaughterer in SS uniform was right – this time there would not be any privileged left.

But we could not remain sitting for long in the police command building. Soon the order came from outside for everyone to come out. No one was to remain inside. Slowly people started to leave but this time I was in no hurry.

The rooms emptied out. We began moving from one room to the next until we came across a small room in a corner. We entered and found Police Kommissar Aster with his family and a few other high brass. They tried to play their ingrained role of superiority ordering us to leave immediately. I remained calm: "Not anymore," I said in a calm voice, "not this time. This time you will walk out first and I will be the last one. Understood?" They did not say anything more.

We stayed in the room for quite a while and nobody spoke. Suddenly we heard a conversation going on between Kittel and Solomon Gens. Kittel asked: "Are you sure that nobody is inside the buildings? If I find anybody inside I will destroy the building together with the people in it with dynamite."

"I give you my guarantee that everyone has left the buildings. There is not a living soul left behind," Solomon replied.

Hearing the conversation, Kommissar Aster and his family and the high-ranking police officers immediately left the room. I remained and had all intentions to remain inside. But my wife and daughter became hysterical, saying that they didn't want to stay. "They will kill us on the spot. If the police left we should not stay here any longer." I could not hold out against them and we went out. As soon as we showed ourselves outside we were surrounded by Ukrainians who led us to join the group of people already in the courtyard. We joined the ghetto privileged whom we had seen earlier through the window.

The drama took place on Friday, September 24, 1943, between seven and eight in the morning. The courtyard of 6 Rudnicka, the first official address of the Judenrat of the Vilna Ghetto, became the address where the last Jews were collected to be sent out of the ghetto. When the other groups had left we were led to the gate guarded by a very large group of Ukrainian military. We were joined on the way by other small groups until in the end we became a group of a few hundred people. We walked along Rudnicka Street for the last time. Two years ago we had been herded into this place. Here we had spent an endless nightmare dreaming of getting out of here as liberated people. Now we were leaving. But to where?

Carrying our few remaining bundles and struggling to stay together, we walked to the ghetto gate for the last time. We had left behind most of the things we had packed and even so we could hardly keep walking. Next to us walked Solomon Gens with his young wife and the little baby in her arms. Solomon Gens's wife Lili Reszanska, a pharmacist, was one of the ghetto privileged. Our group contained nearly everyone who until the previous day had been on top of the "who's who" list in the ghetto. Looking at them, I couldn't help thinking that all of us were now equal. Now everyone had to agree that when it came to the destruction of Jews, the Germans considered every Jew the same. No more differences between Jew and Jew. Poor Jews, rich Jews; academic Jews, illiterate Jews; young, old; healthy, sick. Men, women, children – all Jews were the same to the German killers. All went to Ponary – as long as they were Jews.

The Germans had fooled us to the end. To make the destruction of Jews easier for themselves, the Germans had devised a diabolical plan to create an apparent difference between Jew and Jew. They divided us into "useful" and "useless" Jews. "Deserving" and "undeserving" Jews. "Legal" and "illegal" Jews. Tradesmen Jews and untrained Jews. By this sadistic method they confused us. They made us believe that they had not condemned us all to total annihilation. They made the "useful" Jew believe that the "useless" Jew was the cause of his calamity. They made the "legal" Jew despise the "illegal" one for being the cause of his suffering. They made the "deserving" Jew hand over to death the "undeserving" Jew in the belief that by handing them over the others would be saved and redeemed.

The Germans, the greatest murderers in human history, made their victims help them in their own destruction. Some of their helpers were individuals without a conscience who without any hesitation handed over other Jews for destruction. There were such people. They were common criminals. There were others, though, who believed that by handing over Jews to Ponary they were saving themselves and their families. They were weak characters who wanted to have an easy life while surviving the darkest hours. And there were those who rationalized their actions with the argument that by meeting the German demand for quotas to Ponary, they were saving the rest.

Some of them were now walking next to me. They had usurped the right to decide who should be sent to Ponary and who should remain. The Germans had encouraged them, and they had often used their power to enrich themselves in the process together with their German masters. They released the person who could pay in gold, replacing him with another Jew who had no gold. To the Germans it made no difference who went first and who would go later. If the Germans could enrich themselves while the final destruction of all Jews was taking place they were happy to cooperate with the "legal" Jew and send the "illegal" one first – knowing full well that in the end the "legal" Jew would be destroyed as well.

We were coming close to the ghetto gate. I looked at it for the last time. Would I ever have the privilege to be here again? Would my family and I survive this hell of hells, or was this our last look at Rudnicka Street?

When I was near the gate during the time we were caged there, I had a strange dream that I would one day be privileged to climb up the wooden gate and address the liberated world in a festive celebration speech. Now I was leaving the ghetto without the speech. As I walked out, I turned my head and read for the last time the brass board at the entrance to the ghetto: "Attention! Typhoid danger! Jewish quarter. Entry is strictly forbidden for military personnel and non-Jews."

As soon as we passed the gate, we were surrounded by other Ukrainians who stood ready for us with outstretched rifles. Instinctively we closed ranks a little more and kept walking. We passed the Church of All Saints and kept going through a number of streets. It was a beautiful morning, a time when the streets should have been noisy and full but there were few people around. Obviously the streets had been closed off. On one street we did see a few Gentiles in the distance. They had stopped and were observing our tragedy. What could they have been thinking?

We reached the narrow part of the street. The column became narrower but longer. Suddenly our walk was interrupted. A German officer approached, running and screaming. We halted for the moment. We found out he was chasing a girl who had tried to leave the column as we were passing a building. She ran into the building but had the misfortune to be noticed by the German officer. While we were ordered to resume walking we managed to notice that the officer was leading the girl away. We heard a shot and – that was all.

We walked on and came to the monastery on Subocz Street and suddenly the walk became chaotic. Germans tore into our columns. What was going on? We were pushed in all directions. We could not see anything but felt that something terrible was taking place. I tried to get the family to stay together but when I tried to get hold of my wife and daughter I saw them being dragged away. My daughter managed to hold on to me for a second and kiss me while calling, "Papa!" The Devil's hands tore her away from me as people kept pushing me from behind, calling, "Move on, move on. Hand over your money! Watches! Hand it over, quick!"

It all happened within seconds and it was frightening. Instinctively I took hold of my son and kept him in an iron grip. A soldier was searching me, quickly and superficially and not finding whatever he was looking for, he let go of me. At that moment I saw the women who had been torn away from us being driven into the monastery. Was this going to be forever? Yesterday they took my mother. Today? For two years I had managed to keep them from the hands of the German and Lithuanian demons and today it was all lost. Today, on my wife's birthday, the demons had managed to take her away from me. I was choking, trying to swallow the tears I was holding back. I was unable to keep control of the thoughts racing through my head and the demons in front of us pressured us to the point of collapse.

We were stopped at the monastery. While we tried to make sense of what was going on, we heard rifle shots from one direction. We turned toward them and saw the body of Gerszon Lewin, the watchmaker, hanging on a lamppost in the middle of the street, and next to him the body of Advocate Chwojnik.

An announcement was made that they had been hanged because they tried to resist.

We remained there for the rest of the sunny and beautiful morning, while the soldiers went around robbing us of whatever we had. The Germans kept running in all directions while Kittel appeared to be in charge of whatever was going on. We began whispering to each other and accusing ourselves for our stupidity of having allowed ourselves to be trapped so easily by the German net.

I was angry with myself. How could I have lost my head so completely! After all that we had gone through over the last two years, yesterday I lost my mother, today my wife and daughter and on top of it I had lost everything that my son and I might need if we remained alive. During the last days of the ghetto I had risked going outside the ghetto to our angelic neighbor Mrs. Kozlowski and had taken back from her a considerable fortune that we had left when we were driven into the ghetto. I had brought back jewelry, gold and money and divided it all between my mother, my wife and my daughter, leaving a little for myself, to make sure that whatever happened none of us should be left without some financial security.

We were all worn out and our tormentors let us sit down on the ground for a moment. We had just caught our first breath when the order came: "Form rows of ten! Quick, quick!" As we rose from our places we heard the noise of trucks approaching. A whole column of trucks appeared in front of us. Their appearance made us forget everything that had happened in the past hour. Trucks, not trains! It could have but one meaning – Ponary. So, we were not going to Lithuania or Estonia, we were being delivered by trucks to Ponary. "To Ponary," someone said the words in a dead voice.

My child clung closer to me: "Papa, are they taking us to Ponary, is this how it will end?" I looked at him and saw he had turned white with fear. "I don't know, son, if it is Ponary or not. We will see what will happen," I replied, not believing the answer I gave him.

Once more we were not allowed to think. Again the Germans made effective use of their sadistic plan: Don't allow the victims to think. Don't give the victims time to know what is going on, confuse them as much as possible.

"In rows of tens, and be quick about it!" We made our columns, the Germans and the Ukrainians noticed that no one wanted to be in the first columns. For a few seconds it became a cat-and-mouse game and the soldiers began using the butts of their rifles on our backs. It worked. Let it be what had to be and let us get it over with.

Behind me, someone was already reciting the *Vidui*, the Jewish religious confession recited before death. *God, why do we deserve such a fate? Why do we have to perish like dogs on such a beautiful day, why, God?*

"Forward march!" came the command and we started our last march to the trucks and from there to the end at Ponary. Had they already prepared the grave for us, or would we have to dig our graves before they would kill us? No time to think. "Quick, quick!" We marched along – but we were not being marched to the trucks! We had been diverted to Rossa Street. Is this a dream, a hallucination? There were no trucks and we didn't hear their engines any more. My son and I held on tight to each other; "alive!" we cried in unison. My eyes were damp, although I didn't feel like crying. We were not going to Ponary. We were standing in front of a railway line with trains to our left and to our right.

It was German planning at its highest efficiency. Kittel was standing and counting the rows: "10, 20, 30, 40, 50, 60, 70 – right," and then again, "10, 20…70 – left." We calmed down; wagons were waiting for us on both sides. Kittel kept ordering, "Into the trains!" It had but one meaning. One side was going to Lithuania and the other to Estonia. I wanted to go to Lithuania. It might not have meant much but it was the land where I was born. But how was I to know which was which? Let it be. Wherever fate would take us we would go. With secure steps, passing Kittel and holding my son in an iron grip like soldiers in a ceremonial march, we went to the train. Quick!

I was one of the first to enter the wagon and caught a place in the corner under a window. It was a large, empty freight car. No benches and no toilet. Dirty, with a small window fitted with iron bars and wired up with barbed wire. Now we could at last sit down on our bundles and catch our breath after all we had gone through.

The wagon quickly became full. Seventy-one people and their packs were crammed into it. This would be how we would travel until we reached our destination. In the meantime we looked out and saw the other wagons filling up and the soldiers closing and locking them. Slowly we calmed down a little and tried to make ourselves more comfortable. Somebody noticed that there were a few boards in the wagon. We improvised benches and started to group around.

I looked around trying to find out who were the people with whom my son and I were traveling. I knew a few. Next to me on one side was Shabtai Blacher, on the other side was old Olejski and his son, the sergeant of the ghetto police. Nearby was Woron, the foreman of the sanitary group who had been delivered by the Gestapo to the ghetto on the day the ghetto was liquidated. In another corner was Gurewicz the bookkeeper and a few others. Many ghetto police had entered our car with their packs and cases well prepared beforehand. I looked at my two small bundles and began to ask myself how I would be able to provide for a minimum existence with the little I had brought.

I had a little money and very few jewelry items; our packs had remained in the street. I comforted myself with the thought that at the last moment I had handed over to my wife a very elegant gold watch with a golden chain and a few thousand rubles that would help them in their need.

While I was slowly regaining my ability to think more clearly, the doors of the wagon opened and someone called for five or six men to come and collect the food that had been provided for the journey. The call made us all happy.

Some young men volunteered. They left the wagon and came back with mineral water in bottles – ten bottles per person. But instead of 710 bottles our volunteers had managed to bring in 1200 bottles. We realized that we had found the right people. A few minutes later they were back with loaves of bread. At least that meant we would not die of starvation. The ration was two loaves each but our providers managed to get hold of an additional fifty loaves. A little later they brought in sausage. Suddenly we felt as if we had left hell and landed in paradise!

A few hours earlier it had been Ponary and now the Germans were giving us bread and sausage. How was one to understand the perfidious German mind? The loading of the food for the whole train took a few hours and it was already midday. We had relaxed for an hour or two and our spirits rose.

On Woron's proposal, Olejski was made the commandant of the wagon. We were exhausted and could not care less who would be commandant. Olejski, Woron – let it be anything as long as it was not Ponary. It was decided that we would divide the food as soon as the train started moving. In the meantime I was getting hungry. Gawenda Gerc, who somehow became my neighbor, handed me over some bread. We had known each other for years and I had attended his wedding. Discovering that I had not managed to bring in any bread of my own he handed over a loaf and said I could take as much as I needed for myself and my son. It was most generous of him.

Having eaten, I stood up and looked out the barred window above my head. Some local boys were selling apples to the other cars. I bought a few apples and was about to buy more when the soldiers noticed what was going on and chased the boys away. The apples remained in my hand.

The spirit in our compartment was good. The events of the last few hours, the pain of separation from our wives, children, parents, the uncertainty of their fate were all temporarily pushed aside. We could not afford the luxury of grieving. The two years in the ghetto had trained us to live for the moment.

*   *   *

After the war had ended and my family was reunited I learned from my wife and daughter of how the women had fared. During the hours that we were waiting in the train, the women in the monastery courtyard went through all seven portals of hell.

When we were torn apart, the Ukrainian soldiers drove the women into the courtyard of the monastery with deliberate brutality. The place was already full with thousands of women who had been there since the day before. My wife and daughter met my mother there. They were kept for hours while the Germans were busy with us. After we had been locked away, they started to segregate the women by selection. A German officer and Lithuanian soldiers made the women parade in front of them and began separating them: left and right. When the women noticed that the sick and the old were all being sent to one side, they understood that that was the side destined for destruction. They began pinching their cheeks to get color in them. Those who had lipstick began to use it to make themselves look young and tidy. The most tragic moment was when some mothers began to abandon their small children and walk to the parade before the Germans without them. Some Germans who noticed began calling for the "criminal and heartless Jewish mothers" who were leaving their lovely children. The women hid themselves behind other women to avoid being seen by their little ones. It was a sight beyond anything that could be described or understood except by those who experienced it.

My wife and daughter went to the selection together. When they reached the German officer he sent them both with the whip in his hand to the group of the young ones. The Lithuanian tore my wife away, dragging her to the other side. My daughter reacted by screaming to the German officer and pointing to the Lithuanian soldier, arguing that he was going against the German's decision. The German became angry and called out, "You cursed dog, let the woman go where I sent her!" This saved my wife.

Of the many thousands of women and children assembled in the monastery courtyard fourteen hundred young and healthy women were sent to Kaiserwald close to Riga, Latvia. They worked later in the factories of Riga. All the others were sent to Majdanek; among them was my mother of blessed memory.

*   *   *

We had not yet finished drinking the poisoned chalice to its full. Hours of uncertainty, of fear in the shadow of death still awaited us. One would have to be as sadistic as the Germans to understand to what lengths they went to enjoy their power over us Jews.

When all the products had been delivered to our wagon and our spirits had lifted somewhat, we went to the barred windows and asked the rail workers passing on the platform if they had seen our women and children. We asked if they were being added to our train or were they somewhere else. Their answer was that they knew nothing and they had not seen any women. We asked a passing conductor where our train would be going and his answer cut our spirits to shreds: "The train is going to Landwarovo," he said. That meant Ponary. Our blood froze in our veins. We were going through Ponary. But why? They were sending us to Estonia, so why were we going in the opposite direction. We forgot our food and drink and our brains pounded with one word: Ponary. Having heard the name Landwarovo we stopped every rail worker with the same question. The answer was always the same: "I don't know" or "Ponary."

Our restlessness kept growing with the minutes. The railway workers had all said with one voice, Ponary. One worker said he didn't know if the train would stop at Ponary or if we would be passing through it. We asked a Polish train driver: "Have you ever driven a train through Ponary?" He answered affirmatively. "Did you ever know in advance if your train was to stop there or keep going?" "No," he replied. "The order to stop or not is never given to us until the last moment, not when we leave the station."

So it looked as if we would be going through Ponary and the train would stop there. So why did they play with us the comedy of providing us with food for three days? If we were to end at Ponary why did they give us so much water, bread and sausage? If this was to mislead us at the last moment it was all unnecessary. We had already been locked up in our wagon, the windows were barred and wired and we couldn't run away. The situation was becoming worse than in the morning.

It was no use racking our brains. My son cuddled up to me and I could hear his teeth chattering. He asked me once more: "Papa, are they sending us to Ponary?"

The discussion and interpretation of what we had heard from the railway workers did not stop. "You know," somebody said, "we will know if we are going to Ponary or through it. If the train leaves early in the evening, we will be going through Ponary. They don't shoot people at nighttime. But if we stay here until dawn, we are the next guests at Ponary." We accepted the logic that they don't kill people there at night, but our nerves were now tensed to the highest degree. We had already asked many people and we still kept asking. Suddenly

I noticed an SS officer passing by outside. Having nothing to lose, I asked him: "Is it true that we are going to Ponary?" "No, you are going through Ponary," he answered. "You can be calm, no evil will happen to you." But could we take the word of a German SS officer? It seemed that he had sensed our worry and as he passed the next window he repeated with more assurance that we should be calm, we would be only passing through Ponary. Oh, how we wanted his words to be true.

But we were still waiting for the blessed moment for the train to move. We had exhausted our energy and our patience. How long could we stand the torture? And what about our families, wives and children. The train had been standing for hours. Why?

Dusk was descending and we heard the first noise of the locomotive. We hoped the train would move soon and we would not stay there overnight. If that would happen we would be going, as the German SS officer had said, through Ponary. It was a hypothesis that we wanted to accept. A few minutes passed and our train began to move. We went over to the windows and looked outside at people walking in the street, free, swallowed up by the descending darkness. The train was not going very fast but we were moving. Every turn of the wheels cut into us as like a knife. We stood at the window seeing our end approaching, counting not the minutes but the seconds. We were taking leave of Vilna forever. We were leaving, never to return to Szkaflarne, the large bridge we were crossing. We were under the bridge. And all the while my heart was crying: *Vilna, my dear Vilna. My beloved birthplace. The place where my parents were born. And their parents, my grandparents, before them. I have not even taken leave of them. I have not visited their graves...*

Never in my life had I imagined such an end. To say good-bye to Vilna in a closed, dirty freight car, with bandit soldiers as our company. The people in our car became quieter and quieter as the train moved further and further away from Vilna. The silence became oppressive, choking. The darkness felt like a heavy stone on my chest, preventing me from breathing freely. Each of us shrunk back into our own thoughts. Even my son had nothing to say; nothing to ask. He curled up like a little kitten and his teeth kept chattering loudly in fear. What was my son thinking in those moments? Had the bloodthirsty murderers given a single thought to how people, how little children felt when they were in our situation, as the train drove us to our deaths?

We were looking into the last minutes of our existence. Next to me stood a ghetto policeman; his face touched me as we both looked out the window. I could hear his heavy breath of fear and like my son, his teeth were chattering. In the darkness I could barely make out his face, white with fear.

For two years his colleagues in the Jewish police handed over Jews to the Gestapo to be sent to Ponary. The police had used every trick to provide the murderers with the number of victims they demanded. With their own hands they had hanged six Jews. For him and his colleagues what went on during the last forty-eight hours in the ghetto was totally unexpected. I wondered if his fear now was because of the train and where it was taking us, or did he still suffer from the original shock to the police force. Even the previous night, some policeman were still collecting bribes, making false lists convincing people that they would be sent to Lithuania. And now he was standing and waiting – just like his victims.

I was totally unconcerned for my own fate, though I didn't know why I felt that way. If it had to be Ponary I would accept it – the end. But my heart did not and could not accept that my young child should end this way. I forced myself not to show my feelings to my son as we stood near the wired window and each turn of the wheels kept taking us closer and closer to Ponary.

We reached the tunnel. I recalled that when I was a child traveling through Landwarovo for the first time I was scared during the few minutes that the train passed through the tunnel. How different were my feelings now. I wanted the train to crash and kill us all rather than deliver us alive to Ponary. The issue wasn't the dying any more – it was the wish not to give the Germans the joy of killing us. Not to die by the hands of the Germans!

As the train left the tunnel a voice called: "Comrades, let me have a look out the window. I have worked here recently for the Germans and I know every span of the way here. I will tell you if we are going to Ponary or Landwarovo. Here the rail lines divide to the right and to the left."

We automatically moved away. I jumped down from the bench and let the young man be our last guide to tell us if we would live or die. The young man climbed up, looked out and was speaking as if to himself: "Soon we will reach Ponary. Left, the way leads to the barbed wire. Nobody returns from there. Right, the way goes to Landwarovo. Now let us watch every turn of the train wheels to see where they turn."

The train was losing speed, the wheels were turning slower and slower and we became paralyzed as the train stopped. Our hearts probably stopped beating. Every second seemed like a year. The man at the window didn't say anything. At the other windows two of the "strong ones" grabbed the iron bars in their hands, like Samson at the last building of the Philistines. Seconds passed, dragging on like years.

And then the train started moving again. All eyes were on the man at the window. The train moved slowly, very slowly. I pressed my son's head to my breast; I stroked his face. Dear son of mine.

And what was happening right then with my wife and daughter? And my mother, my old trusting mother, it would all be over soon. This was my wife's birthday. The irony of our fate. Suddenly we heard a shout: "The train has turned right, we are saved!"

The train turned right! Hot tears burst from my eyes. My son fell on my face and cried. His tears mingled with my own. We hugged each other with all our energy. The people in the wagon were still waiting in suspense for confirmation from the others. The right turn was confirmed.

We had come close to Ponary but we were going to live. We were traveling to Estonia. Now we fell like cut trees. Our energy had been totally drained during the previous hours. We fell on our bundles thinking of the future. Would we survive to the end, to take revenge for the thousands who had gone to Ponary and remained there… For our near and dear ones, for the years of sadistic torture we suffered from the Germans…

We had survived Ponary twice within one day and we were still alive. With renewed hope, we watched as the train left Ponary behind. We were going to a new destination. What was awaiting us there? What was next in the German plans for the remnants of Vilna Jewry? We could no longer think. I found a little space on the floor, took my son in my arms and we fell asleep.

◆

PART FOUR

In the Concentration Camps of Estonia

CHAPTER 13
The Klooga Concentration Camp

Our Journey Continues

Worn out by the events of the last two days we had fallen into the first heavy sleep in the locked train that took us to Estonia. Suddenly, in the middle of the night, the doors of the wagon were ripped open and three armed Ukrainian soldiers in German uniform tore into the wagon. Treading on us with their heavy boots, they shone their torches in our faces and demanded: "Hand over your money, watches, jewelry and razors – and be quick about it!"

We had placed the bucket that was our toilet right at the door. As the three Ukrainians entered, they turned over the bucket and its contents spread all over the floor. In a single moment the car became unbearable by its offensive stench. Seeing that there was no place to make themselves more comfortable, the one in the front with the outstretched rifle ordered: "All of you move over to one side and leave the other side for the goods."

The sudden situation that had taken us out of the first quiet rest caused pandemonium and in an automatic reaction each of us took hold of whatever we had managed to save. The Ukrainians were ready and obviously experienced. They started using the butts of their rifles left and right in a murderous way. Their beating had its effect. We threw away the bundles to one side of the wagon as we tried to squeeze ourselves into the other end. In the rush to move over I heard my neighbor say: "Don't worry, we will survive this as well."

Having dispatched us to one side and our goods to the other side the three Ukrainian began a body search of each one of us. From the way they went about it, it was obvious that they had practiced their technique on many others before us; they were real professionals. They profited quite a bit from our car, particularly from their search of the Jewish policemen. It turned out that at the last moment, as the ghetto was in its death rattle, the Judenrat divided whatever was left among its workers. Ordinary policemen had received 5,000 rubles each; the higher ranks received more. What the top leaders took for themselves remained unknown. Workers of my department were apparently allocated 350 rubles each but where the money had gone no one knew. Now, during the body search each policeman revealed a full bundle of untouched Russian rubles. In addition, each of the policeman had a considerable sum of "private" money, watches and jewelry collected from bribes. Now it all fell into the hands of the three Ukrainians and into the suitcases they had opened for their collection. In the unlit wagon it was impossible to estimate the worth of the valuables the bandits were collecting, but the shocked reaction of the police was obvious. "Such a fortune and all gone in a matter of minutes!" The much-used proverb was confirmed once more: "Easy come – easy go." It remained unclear how the Ukrainians knew the policemen's identities but the police were all searched first.

When they had finished with the police it was our turn. I had 2,800 rubles, which I was not ready to hand over to the Ukrainians. On the advice of my friend Gawenda I put the money in an empty bottle of mineral water and dropped the bottle behind me under the improvised bench. I was not going to risk keeping the money on me and be beaten to a pulp for it. They searched me and my son and found nothing on us.

Having finished the personal searches, they pushed us over to the other side of the car and began checking out the half of the car where we stood. They found some jewelry, watches and money. Apparently there had been others just as wise as I was. It all went into the open suitcases before they ordered us back to our original position and began to search our parcels. They opened each bundle and searched each piece of clothing, taking away anything they liked and throwing the rest into the car. They collected enough suits and dresses to fill a small clothing shop.

The bandits had done their work very systematically. They obviously knew the distance to the nearest stop of the train as they spent a long time in our wagon. Meanwhile we were choking in our corner without food or drink or the opportunity to use the bucket. In the end they packed a number of suitcases with jewelry, money and clothes and as the train began to slow down they left the wagon, locking the doors from the outside.

The train stopped within minutes after the Ukrainian bandits left. We looked out of the barred windows and found that our train had stopped on a siding. From the signs we learned that we were in Lithuania. The place was as quiet as a cemetery. Some of us had been hardened enough to disregard the horrible stink of the wagon and began eating while others knocked out a hole in the floor to clean the wagon a little and to create a natural toilet. After we gained back our equilibrium we began talking about our families, wives, children, parents. We shivered imagining how the same kind of murderous searches must have affected our womenfolk.

It was already daylight. We ate and began to restore some order in the wagon by collecting and sorting the things that the Ukrainians had thrown all over the place. Woron, the foreman of the sanitary group in the ghetto who had made a fortune together with his "good" Germans arranging the release of imprisoned Jews, became the keeper of order in the car together with Blacher and Olejski. It took the rest of the day to hand the things the Ukrainians had thrown away back to their owners. Among the items collected was also the bottle I had thrown under the bench. After providing identifying details the money was returned to me.

We were able to sleep through the next night without any more surprises from unexpected visitors. The trouble started early in the morning of the third day when somebody remarked that the stack of bread loaves that had to last us for the rest of the way looked too small. Taking advantage of the chaos that had gone on the day before, a few passengers in our wagon had helped themselves to the communal supply of food to restock their personal food supply. This time Hertz, Gawenda and I went through the wagon searching for the loaves. A number of loaves suddenly rolled on the floor unnoticed by us; others we took back directly. The only loss was of the loaves that had been consumed in the meantime.

Our train remained in Shavel for a considerable time. The guard opened the wagons and we were allowed to step out, remaining under guard on our platforms. While I was standing outside, a German Gestapo officer came over and handed me a small piece of paper, asking me to read it aloud. Glancing at the paper I noticed that it had been written in Yiddish: "To the Jews of Shavel! I, Israel Segal of Shavel, am traveling now in a deportation train from Vilna to Estonia to work. The Vilno ghetto has been liquidated."

The note had been written by the stage director of the Yiddish theater in the Vilna Ghetto. He was originally from the Jewish community of Shavel. He had thrown out the note to let the Jewish workers at the Shavel railway know about the fate of the Vilna Ghetto. How the note came to be in the hands of the Gestapo officer one can only imagine. The man asked me, "Have you read it properly?" "Yes," I said, "I can read Yiddish very well." "Then it is good," he replied and went away.

After a while we left Lithuania on our way to Estonia. We spent more time stopping and waiting on sidings than traveling. We passed through Latvia, stopping at Riga for a considerable number of hours and came at last to the end of our journey in the small hours of the following Tuesday. We remained in our locked wagons until dawn, at which point we discovered that we were at the sadly famous station – Vaivara.

At the first full daylight the area around our train came to life, with a large number of German SS and military surrounding our train. Through the windows we saw wives of our people from Vilna and the first sigh of relief escaped from our hearts: They were alive and working in Estonia! From a few short exchanges we managed to have with people outside we learned that we were at the main camp and the head office of all the work camps in Estonia.

The door of our wagon opened and we heard a conversation: "Here, we are the authorities and we decide what to do with the people. You have nothing to say here." To which the Gestapo officer, who we could now see outside our open doors talking to a Wehrmacht officer, replied in anger: "As long as I have not handed over the transport, we are the authority over these people. I am the head of this wagon." It was a nice welcome and we enjoyed the free spectacle. They were fighting over us! It means we had some value. At the same time we worried that the fight and anger between them might cause us serious damage.

While this argument was going on, I noticed that the children who had come with us on the train were being separated from the men. My blood froze. What was I to do about my son? I grabbed him and pushed him behind me. The angry Gestapo officer started counting us by pointing at us with the tip of his whip and said nothing when he passed me and my son. When he was satisfied that he had brought all "his people," seventy-one men, he said, "It's all accounted for," and left.

We stood near the wagon that had been our home for days for a long time and used the opportunity to breathe in as much fresh air as we could. Our senses of vision and sound had become very acute. From each movement around us we sensed that our fate was now being decided. It took some time before we heard the command: "Back in the train." I quickly took my son and moved back into our wagon, with the distinct feeling that we had just been saved from a looming tragedy. From the small barred windows we saw many Vilna Jews walking around, making out as if they were working, but we did not like their "work." It was obvious they were not performing any real task, but they did look healthy and lively. Among the workers we saw the son of Haim Bakaturski and the son of Abraham Kac. We also noted that many people from other wagons in our train had been taken away somewhere.

Once it was all sorted out the train pulled out of the station. After we had been traveling for some time people noticed that we were moving back the same way we had come. Although we were no longer as fearful as we had been when the train was passing through Ponary, going backward disturbed our calm. Someone comforted us with the thought that there were many working camps in Estonia; we had probably been moved from the central camp in Vaivara to another camp.

We traveled that way the whole day and part of the night. We stopped sometime in the middle of the night and waited impatiently for the first daylight to see where we were. By the first light we noticed large white buildings in the distance. A little later we saw a number of white buildings in an open stretch of land filled with masses of timber boards and uncut wood. Around the place a few men with white armbands were moving around; we assumed they must be the camp police. Within a short time we knew that we had come to a camp called Klooga. Around eight in the morning the doors of the car were opened and we stepped down into the Klooga Concentration Camp.

We were directed to a large barrack. It appeared as if it had been dropped accidentally in the middle of nowhere in an open field. In front of us walked two groups from other cars. We all stopped in front of the barrack that we had noticed from the train. The German camp leader, a Gestapo officer, and the Jewish camp elder waited for us at the barrack together with a few policemen. We received the usual welcome from the German camp leader: "All that you have in money, watches, jewelry and other valuables must be handed over immediately. Leave all other belongings here." He pointed to the side. Standing in the first row, Woron became the immediate translator and the German Gestapo officer asked: "Did you understand?" "Yes," we responded very loudly.

The Gestapo officer added: "For not handing over everything you have, you may end up the same way as this man." With his boot he kicked a dead body we had not noticed lying behind him. The Jewish elder who introduced himself as Melcer explained: "The dead young man whose body you see was shot by the camp leader a few minutes ago because after the order to hand over everything, it was found he still had money on him." We listened and understood the "friendly" welcome.

Row after row we went forward to the table in front of us. The German was standing at the side making sure that anything still left after the robbery in the train was handed over. Standing in the row together with my son I was considering the situation: "How do I get out of this fire?" I was wearing a costly watch, a gift that friends and colleagues had given me in Lodz on my wedding anniversary. (I realized that I had left it on my arm in the train when the Ukrainian bandits robbed us of everything and wondered about the miracle that had prevented them from noticing it.) I decided I could not keep it but I would not hand the watch over to the new robbers. Slowly I removed the watch from my arm and dropped it, stepping on it and crushing it. I also had the twenty-eight hundred rubles I had managed to save when I put it in the bottle. I was not willing to hand it over but was I ready to risk my life and be shot in front of my son? I decided on a quick Jewish compromise: I would hand over the eight hundred rubles and would put the four fifty-mark banknotes up my sleeve and let it be the way the Almighty may decide.

The parade was moving forward; the heap of gold, jewelry and money kept growing in the box at the side of the table and the mountain of other items in the designated place for it. My heart was pounding as first I and then my son passed the table inspection – and nothing happened. At the last moment, I did the same with the bundle of goods: I gave away some of it and kept some for us – it also passed. *At least we will have something left to put on*, I thought to myself. Before the parade was completed I found out the name of the first victim: it was the ghetto policeman Nosikov.

The next day the German camp leader came to the registry room and ordered Melcer and his clerk Niderman to make out a protocol that Nosikov died a natural death. On the command of the German the two had to sign the false death certificate. The ordinary prisoners interpreted the case as a sign that Jewish life could no longer be taken without an accounting. Even the German camp leader had now to account for the death of a Jew.

Compared to the risk and worries of others, my worries were minor. Not all cars in our train had been robbed the way our car was. Some people had managed to keep gold, jewelry and other valuables all along. At the last moment before the parade they buried their fortunes in the ground before passing the collecting inspection. Nearly all who did so lost everything. The police and other experienced inmates removed the buried goods before the owners came back to dig them out.

The stealing of the buried goods caused a major scandal in the camp soon after our arrival. A policeman named Gurewicz noticed the place where a father and son named Kliaczka had buried their bundle of gold coins and diamonds. Being able to move around as a policeman, he removed the buried goods and refused to hand them back. He would not even agree to hand back part of the fortune he had stolen. At a later stage when the Kliaczkas were totally destitute they turned to *Die Sharke* in the camp to help them. The *Die Shtarke* forced the policeman to hand back to the Kliaczkas at least some part of the stolen goods. But the case reverberated throughout the camp.

We arrived at the Klooga Concentration Camp on Wednesday, September 29, 1943, on the eve of the Jewish New Year 5704. The search at the welcome parade took some hours, after which we were marched to a large empty place and ordered to stand in rows of fives. We were now facing a building that did not look like either a prison or a concentration camp. It was an impressive white concrete structure with two entrances and large windows. Nearby was a small kitchen that gave the impression of being a temporary structure equipped with large kettles. Here we waited until all the wagons were searched. As long as we did not leave our rows we were not harassed and had a chance to exchange a little information with earlier arrivals who approached us. We learned that before our arrival the camp accommodated fifty-five men and six hundred women brought from Vilna and the surrounding areas. The men were living in the block in front of us and the women were accommodated in another block. The elder of the camp was Melcer, the man who had welcomed us together with the German leader. He was assisted by two policemen, one named Gurewicz and the other named Straszun. The men and the women worked at all kinds of tasks but what the work was we could not immediately discern. We only learned that the kitchen employed many women. The general spirit was not bad but nothing was clear. After all this information we were left with the nagging question: "What is going to happen to us?"

It was after midday before Melcer arrived and made us stand in our rows of five with twenty rows to each column. He told us to remove our caps when the Germans arrived.

Quite a number of Germans soon arrived. The camp commandant was obviously the head of the German group. Next to him was the building chief, Kurt Stacher – a man the size of a fat bear with a large bloodhound at his side. Originally a lawyer from Wilhelmshafen, we were soon to discover his cruel nature. An assortment of SS men and members of the Todt organization stood next to them. The camp commandant addressed us: "Your incarceration in the ghetto is now over. You are not here as Jews. You are here as inmates. You may now remove the yellow stars that mark you as Jews. You are here as working inmates like other nationalities. You'll be working here, you'll receive your deserved nourishment and you'll be able to work well."

Standing stiff like soldiers and listening to the short welcome speech we asked ourselves: "Are we not dreaming? Is this really true? No yellow star, no longer Jews, simply inmates, workers…"

The commandant turned to Henekhke Szapiro, the Vilna Ghetto Gestapo agent, and asked him to translate the speech. Henekhke stepped out of his row and turned toward us saying in Yiddish: "Comrades! The master here says that we are free people. No more ghetto, no more misery, we are to take off our yellow stars, we are workers. We will be well treated! We will have a peaceful life and plenty to eat." At the last word he moved his hand across his throat and cried out aloud: "Understood?" "Yes!" we called out in unison.

The commandant was satisfied and in a jovial mood. He ordered us to sort ourselves according to our trades and professions. This created a stir as each of us tried on the spur of the moment to decide on the right trade in order to join the right trade group.

The group of free professions remained isolated from the others. Among us we had fifteen medical practitioners and quite a number of lawyers, pharmacists, engineers, and other such professions. The building chief noted down the various trades without any remarks. Having finished with the people he turned to our group. He asked Teitelbaum: "What are you?" "I am a lawyer," Teitelbaum answered. The building chief burst out laughing as if he had just heard the most hilarious joke: "Oh, you are a law twister…ha, ha." I was the next one: "And you are what?" "I am a pharmacist." Again he laughed, but a little less: "You churn out pills…ha, ha."

He turned to the commandant: "Who needs so many doctors? Let them start working for a change." His friend could not agree more. "Of course," he responded and started asking the doctors about their individual specialty. Suddenly each doctor had been a specialist of one kind or another. Everyone had been practicing surgery or internal medicine as a specialist. The commandant noted down two doctors, one surgeon and one women's specialist. From the pharmacists he noted Isaac Frumkin who stood in his white coat with a medicine box marked with the Red Cross in his hand.

It was already afternoon when the induction ended. After the Germans left we were each given some bread and margarine and hot ersatz coffee. We were famished and made a quick meal out of it. A whole week had passed since we had had anything warm inside us – a week that had put us through the mincing machine but we had managed against all odds to come out alive. We were left in peace for some time and sat down on the grass where some old inmates joined us and gave us some additional information.

On his own initiative, Dr. Epsztajn organized the physicians to stay together in one room, so they would not have to join the others in the large hall. Melcer, who had joined the group for a while, promised to give the group of intellectuals separate rooms.

At last we were led into the building and found it to be in good condition. It consisted of two floors, with most of each floor consisting of a huge hall that was to accommodate most of the inmates. At both ends of the hall were four separate rooms. A group of around forty of us took over one of the large rooms. It was full of light but except for a small table there was nothing in the room. We immediately marked out our places on the floor like in the hideout in the ghetto. When night came, we sat in our places in the dark. We could not turn on the lights because there was nothing to cover the windows with and the Leningrad front was not far from us.

From all outward signs the camp was in the first stage of being organized. Our arrival of 750 males caused a minor revolution in the camp. Advocate Muszkat, the police inspector of the Vilna Ghetto, replaced Melcer as the new camp elder. Five policemen were added to the camp police force, including Former Chairman Fried and Henekhke Szapiro. A sixth policeman, Dr. Misha Rat, lasted one day only before he joined the ordinary working column. Solomon Gens, the surviving brother of the Vilna Ghetto representative, became camp scribe together with another man while an inmate named

Laybe became leader of the working column. All this was accomplished in a single day.

The next morning, Germans came at around seven o'clock and took us to work. There was no real work for us at that stage. We were ordered to clean the area around the building and of the open camp. We worked from 7:00 a.m. to midday, and then again from 1:00 p.m. to 6:00 p.m.

At 6:00 p.m. we came together in front of our building for roll call. Unlike the torture and torment which made up roll call in all German concentration camps, the roll call in Klooga was simple. We stood in columns and as the commandant arrived the Jewish elder Muszkat called: "*Muetzen up* (Form lines of ten)!" The commandant counted us and we were released to our building, "the block."

Our first impression was that the camp was organized by clever Germans who had found a way to avoid being sent to the Russian front. The camp, established by the Todt organization and the building chief, had for the moment not reached the stage of being closed off by a barbed-wire fence, as was the system in German concentration camps. And although the men and women were located in separate blocks, the usual strict separation of German concentration camps did not exist in Klooga.

For a few days we believed that the words we heard from the commandant on our arrival about no longer being Jews but inmates in a labor camp had some meaning. This illusion came to an end within less than a week. On Saturday, October 2, we finished as usual at 6:00 p.m. and arranged ourselves in columns ready for the roll call. This time the commandant appeared in the company of the building chief. The building chief approached our group and stopped in front of Dr. Epsztajn, who was standing next to me, and began abusing him: "You cursed, filthy Jew! You believe you can go over my head to the commandant to give you work as a doctor, do you? I am here to decide about work!" With that he began to beat Epsztajn on the face with his stick. The poor doctor began bleeding and asked: "Why are you hitting me?"

The building chief became enraged, wild like an animal. He continued beating the doctor until his stick broke. He was still not satisfied and took the commandant's whip out of his hand and continued his murderous attack. We stood head to head and each time the building chief swung his whip I turned my head aside not to fall victim to his rage. Epsztajn fell to the ground and stopped screaming. No one dared to do or say anything while the German was raging. But we learned what our position as "inmates" was worth. Slowly the anger of the German evaporated and the roll call was over. We lifted Epsztajn off the ground and took him to the infirmary. The remark made by his colleagues was not flattering: "He deserved it. In the ghetto he would not register anyone on his yellow document and thus let three Jews that could have been saved go to Ponary. Here he tried the same. He wanted to be something special, so he is something special."

All through Sunday Epsztajn was left to rest together with us. On Monday morning he was sent to special hard labor on the order of the building chief. By then we had well absorbed what kind of inmates we really were.

Getting "Settled"

Unlike other concentration camps where communication between men and women did not exist outside the workplace and always took place under the supervision of German guards, contact between male and female inmates at Klooga was a daily occurrence. During a visit to the women's block I met an acquaintance from Lodz who had arrived with the first transport and was already "settled." When I told her that I had my young son with me and had no clothing for him, she took me to the head of the women's block and introduced me, asking for help on my behalf.

The woman was very helpful. She gave me a towel and some pieces of clothing from her own belongings. In addition she ordered the woman who worked in the clothing store to provide some warm clothing for my son. The help was a life-saving gift for my son and myself.

From the head of the women's block I learned that the Germans had confiscated the many large parcels of food and clothing that the people of the ghetto had sent to their family members who were the first to be sent to Estonia. They selected the good items for themselves and let the rags be delivered to the inmates. They did the same with the bundles we brought. In order to obtain anything at all of our own clothing one had to have very close contact with the new rulers of the camp. Within days the newly appointed policemen appeared well dressed in new jackets and high boots, while many of us recognized the clothing we had managed to save until our arrival in the camp. But I must admit that the seventy youngsters who entered the camp with us received decent, warm clothing. As a special gift, the lady I knew from Lodz managed to obtain for me a large, two-liter food container and two spoons, one of them a silver one.

During the following days I managed to collect a few necessary items for our daily needs. The only thing that I could not manage to provide for myself or my son was food to supplement the starvation rations that we were given by the Germans. These included a liter of ersatz coffee in the morning, a liter of soup (i.e., water with a hint of some vegetable in it) at noontime, and 350 grams of bread with a few grams of margarine or marmalade at 6:00 p.m. On Sundays we would be given a few grams of sugar or cheese or some other "treat." As always, there were possibilities of buying bread in the camp. But the price was 1400 rubles for a kilo of bread, which put it out of reach, and slowly hunger became a permanent condition.

One day my friend Minker came to me with an idea of how to make life a little easier. The camp was still in its building stage; the timber that was being delivered was used to build living quarters for us and those who were still to come. Minker, like myself a veteran pharmacist , had thought of a way to use his background in chemistry to get us out of the regular forced labor and asked me to join him.

He presented himself to the building chief as a chemist with experience in industrial chemistry and offered to make putty for the windows of the new buildings. All he needed, he said, was a place for a laboratory. It didn't take the German much time to see the benefit of the offer and within a single day Minker had at his disposal a large, lit room and permission to take on two assistants. I was happy to be one of them, because it kept me out of the cold weather and the work was more in my field. But I could not understand how we could make putty without linseed oil. When I asked Minker about it he replied: "That is my problem; I'm the chemist. You just follow my instructions and see."

We started our work filling wheelbarrows with clay that Minker found behind the camp. From the sawmill we brought loads of sawdust and from the building supervisor Minker obtained ten kilos of carpenter glue. Out of these materials Minker was going to make putty for the many windows of the new barracks. For a full month the building supervisor left us in peace while we enjoyed the warm, calm and peaceful atmosphere around us.

Minker was a pleasant man and a good boss. First of all he let the German women in charge of the female section know that he was making facial and skin creams. The German women brought him butter, margarine, perfumes and powders. Minker skimmed off three quarters of the material and made some quite acceptable creams from the rest. We quickly learned from him the art of cream making and made creams for Jewish female inmates. The "chemical brigade," as we were soon called, was considered by the others as a kind of a joke and when Melcer called the brigade's name in the morning's roll call we were greeted with some gentle laughter. But we soon realized that our work instead of being a joke could end up in tragedy. Minker's intentions were good but his expertise in making putty was very questionable. A few times we warned him that the building chief was looking at our work with a great amount of distrust. When he came to visit our laboratory we went on kneading the clay and dust and poured oil over it to turn it into "putty."

Toward the end of the month we delivered our product and the glaziers began using it. We were all happy with the results. But our happiness didn't last very long. After a week, the glazier came back with very bad news: our "putty" had failed and all the panes they had put in had fallen out. To our misfortune the bad news also reached the ears of the building chief

The next time the building chief met Minker outside the laboratory, he stopped him and addressed him in the usual German way: "You cursed filthy Jew! You dirty liar! You call yourself a chemist? You're scum!" With this he began using the stick that he never let out of his hand on Minker. The screams of the little man were heard over the whole area. And when Minker fell to the ground, the building chief let his large dog loose on him. Bleeding and half-alive, Minker managed to crawl away from his tormentor. We heard the screams in the laboratory but did not know what was happening. We were lucky that Melcer came running and screamed at us: "Get out of here while you can! The bluff is over, get lost!" We escaped as fast as we could, thanking God and Melcer who protected us from meeting the building chief. But Minker paid dearly for his attempt. He had our sympathy. He was a good man, a very good colleague and had meant to help us as much as he helped himself.

At the time we arrived in Klooga, Nehemiah Melcer was the camp elder. He was a man in his early forties from the Vilna area, well known in the timber industry. He was an honest man, straightforward in his actions and helpful – as much as he could be – to other inmates. With the arrival of the former leaders of the Vilna Ghetto the intrigues started. Within no time at all Melcer was removed from his position and his place was taken by Advocate Yosef Muszkat, the former police inspector of the Vilna Ghetto. But the new leaders didn't last very long. With the help of the elder of the female block, Muszkat was quickly removed from his position and Melcer once again became camp elder. He held that position until the camp's liquidation.

The plotters received their due on November 5, 1943. During roll call 150 names of inmates were called out. They were to be transferred to another camp. It was the first "cleansing" of the camp. Among the men selected for transfer were Fried, Muszkat, and Epsztajn. We all knew that Melcer and the elder of the female block had managed to get rid of the Vilna Ghetto "aristocrats" without sending them to their death.

As soon as we completed the preparatory work of organizing the camp the Germans began to implement a massive program of industrial development. The labor force at their disposal included the twenty-five hundred Jews in the camp and a large number of Estonian prisoners, all serving sentences for criminal activities. Some of the skilled tradesmen were Russians who had found themselves in Estonia when the Germans arrived and had switched sides. The first priority of the Germans was to construct all the buildings and structures that were needed to accommodate their various operating units. The German in charge of this construction group was Karol Dugarden from Aachen. He was a giant of a man, given to sudden attacks of insane bestiality that always ended in indiscriminate beatings of whoever was near him. It was to this group that I was assigned after the unsuccessful chemical laboratory experiment. It was not very long before Karol noticed my lack of building skills and I became his favorite object of rage. That meant almost daily beatings and assignments to the most difficult tasks.

One day he called me and another Jew, a tailor from Vilna, and ordered us to remove a huge boulder from a spot in the ground that was to be prepared for a building foundation. The two of us looked at one another and at the stone and knew that this would not end well. But having no choice, we started hammering away at the stone with our pick-axes. We did this until we were left breathless, but barely managed to scratch the surface of the stone. When Karol returned after an hour or so and saw how little we had accomplished, he fell into his typical rage and started hitting us indiscriminately with his ever-present stick. And the more he hit the greater became his rage. We thought the end had come and we would not survive this beating. Fortunately, a young Jew who heard our screams and saw Karol's rage came running and yelled at us: "You stupid fools, that is not how you remove a boulder – you need to dig a hole next to it and bury it." With this he threw some spades at us and told us to dig. Seeing this, Karol left us alone and went away. Now we had to dig – the tailor with a broken arm, the result of Karol's beating, and I in terrible pain. Some of the Jewish inmates who saw our predicament came over and helped us out. Within a short period of time the boulder was buried.

Within a few short months the intensive construction activity provided accommodation for Estonians and non-Jewish prisoners, warehouses and various workshops. These included a carpentry workshop that manufactured all the beds, tables and benches needed in the camp; an electrical workshop that took care of all the electricity problems; a mechanical workshop; a paint shop, a radio-repair shop, a laundry; and a tailor shop and shoe factory – both of which were used by the Germans for their personal needs. All of the shops employed Jewish tradesmen, many of whom had years of experience and were therefore able to meet German requirements. In addition, Jewish slave labor was used in a plant producing concrete blocks used in the various construction projects. Unlike the generally reasonable conditions in the various workshops, conditions in the concrete-block manufacturing plant, where I was assigned after my boulder incident with Karol, were inhuman. Due to the constant need for concrete blocks, the Jews were required to manufacture ever-increasing quantities of blocks. This meant hauling ever-increasing numbers of cement bags – each weighing fifty kilograms – and ever-increasing amounts of reinforced iron and mixing ever-increasing amounts of concrete. Doing this day and night with very little rest and on the verge of starvation took its toll. Any deviation from the daily production quota resulted in cruel beatings and punishments and I considered myself lucky if at the end of the day I managed to return to the camp alive. But my physical condition was deteriorating rapidly.

Estonia is blessed with forests and the Germans decided to take advantage of that fact to set up a sawmill to supply all the timber needed for construction. All the machinery was in the warehouse and German technicians and Jewish slaves installed it in record time. The Germans were so pleased that they doubled the food ration of the Jewish workers.

In the spring of 1944 a new manufacturing plant was established in Klooga. We did not know at first what it was to be, but from the intensive interest shown by the senior German staff we assumed that it was something rather important. We soon found out. The new plant was to manufacture underwater mines to be used off the shores of the Baltic Sea. It was to be a top priority, to be completed as quickly as possible. Work was to be done around the clock. Several hundred Jews were assigned to this project, my son and I among them. Once the location of the plant was decided, we went to work preparing the ground and laying out the foundation.

The mine consisted of three parts: a steel structure, steel boxes filled with concrete and explosives. Our function was to manufacture the steel structure, place it in the steel boxes and pour the concrete around it. When completed, the mine was about seven feet high and weighed nearly a ton. When our work was finished, German technicians would install the explosives and the mine would be moved to a storage area. Men, women and children were used in this plant and the working hours were from 2:00 a.m. till noon and from noon till 10:00 p.m. My son was in the group of children who were assigned to the steel-structure section. Their task was to carry the steel rods from the warehouse to the site and to tie the steel rods together to form the structure's frame. They worked day and night, exposed to extremes of weather, in deadly fear of what might happen to them if they didn't meet the daily quota. From time to time, during a short break, my son and I would meet and comfort each other. Supervising this work was a German whose insane rages and cruelty surpassed anything that we had witnessed in the Klooga camp. The production quota he demanded was impossible to meet, neither the men nor the women and children could mix the concrete, manufacture the steel structures and pour the concrete at a rate that would meet his demands. That would bring into action his steel rod, which he used mercilessly on the helpless prisoners.

My own condition was becoming very difficult. I was extremely weak, my feet and legs were swollen beyond recognition and I felt that my end was near. I was becoming a menace to other workers because I couldn't keep up with their tempo. One morning while I was hauling one of the steel boxes, it slipped from my hands and fell on my foot, smashing the big toe. I fell down in excruciating pain and saw a German running toward me. My only thought as the German approached was *what will happen to my little boy, how will he survive when I'm gone?* But the German was unusually quiet. He looked at my foot, looked at me as if to say, "Well, you are no longer of use to me," and sent me to the camp infirmary.

In the infirmary, the doctors looked at the foot, saw the damaged toe and swollen feet and did what they could but would not give me a release from work even for one day. "It is against regulations," they said. However, they gave me permission to stay in the infirmary. When I got up in the morning to go to work I realized that I couldn't use my leg, the pain was agonizing and that if I went to the plant I would not come back.

At that moment the German we knew as Antosch, the man in charge of all medical and sanitary problems in the camp, entered the infirmary. Seeing him and realizing that I had nothing to lose, I quickly removed the bandage from my foot, turned to him and showed him the open wound. I told him about the accident and said that I couldn't go to work in such a condition. Antosch was taken aback by my direct approach (only the head of the infirmary was entitled to speak to him directly) and by my request but did not say anything. He looked at me and then at my foot, turned to Dr. Pomeranc who was in charge of the infirmary and said: "Release him for two days." Dr. Pomeranc immediately took me to another physician who set the toe, bandaged it and told me to rest. I have no doubt that my request to Antosch and his order to give me two days' rest saved my life. After two days I returned to work and continued in the underwater mine plant until my transfer to another camp.

During the several months that the mine plant was in operation, several thousand mines were produced. The plant was considered of strategic importance, as witnessed by the many official visits of high-ranking German officers. Yet after liberation we found many mines where we had placed them during production – in their original storage area.

The Struggle for Survival

During the first few weeks after our arrival to Klooga we were ordered by the Germans to rehabilitate the buildings where we were to be accommodated and, above all, to provide all the required sanitary facilities, including showers. The question of showers was of particular importance to us since we wanted to make certain that all camp inmates would take a shower at least once a month to avoid any possibility of disease and contamination. The Germans also insisted that all men shave, and a small barber shop was established with several Jewish barbers to take care of our beards. The buildings themselves were equipped with double-decker bunks, tables and benches so that at least as far as accommodation conditions were concerned we had the basic minimum. But we very soon realized that the threat to survival, apart from the backbreaking work, was starvation. The food rations provided by the Germans were starvation rations and only those who could supplement these rations with additional food had any chance of surviving. This quickly led to the development of a black market, with many entrepreneurs establishing flourishing businesses, dealing with Estonians and Germans, obtaining provisions that they then resold at significant profits to the Jews in the camp. For those who had the money or other valuable items, everything was available: bread, butter, eggs, cheese, meat, potatoes, even alcohol. The exchanges took place in the evenings, outside the buildings, although in some cases the traders set up a display "shop" near their bunks.

With my limited resources (the two thousand rubles that I had hidden when we arrived) I could not afford to buy much. During the first three months, when hunger and hard labor reduced our strength and ability to function, I spent a third of my capital and bought one loaf of bread. That helped us for a few days but when, one evening, I saw my little son place his head on the table saying, "I'm hungry," I almost cried with anguish. I realized that I had to do something to obtain more food. By lucky coincidence, we found out that a camp of Russians located not far from us had been evacuated and they had left behind a large quantity of potatoes in storage. We decided to go there and get some of the potatoes. We smuggled ourselves past the camp guards and got to the Russian camp without incident. We found the potatoes, frozen in the December frost, filled our pockets as much as we could and returned to camp. Our joy knew no bounds! We had some food.

When I returned from work on Christmas Eve, I again realized that we had no food left. Without saying anything to my son, I left the camp to go to the Russian "turncoats" to try to get some food. These were Russian soldiers who switched sides and went over to the Germans. One of them, named Fedka, was my working companion. When I arrived there, I walked into a small, dark room expecting to find the Russian, but to my horror I found myself in front of the Estonian officer who was in command of the Estonian prisoners. *What have I done?* I thought to myself. *How do I save myself from this situation?* Without thinking too long, I turned to the Estonian and said: "This is Christmas Eve. You are away from your home and family, all alone. So are we. I am here with a young son and we are dying from hunger. Please help us. You too probably have children…" The Estonian stood as if frozen, unable to speak.

"What are you doing here?" he mumbled. "Yes, I do have a son and he is now on the Leningrad front. I, too, was there and barely managed to stay alive and come to this camp. But what can I give you? I haven't yet received a package from my family. All I have is bread." With that he went away and in a few moments came back with a large loaf of fresh bread. "Take it and be careful as you go back to the camp." I thanked him profusely and left feeling on top of the world.

But I did not go to the camp. I decided to try to find Fedka and was successful in finding his room. Just like the Estonian, Fedka was surprised to see me but immediately gave me some bread and a fistful of sweets. "Go quickly, go," he said in some panic and I left.

On the way back to the camp I had to pass by the German kitchen. "Well, why not?" I thought to myself. I had risked leaving the camp and had been lucky so far. Why not stretch my luck a bit further? With this thought I walked into the German kitchen.

They were in the middle of preparations for Christmas dinner. The tables were decorated – they even had flowers. Jewish women were running in and out of the kitchen preparing the tables. The first Jewish woman who saw me was stunned: "What are you doing here? Please run away, the German is here."

"I would like to talk to him," I said. In a few minutes the German officer, elegant and smiling, walked into the kitchen. Without any hesitation I immediately told him that my son and I were very hungry, we had no food, and on this holy day of peace I would like him to give me some food. He looked at me and without saying a word, he left and immediately came back with a half loaf of bread. "Go back to camp and be careful," were his parting words. Filled with happiness I went back to camp, crossed the wire fence without being caught and went to our room. Seeing me, my son burst into tears. He didn't know where I had been for the past few hours and was very worried.

I gave him the sweets and told him about my adventures. For the next several days we had a feast! I realized, however, that not every day is Christmas and I could not take the kind of risks that I had taken that night. I therefore

decided to try my luck at trading. I was helped by the fact that a distant relative of mine incarcerated with us in Klooga had a candy factory in Vilna. He
was ready to manufacture sweets that I could then sell and make a profit. This
became a successful business.

Every day, after work, I would start the rounds among my customers,
many of whom were eager to have sweets with their tea or coffee. My son also
contributed in his own way. He used his skills in the mechanical workshop in
the camp to manufacture small chain scales for weighing food products, and
a number of women's hair pins. I sold those as well.

There was, however, a very dangerous side to my new "career." My trading
activities meant that returning to camp after a day of hard labor, with every
shred of my body in excruciating pain, I was unable to catch my breath and
rest for a few hours. I had to start my rounds in the camp and seek out customers for my goods. Within a few weeks my health had deteriorated to the point
that I could no longer continue. I became very sick, with high fever and barely
managed to go to work and return alive. Since my temperature did not exceed
forty degrees centigrade, the infirmary would not give me any medication. Nor
would they give me a release from work. During that period my son tried to
collect some of the money that was owed to me and that enabled us to supplement our daily ration with an occasional additional ration of bread. One day,
however, we had a wonderful surprise. One of the German guards killed a dog
and as a sign of his generosity he gave it to his workers. They immediately cut
the dog into meat portions and divided it among themselves. Some of them
were willing to sell it and I bought two portions for 150 rubles. I used them to
cook a stew of meat and potatoes and for the first time since we came to Klooga
we had a hot meat meal. We feasted for two days.

In addition to the backbreaking work and starvation diet, the Germans
introduced another means of torture: roll call. Every day after we returned
from work there would be a roll call in front of the camp building. We would
be placed in columns and counted off to ten. In the early days of the camp after
count off we would be allowed to go inside. But with time the Germans forgot
their "welcome speech" when we were informed that in Klooga "you are not

here as Jews. You are here as working inmates…and you'll be able to work well"
and converted the roll calls into sadistic exercises of brutality and cruelty. They
would use the roll call to punish "offenders" by strapping them to a specially
designed bench and beating them to a pulp while we all stood and watched in
horror. At times they would have us sit for an hour or two with our hands up for
no apparent reason in spite of the freezing winter weather. At other times they
would have us run, fall, run, fall for an hour or two threatening to kill anyone
who would not be up to it. On those occasions, knowing that I wouldn't last
very long, I managed to hide in the washroom. My son was not so lucky and
had to suffer the whole routine. Women's roll calls were not much different,
with the female German guards showing even greater cruelty than the men.
The officer responsible for this brutality was S. Barde, nominally in charge of
health and sanitation. That same Barde brutally murdered three babies born
in the camp by throwing them alive into a flaming oven.

In spite of the hard, inhuman work and the cruelty of the Germans we
succeeded in maintaining our humanity, morality and dignity in the best Jewish
tradition. It would have been so easy, under the prevailing conditions, to lose
hope, to let oneself fall into the abyss of degradation. But we did not. It is to the
credit of Melcer and his group of orderlies that the camp was clean, sanitation
facilities were maintained in good condition, washrooms and kitchen were
spotless and a certain degree of disciplined behavior was enforced. Cultural
discussions and discussions of political events helped to bring people together
and, especially when the war news from the fronts became positive and the
Soviet advances became a daily occurrence, the mood became much more
hopeful. The religious element in the camp made a serious contribution to the
manifest will to survive and to the determination not to succumb to adversity. I
do not know how they were able to smuggle *tefillin* (phylacteries) and *taleisim*
(prayer shawls) into the camp but as soon as we were settled one could see many
Jews saying morning prayers before they went to work and reciting evening
prayers after they returned. We arrived to Klooga on Rosh Hashanah (the
Jewish New Year) and several days later a Yom Kippur service was organized
in one of the big halls. Some of the beds were moved aside to make room for

the rabbi, and the cantor, Szlomo Szarf from Vilna, sang *Kol Nidrei*. After the service I was asked to say a few words. I spoke of our condition, of the fate of our families who were separated from us and of the thousands of Jews who were murdered for being Jews. Never in my life have I spoken to Jews under such tragic circumstances. Tears were streaming down my face and down the faces of many in the hall. The next day, Yom Kippur, we went to work as usual, many of us fasting.

Hanukkah and Passover were also observed in the camp and for Passover some enterprising people managed to bake some matzahs. These were sold for fifty rubles each and many people bought them. Several groups in the camp organized Passover seders, including one in our room. Watching the observant religious element in the camp it was difficult not to be impressed by their stoicism, their apparent tranquility in the face of the most savage cruelty man has ever known.

Their faith in the Almighty gave them the strength to cope with any adversity and the hope that, in the end and in spite of all, Jews would survive this latest attempt at their destruction. They were truly a fountain of strength to us all.

CHAPTER 14

The Carnage in Lagedi and Klooga

The End Is Near

During the early summer of 1944 we received worrying rumors from outside our camp. The advances of the Red Army on the eastern front made the Germans restless and more dangerous to us. We were informed that transports of Jewish prisoners were arriving in Tallin from Estonian camps that had been liquidated. Despite our wishful hopes we were under no illusions; we knew that at the last moment the Germans would liquidate us. Our worries became more pronounced when on August 22, 1944, we learned that 250 women had been taken out of the women's barrack. We had no idea why they had been taken or where they were to be sent.

As we were about to begin our usual march to work on that fateful morning, our camp was surrounded by armed guards. We remained standing in our columns while the Germans called out our numbers from prepared lists. It caused immediate panic within the columns. We knew that the lists were prepared by our foremen as the numbers called out were of people who were least useful to them. My number was called out and I was not surprised. My deteriorating physical strength made my contribution to the work in the underwater mine factory rather limited and the foreman was probably looking for a more suitable replacement. But I became terribly worried about my young boy. How would he manage without me? How would he survive this hell all alone? Until now I had managed to save him during the liquidation of the Vilna Ghetto, shelter him from starvation in the camp and give him some of the warmth that a father can give during even the worst of times.

My young son had obviously the same thoughts. As soon as the number calling came to an end and without saying anything, he went over to the German with the lists and asked to be allowed to join me. The German he asked allowed him to do so but another German chased him away. I now had a terrible dilemma. On the one hand if I was sent away by myself who would look after my child? On the other hand how could I be sure that the numbers called out did not mean death? In that case if I went alone at least my son would stay alive. Who could tell what the Germans had prepared for us? While I was struggling to decide what was best, my son did not rest. Once more he went over to the German with the lists and this time managed to join our group. Now we were in God's hands, with whatever fate was to offer. For the time being at least, we remained together and in my heart I thanked God for the gift.

As soon as the people whose numbers had been called were assembled we were surrounded by guards with their guns at the ready. No one was allowed to approach us or talk to us. We were not allowed to leave our place to enter the barrack to retrieve our possessions we had left there. Not expecting the sudden development, we had left our bread, money, underwear and clothing in the barrack. I had hidden some money and bread and now I was standing together with my son – with nothing. Moreover, the day was quite hot already and we had gone out to work half-naked. But there was nothing I nor anyone else could do about it. As we waited, we were given bowls and spoons but nothing else. We stood and waited and watched as the others went to their usual work.

We did not remain standing for long. Whipping and beating us, the Germans drove us out of the camp to trucks already waiting for us. The inmates who managed to see us on our way waved to us – but nothing more. For a very short moment I tried to imagine what was going on in the camp we had just left, after 250 women and 250 men had suddenly been taken away. The whole operation, the sudden German decision, the way we had not been allowed to take our things with us did not auger well for our future. After nearly eleven months the sudden uprooting was particularly difficult. We had accustomed ourselves to the labor camp's terrible conditions and we had hoped to leave the place as free people, though with my state of health and lack of energy I wasn't sure that I would make it. But now it was as if any illusion we might have had had been taken away. We were transported once again into the unknown.

The trucks didn't give us much room. The Germans pushed the 500 people into four trucks. In each of the first three trucks they loaded up to 150 inmates. The last ones had to share their truck with the German guards. The trucks were not covered but they could not accommodate the number of people the Germans loaded into them. Seeing that, one of the guards jumped on top of us and with his heavy boots started kicking and pushing. To avoid being trampled by the German's boots we had to contort our bodies and squeeze ourselves against each other until enough room became available for the guards.

As the trucks began to move the bones in our emaciated bodies rattled at every twist and turn. Even now I sometimes ask myself the Talmudic question: We Jews survived the journey because we had been conditioned to everything, but what power enabled the trucks to survive? We traveled some hours and were unloaded at a small railway station. Some of the inmates in our truck needed help to straighten themselves back into human shape. Someone still had sufficient humor left to say, "After this road, we'll survive the coming of the Messiah. We're strong enough for it." From the station we were taken to a nearby field with some wooden huts on its periphery. We met a few Jews there who had held high positions in the Vilna Ghetto. From them we learned that we had landed in a German camp in a place called Lagedi.

The prisoners we met told us that a week earlier the camp had around twenty-five hundred Jewish inmates brought together from camps that were being liquidated in Estonia. They were held in Lagedi for a very short time and were sent by ship to Germany proper. Only ten inmates had been left on the advice of German medics. The transferred inmates left behind all their belongings. The Germans took away whatever was still in good condition, leaving the rags and a considerable number of blankets. The first piece of good news we were told was to feel free to select whatever we might find useful.

There was no real camp in Lagedi. In the field where we had been unloaded the Germans had put up huts hammered together from thin boards – like for dogs. Each hut was to hold twenty inmates. The huts had no floor and during the rain the ground inside the huts became waterlogged. For the Germans it didn't matter much as the huts had no furniture and the inmates slept on the bare ground. Water was also not available in the camp; it was brought in from outside. There was also no kitchen. We concluded from all this that we would not remain in Lagedi too long. The inmates knew that a ship was due in a few days to take us away as it had taken away the inmates before us. There was no roll call or handing us over in any formal way; we were left for the first few hours to our own devices.

I immediately rummaged through the pile of rags to find something for me and my son. We were nearly naked and had to find a little underwear and some clothing to cover ourselves. I found a number of women's shawls and kerchiefs and a pair of nearly new women's trousers made from a blanket. The clothing was like a treasure given the condition in which we were when we had arrived. We were given a few blankets but no food. The first night there was a nightmare to which we, seasoned inmates, had yet to get accustomed.

We were not called to work the next day. The day was reserved for "settling in" for us and for the newly arrived women. My son and I were assigned hut no. 27, which we were to share with eighteen others. Again, for the second day in a row, we were given no food. "No work – no food," said the Germans. By the end of the second day we had solved all our "accommodation" and "settling in" issues. On one side of the field there were huts for males and on the other side the huts were given to the women who came with our transport. The open space in between belonged to both. Nothing in the camp had been prepared to accept workers and the whole environment was not one of a prisoner camp. Whoever had some courage and was willing to gamble with survival against outside guards could walk away into freedom. But there was no freedom to walk away to in the vicinity.

The next morning our German tormentors remembered why we had been brought to Lagedi – we were meant to die as exhausted animals killed by labor without food. Our work was purely military. Officially we were meant to built dugouts, fortifications and camouflage areas but we and our supervisors had the same idea – not to finish the job too fast. The Germans of the Todt organization were our supervisors. They did not push us to work and we obeyed. They all seemed to have come from East Prussia. To this day I cannot understand the situation at Lagedi. For entire days we did nothing. We stood around talking among ourselves while they walked around us without saying anything. They sprang into action only when they saw a ranking officer approach and we obliged by becoming very active. But the officers also seemed not to care too much. After the excruciating slave labor conditions in Klooga, the relaxed atmosphere in Lagedi was difficult to understand. Were they aware that our end was near and was this part of the plan to keep us tranquilized and passive? We tried to talk to our Todt supervisors but they wouldn't say much. I believe that they did not know what the SS planned for us and their main concern was to keep the work going as long as possible. A few times my Todt overseer gave me his breakfast and offered me some wine from his container.

Most of the Todt supervisors behaved with a degree of humanity but even among them there were one or two sadists who gave vent to their cruelty at every occasion they could. I fell victim to one of them. I was in a field digging trenches and stopped to catch my breath. A Jewish woman standing near by said in Yiddish, "Why aren't you working?" Before I could answer I saw the German sadist running up with his ever-present stick in his hand, yelling, "Who isn't working? Who isn't working?" The woman pointed at me. The German turned to me and started pummeling me with his stick without mercy. Knowing that if I cried out in pain his fury would only increase I kept quiet and only hoped that my son standing nearby would not start crying, causing the German to turn on him. I also prayed that the German would not make me an invalid. He continued beating me until I fell to the ground. I was half-dead but fortunately nothing was broken and with the help of others I was able to return to camp.

The best part of the "idyllic" situation was going to bring water. The camp had, as already mentioned, no kitchen and no water and we had only to ask for permission to be allowed to wander off with a human-drawn cart and a barrel to bring water. Four people usually went on that expedition. As there was no hurry for anything, the water carriers used to disperse to visit the houses of the surrounding Estonian small landholders. The farmers gladly sold us vegetables and fruit and sometimes they handed us food without asking for payment. Each of us established his own group of "farmers." The prices were not much different from what they charged in the market and the time was just right for the village harvest. All in all we no longer went to "work" hungry.

I had established friendly relations with a lady who understood our situation and was willing to help as much as she could. When I told her that in my normal life I was a pharmacist she immediately told me about her young daughter who was suffering from tuberculosis and showed me the prescriptions. She asked for my help but understood that I could only confirm if the medications were good for her sick daughter or not. I sympathized with her situation but what could I do for her?

The house belonged to a prosperous farmer. Like at other farms I was offered food not only for myself but also for my son. I visited the place a few times. However the house was outside the camp perimeter and every visit was dangerous. Once a guard shot in my direction and I was lucky to escape. Another time I did not manage to escape from an Estonian guard who caught me on my way back to the camp. He poured out the milk soup I was carrying for my son, threw away the few potatoes I had been given and I had to clear my pockets and drop the bread I had hidden. Another time an Estonian guard who saw me entering a farmer's home came after me, gave me a very painful beating and told me to thank him that he had let me off alive.

After my experience with the sadist, I decided to try to find work in a different place. I took advantage of a visit to the fields of one of the supervising engineers with whom I had conversed on previous visits. I walked over to him and asked if he could help me to find another working location for myself and for my son. He asked a few questions about my background and promised to try. He kept his promise. The next morning, when I arrived to work, he walked over to me with another German and pulled my son and me from the working column. He said something to the German, who told us to follow him. After a short while we arrived at a large wooden house surrounded by a beautiful garden and were led to the back of the property. A door opened and a young man, an Estonian officer, appeared, told the German to go away and showed us a pile of wooden logs. "These logs need to be cut and arranged in the storage place, ready for the winter," he said and left. After a while, an older lady, who turned out to be his mother, came out from the house and brought us some food. We were overjoyed with our new situation and only wondered how long it could last. The number of logs we had to cut and saw was not very large but we could see that the house owner was not in a hurry to get this done and we obliged. Every morning a German guard used to bring us to work and in the evening the same guard brought us back to camp.

The conditions in the camp were miserable. We were still living in dog huts, sleeping on the ground and had no sanitary facilities. There were no chairs or tables and we had to eat either standing or sitting on the ground. There was an infirmary but no medication. In spite of that, the relaxed labor conditions, the food we were able to obtain from the surrounding farms and the nice weather enabled us to recuperate and gain a little strength. We did not know what was to come after Lagedi but the fact that the ship we were expecting did not arrive led our optimists and pessimists to extreme interpretations. The optimists were sure that together with our Todt supervisors we would leave there alive with the roles changed, while the pessimists said we would not be left alive. "At the last moment…," they said. Despite all our experience we preferred to trust the optimists…

The days passed, and the Jewish New Year arrived. Rosh Hashanah that year fell on Monday, September 17, 1944. After the day's work we assembled in one of the huts and welcomed the New Year by candlelight. We greeted each other with the customary Jewish wish, "May you be inscribed in the book of the living," only half believing the words that came off our lips as we separated, each to his own hut. None of us had any inkling of what the German perfidious mind had prepared for us as a Jewish New Year gift.

The next morning, Tuesday, September 18, 1944, we went to work as usual. At the end of the first day of the Jewish New Year the Estonian officer in whose home we were working came over and asked if I would be coming to work the next morning. I assured him that I would be there as long as he would want me. I began to worry that he might have tired of me, but as he had not dismissed me I was happy to keep the job.

Together with others who were working in the area we marched back to the camp as usual. But we were not allowed to enter the camp. We were stopped on the road and told to wait. We realized that something unusual was happening – but we did not know what it was. The talk was that we were being taken to a ship waiting for us in the port. In spite of our expectations that one day such a ship would arrive the sudden change in the daily routine made us restless and frightened. "What have the murderers prepared for us now?" somebody asked as we saw trucks waiting outside the camp perimeter. "Trust the Germans," somebody else said sardonically.

Armed Germans were standing near the trucks. While we waited at the roadside, the guards kept bringing groups of twenty to thirty inmates from the camp and loading them onto the truck. When a truck became full it left and the next one was loaded. Within a short time the empty truck returned and took on a new load from inside the camp while we were ignored.

I was standing close to an empty truck ready to step in but withdrew at the last moment. One of the loading Germans noted my hesitation. He punched me and hit me with his rifle butt – but instead of going forward I withdrew as he became busy loading others. My son began crying: "Why are you carrying on, Papa? Do you want to be beaten again? Let's get on the truck and be done with it." But I remained reluctant and withdrew to the back. I kept on moving back until night fell and only four people remained on the road. The Germans asked our group to enter the camp.

In the center of the field that divided the male and female huts, the last prisoners stood around talking freely. The ones who had remained in the camp told us that all the workers who had returned to the camp before us had already been taken away. The camp commandant and two Germans were present and kept talking in a very friendly way with the remaining Jewish workers. We used the opportunity to collect the things that were strewn on the road. The crafty ones found the food store and took out as much bread as they could manage to carry. In the meantime another truck arrived and again it was loaded and left. Another truck arrived and the last women were taken away. We were the last thirty-four men left when a truck arrived with a canvas cover over its metal frame. It was already quite late at night and we could no longer hold back. We climbed in and when the last guard came after us the truck moved. We traveled a short distance and our truck stopped. We couldn't see what was going on outside but from the conversation that reached us we learned that the truck before us, the one carrying the women, had broken down and our driver had stopped to help his colleague. It took quite a long time before they finished the repairs and the two trucks moved forward. After some time the trucks stopped once more and again we heard a conversation between Germans: "Yes, you came too late. For today everything is finished. Come tomorrow." The trucks moved again. This time we traveled for what seemed to be an hour or so and stopped again. The canvas cover was removed and we were told to get off the trucks. Surrounded by German soldiers we were herded through a large gate into what turned out to be the Tallin prison. The men were driven into one cell and the women into another. We remained there until dawn.

* * *

The few of us who survived the last moments of German occupation had to wait until after the liberation to learn how fate shielded us from death. Uriel Szymanowicz, a watchmaker from Vilna and an inmate in Lagedi told the story of his own survival:

"Together with my thirteen-year-old son I was in a truck that took us away from the camp. We were brought to a small forest where a group of Germans equipped with automatic rifles took over. They led us to a clearing in the forest where they shot each one in the back of the head. It had been going on for hours already. My son and I fell on bodies that had been shot before us. Feeling pressed by bodies that fell on top of me I realized that I was alive. Not long after, night fell and the shooting stopped. The Germans left.

"When it became quiet around me I decided to risk it and got myself out from the bodies lying over me. Crawling on my belly I managed to move away and reach the nearby forest. I was lying down to gain back my energy when the place I had left exploded in one huge pillar of fire that kept on burning throughout the night. In the morning I saw the Germans returning. They collected and buried the remnants left after the fire, cleaned up the place and brought trucks with clean soil that they spread over the area. When they left one could not tell that a few hours earlier the place had been a slaughterhouse where innocent humans, the last Jews of the Lagedi Concentration Camp, including my son, had been killed."

Szymanowicz was hidden for the next few days by friendly Estonians. When the Red Army arrived he was taken to a military hospital and underwent an operation. His survival story was published in the military daily paper *Zashtshitni Rodini*, under the heading "A Night of Horror."

Yes, fate shielded seventy-four people from death, my son and myself among them. The truck that broke down, causing our truck to stop and help it, had made us miss the appointment with our executioners. We had come "too late." The German murderers were not willing to work overtime and had decided that we would have to wait a few more hours for our liquidation. The same murderers were to execute the prisoners at Klooga the following day and we were to be among them. Once more fate intervened to save us from arriving at the slaughterhouse for our execution.

The Final Hours: Death in Klooga

Exhausted from the day's events, we lay down on the floor of the prison and quickly fell asleep. We had no idea how close we had come to being executed. At daybreak we were awakened by shouts, "Quick, quick," and were led to the two trucks waiting outside. We were loaded into the trucks, the men separate from the women, and the trucks started moving. We traveled for some time before we realized we were not being taken to the port. Looking out through the cover of our truck we realized that we were on our way back to Klooga, but when we arrived there we were not allowed to enter the camp. We remained in the two trucks for a considerable time. Finally, the gates were opened and we were told to get off the trucks and enter the camp. The executioners had probably discussed whether to take us directly to the slaughterhouse or to let us back into the camp. They must have decided that seeing us back alive in the camp would have a calming influence on the prisoners inside the camp. To achieve efficient execution of their plan it was worth granting us a few more hours of life.

As we entered the camp we noticed two columns of prisoners sitting on the ground close to the entrance. No one was allowed to stand up and greet us. Those who tried to stand up met with the brutal fists and rifle butts of the guard standing close by.

A little distance from the two columns were other columns of one hundred inmates each, both male and female. They showed surprise and relief seeing us come back alive from Lagedi and from brief exchanges of words we learned of the day's events.

Early that morning the inmates came out for roll call as usual but instead of going off to work they were told to stay in the camp. Some minutes later, the Germans took away three hundred men, all young and strong, saying that they needed them for work in the nearby forest until midday. Three Germans remained in the camp and Estonian guards were posted all around the camp with automatic weapons in their hands. A little later the prisoners inside the camp saw the men outside carrying heavy long logs from the forest to some place invisible from the camp. The camp kitchen was in the meantime preparing an unusually rich soup for the midday meal. Close to midday the commandant ordered the kitchen workers to prepare buckets of soup for the workers who had gone out to the forest. Sometime later we were given our soup; it had a calming effect on us. A few times the commandant repeated that the workers, "will soon be back from their work." Midday passed and the workers had not returned. After about an hour we became worried. Where were they? We were told that they would be back by midday! What did it all mean? Our anxiety rose from minute to minute. But even in our darkest thoughts we could not imagine the horror that was already taking place.

About an hour and a half after midday we heard the first volley of machine guns. We instinctively felt death approaching. Looking at each other in fear we did not dare to say aloud what we knew to be the tragic truth.

The shooting went on for a short time and then stopped. I pressed my son close to my heart the way I had done when we were passing Ponary that first night on the train. Was this going to be our end? It did not take long before the Germans came and took away twenty-five men from the group sitting on the ground. Soon after that the shooting was heard once more and there was no longer any doubt about what was taking place. The Germans were killing the inmates of the camp.

Now we knew we were facing death. We were looking right into its eyes without any way of escape. Even if we decided to run, we wouldn't get very far. The camp was surrounded by barbed wire with a heavy ring of Estonian soldiers bearing automatic weapons. But there had to be a way… My mind was working furiously trying to think of a way out. There had to be a way out! My son and I survived until now, Germany's defeat is imminent and we are to end our lives in the forests of Estonia? I looked around the ground where we were assembled and saw only one way to escape – to force our way back into the barracks. Some of us tried but the Germans noticed and pushed us back with clubs, whips and sticks. After the failed attempt we returned to the grounds. Two Germans came in to the camp riding a motorcycle and took away five young healthy men. The men returned after half an hour. Very carefully we managed to find out that the five men had pulled a car loaded with two drums of gasoline to the forest. Now we knew precisely what was taking place.

Again and again the Germans returned and took away new groups of inmates. Each time we measured the interval between the groups leaving and the shooting taking place. After the general automatic firing we could hear single shots and we knew their meaning. As the hours passed and the murderers continued their barbaric task, the camp became more and more empty. Every time my son and I came close to the group that was near the gate from which the groups of inmates were being taken away I took his hand and moved as far away as possible. Daylight was fading fast and it was becoming quite dark. There were few people left on the ground and I knew that another few minutes and we would have no choice but to join the march of the dead… The darkness meant that the visibility of the Estonian guards surrounding the camp was poor… The Germans were busy counting out one of the groups to be taken away… I grabbed my son and with all my strength sprinted into the camp building, ran up to the top floor and crawled under the bunks in the big hall. A few others followed us and hid under the bunks on the ground floor. I pulled my son far away from the entrance, close to the window and hid together with him in a niche under a bed. I pulled the bed as close as possible and tried to press ourselves into it as if we would be nothing more than worms. I wished at the time that we were worms, small enough to crawl under a stone or hide in a crack in the wall. There we remained listening to every sound that was coming from outside the hall.

Every few minutes we heard the screaming voices of the Germans yelling, "*Schnell, schnell* (Quick, quick)!" They must have already taken away the last inmates. The commandant was busy calling the sick inmates, doctors and nurses out of the infirmary. We could hear the orders to get the sick ones onto the trucks and the impatience in the German voices sounded to us as if they were in a hurry to end it all quickly. There was one voice above all the others repeating every few seconds: "Where are the other men? Where are the other men?" I shuddered – that meant that they realized that a number of men had run away and that they would enter the building searching for us. We pressed ourselves as hard as we could into our hiding place, waiting for the end and hoping at the same time for a miracle.

Suddenly the dark hall in which we were hiding exploded in a flood of light. A wall of fire spread over the area, illuminating the camp buildings and spewing out burning timbers… Over the noise of the crackling fire we heard the impatient calls of the Germans shouting again, over and over, "*Schnell, Schnell!*" Each minute that passed was like an eternity and in the bright light of the fire we waited for the German murderers. The forest was on fire. After completing their unforgivable crime the German murderers were now burning down the forest with their victims trapped inside

Minutes passed before we realized that there were no sounds coming from outside. There was total silence. Only the flames, the bright gruesome flames of hellish light and the huge sparks flying by the windows. Flames that consumed the bodies of thousands of innocent men, women and children. Flames that brought eternal shame and dishonor to the nation of vile murderers. I was lying pressed in my niche together with my son and in our minds we saw the faces of our friends in the pieces of fire that kept flying by. Human flesh. Now all that remained were the German murderers and us – wrapped in the final shrouds of fear, without the possibility of escape. And within those endless seconds when eternity had suddenly stopped, we thought about home, wife, daughter, brother. *Where are you? Are you still alive...?*

In the dead silence I realized that the infamous German precision had for once worked in our favor. The Germans worked within defined "working hours." They had finished their work for the day; in the morning they would return and finish what they had failed to finish today. Maybe we still had a few hours of peace left before the end. Maybe we should go find a better hideout. But where? I fell asleep. It was still dark when I woke up. So far my son and I were alive, but for how much longer?

In the silence surrounding us I heard voices as if coming from the other side of the wall. Was that possible or was I hallucinating? I was not hallucinating. The voices spoke in Yiddish and among them I recognized the voice of Henekhke Szapiro. Obviously there was a hideout close by but how was I to reach it? And if I could reach it would the people in it let us in? In despair I began pulling at the wall that separated me and my son from the other side. As soon as the first noise of my attempt was heard the voices stopped. I knocked on the wall: "Friends, I am here with my son. Can we join you?" Henekhke Szapiro answered immediately: "Come to us but don't touch the wall." I replied: "Here I see the bright light of the fires but how would I find you in the dark? Send somebody to guide us." Henekhke agreed and within minutes somebody came and took us to the hideout. It was on the same level as the hall, an attic stretching out over the outer wall of the building. We crawled in on our bellies and felt relieved. Thank Heaven we were no longer alone. We were with other Jews and if Henekhke was there we had a chance... There were quite a number of others in the hideout, though there was no place to stand up. We had to lie or sit on the floor. In the darkness we didn't see each other but I recognized some of the voices. Here we felt less tense than when we had been on our own.

As dawn approached and daylight started seeping through the cracks in the wall we became frightened. Without speaking to each other we felt the fear that permeated the hideout. If we could only stop the sun from rising!

But the sun rose. An hour passed and then another hour and nothing broke the silence outside the building. No voices, no shouts, no motorcycles. Now the deadly silence began to worry us. What did it all mean? A few of the younger men dared to approach the small window and looked out into the camp yard. They gave us the first report: "There are no Germans around. There are only uniformed armed Estonians in the square." The information confused us: "Where are the Germans? And if the Germans have left what are the Estonian guards doing?"

With mixed feelings of hope and fear we spent the first day in our hideout, sharing what little food there was. The next night a few young ones dared to leave the attic. They came back with some provisions and for the first time since our arrival at Klooga we ate bread with honey.

The next morning we were woken up from our slumber by noises from the camp yard. Our observers informed us that they saw Russian prisoners from the nearby camp for prisoners of war. The Russian prisoners had come with horse carts and were looting the German storehouses. The observers kept up a running commentary. First it was the food stores, after that came the German stores and in the end they were looting our block. They removed the little bedding that was left, the clothing, underwear, everything that they could take away. The report gladdened our hearts. The Germans were no longer around and we were alive! We had survived! But the Estonian guards were still there, so we could not celebrate prematurely. On the third night a large group of people left the attic and brought back a treasure they had found that the Russian prisoners had not touched: the German kitchen food supplies. They collected and brought back foods that we had not seen since the war began. The food was distributed to everyone and that morning we ate our fill.

On the fourth day, the Estonian guards disappeared just like the Germans. From our hideout we saw a Soviet plane passing over our camp. Some wanted to give the plane a sign of some kind but decided against it. Once more fate acted in our favor. A few days later after the liberation when the Russian pilot visited our camp, he told us that he flew over the camp and saw people. He was ready to drop his bomb on us but something made him hesitate and he held back. He had concluded that the people might be prisoners. Seeing the Russian plane was a tremendous boost to our hopes but our joy soon turned to sorrow when we heard that the ground floor of our building was filled with the dead bodies of camp inmates. From one of the few survivors, Dr. S. Seidler, we later learned that after the Germans completed their work in the camp and all the inmates were already taken away to their deaths, the Germans came into the building's ground floor and fired volleys of machine-gun fire under the bunks of the big hall. They knew that people who had escaped from the camp meeting ground were hiding there. But they also knew that their time was short; the Russians were near and they had to flee. That is why they were in such a hurry. The murderers had no time to repeat their blood-thirsty exercise on the top floor but every second they had, until the very last moment, they filled with their thirst for Jewish blood. Dr. Seidler was spared the bullets and during the night he escaped into the surrounding forest. A few days later he returned to the camp to tell his story.

On September 25, 1944, at 10:00 a.m. the first five Russian officers entered the camp. Very carefully we crept out of our hideout and walked onto the camp ground. We had to be certain that the Russians were really there, that it was not a mirage, a figment of our imagination. We watched them approach us, we saw the red stars on their uniforms, we heard them speak Russian and we knew that our liberators had arrived.

One of the officers, as if reading our minds, said in Russian: "The German murderers are no longer here. But we will catch those animals." On hearing this I pulled my son tight to my heart. Tears were streaming down our faces. They were tears of joy and happiness that in spite of years of the Germans' heinous attempts to destroy us, to murder us, and in spite of all the pain and suffering they inflicted upon us – they had not succeeded. We had survived. We were free.

The Carnage in Klooga

The joy at our freedom was soon replaced by a return to the tragic reality. Accompanied by Russian officers, my son and I and a group of other survivors reluctantly left the camp grounds and walked along a path in the direction of the forest. We knew that several hundred yards away, past the railway lines and surrounded by trees, was a wooden hut that apparently served as living quarters for the camp guards. As we rounded a bend in the road and crossed the railway lines, we saw the hut. As we realized what we were looking at we stopped as if riveted to the ground. Nothing was left of the hut but its concrete foundation and a brick chimney in its center. Covering the foundation were the half-burned bodies of hundreds of Klooga inmates, both men and women. Scattered throughout the area were dozens of bodies of victims who were shot while attempting to escape. The few who survived told us the horrifying story of this butchery. The columns of people taken by the SS guards from the camp grounds were led directly to the shed. There they were forced to lie on the ground while waiting their turn to be led inside. Once inside they were shot. Most were killed outright; some were wounded. A few actually escaped injury. When the floor of the shed was covered with bodies, new victims were herded in, forced to lie on top of the dead and the carnage started again. This continued until the shed was completely filled with dead or wounded bodies. The doors were then locked. Toward evening the Germans opened the windows of the shed and poured in drums of gasoline which they then set on fire. The structure burned down and with it the bodies of the victims. Many were burned alive. The few people who were not dead and who were able to move took advantage of the open windows and the darkness, crawled out from under the dead bodies and escaped into the forest. Three or four survived to recount this barbarous act.

Stunned by the satanic atrocity we had just witnessed, we continued along the path into the woods. We wanted to see what had happened to the thousands of camp inmates taken from the camp grounds. I believed that we had already witnessed the ultimate depravity of the twisted German mind. What else could they do to satisfy their thirst for brutality? We didn't have to wait very long to find out. Our path through the woods took us to a clearing in the forest and an indescribable, horrifying scene. Spread in the clearing were the remnants of three platforms, about six meters by six meters each, made out of wooden logs. Each platform was formed by three or four layers of logs and in between each layer were half-burned bodies of people. In the center of each platform were openings for barrels of kerosene. The victims had been forced to lie down on the logs and had then been shot in the head. When the platform had been filled logs were placed on top of the bodies, creating another platform that could be filled by more victims. This was repeated until all the platforms were full and there were no more victims to be led to the slaughter. The barrels of kerosene were then set aflame. Now I realized what had caused the huge burst of light that we saw while hiding in the camp barracks several days earlier. The purpose of the fire was to burn the victims to ashes and conceal the crimes committed. But in their haste to complete their task, the murderers apparently miscalculated the amount of kerosene they would need and the platforms were only burned in the center.

Even now, on the sixth day after the atrocity, some of the timbers and body parts were still smoldering. The bodies of victims lying on the outer edges of the platforms were only half-burned with their faces being recognizable. I could see among them a number of people I knew well, old friends from a different era, a different world. They did not survive. Their lives were taken in the last, desperate moments of German occupation and their smoldering bodies will bear witness to the enormity of German bestiality for generations to come.

Two thousand five hundred Vilna and Kovno Jews were murdered in the death camp of Klooga. Eighty-seven survived.

After the discovery of the atrocities committed by the Germans in Klooga the Soviet authorities established several commissions of inquiry. I was asked by the Soviet chief prosecutor to write a detailed account of life and death in Klooga. I wrote it in Russian and gave it to him. Before I left Estonia he was kind enough to return it to me and I used it in the writing of this work. While the commissions of inquiry were doing their duty, news of the carnage in the

Klooga camp spread around the world and groups of foreign correspondents started visiting the camp. They published articles and photographs, providing the world with early testimony of the Germans' heinous depravity. After four weeks of investigations the Soviet authorities gave us permission to bury the remnants of our martyrs in a mass grave. To help us, they brought in German prisoners of war and had them dig the graves and then collect all the body parts from around the murder sites and lay them out alongside the graves. We built a small fence around the grave and recited *Kaddish*, the prayer for the dead. May their souls rest in peace.

Our task in Klooga was finished. It was time to go home. By the middle of November we were informed that the commission of inquiry had completed its work and we were free to return to Vilna. We were given the necessary travel documents, some basic provisions and train passage. The day before we were to leave, a group of survivors went back to the two mass graves of our brothers and sisters. With tears pouring down my face I recited "*El Malei Rahamim*," a prayer for the remembrance of the dead, and with a few words I took leave of the thousands of martyrs buried in the graves, innocent souls who heroically survived the ghettos and the camps only to have their lives taken at the very last moment. In their lives they were a shining example of an unshakable will to survive and live in dignity. In their deaths they joined generations of martyrs who throughout the ages lost their lives because they were Jews.

*   *   *

Several months after our return to Vilna I was informed that my wife and daughter had survived their hell and were now in Poland. As soon as possible we packed up our meager belongings and traveled to Poland where we were reunited. Soon after, we left Poland to start a new life in Australia.

About the Author

Mendel Balberyszski was born in Vilna to a well-known Jewish family. He studied at a heder, an elementary school and the Vilna Gymnasium (high school). He went on to study pharmacy at the University of Vilna, and completed advanced studies at the University of Warsaw. From his early student days he became active in the Jewish community, in both professional associations and communal organizations. He served on the editorial board of the Yiddish newspaper *Der tog* (The day), was a leading member of the Democratic Party, the Jewish Democratic Folkspartei and the Association of Jewish Artisans and Small Businessmen, and served as chairman of the philanthropic organization Notein Lehem and of the Polish Pharmaceutical Association. Balberyszski was an expert on the Yiddish language and an outstanding orator. After surviving the Vilna ghettos and the Estonian concentration camps, he returned to Vilna. When he learned that his wife and daughter had survived the Holocaust and returned to Poland, Balberyszski and his son left Vilna and the family was reunited in Lodz, Poland. Soon after they emigrated to Australia. In Australia Balberyszski returned to active Jewish communal activities, founding the Association of Partisans and Camp Survivors of which he became the president. He was also president of the Carlton Hebrew Congregation and a member of various organizations, among them the Jewish Board of Deputies. He was a contributor to the Jewish newpapers and a sought-after guest lecturer. The Balberyszski Jewish Bookstore, which he acquired and expanded in the early 1950s, became the center for the Yiddish-speaking intellectuals and a communal institution. Mendel Balberyszski died in Melbourne, Australia, on November 19, 1966.

Index